In the Shadow of My Guardian Angel

Henry Czajewski

Strategic Book Group

Strategic Book Group
P.O. Box 333
Durham CT 06422
www.StrategicBookClub.com

ISBN: 978-1-60976-412-8

Flickering, a flame may go out, but the spark of hope remains.

To my wife, children and grandchildren
May my particularly difficult life experiences be an
indication to never give up fighting the adversities in
life.

April 27/2017

Contents

Foreword

A FEW OPINIONS

Dear Henry,

You have created a splendid piece of work, a testimony to your colorful life and personal story. It is written with diligent attention to historical truth and enriched with innumerable photographs and relevant documents.

You write in a simple, yet beautiful manner about that which you deem most important in your life, God, Family, Love, Work, Joy, and Suffering, both spiritual and physical, with which you constantly struggled as you created this book. In spite of these challenges, you never resigned yourself to doubt or apathy, but heroically fought for your life. This suffering motivated you and gave you extraordinary strength to be able to bring this ongoing project to fruition.

As you depict the path your life took in the midst of the Communist era, you reveal the workings of communist subjugation, repression, and corruption, issues which remain fresh in our minds to this day.

Personally, I am in awe of your work. In it, I came upon many familiarities from my own life, especially from my childhood experiences. I readily identified with your descriptions of the hardships of working in the fields, the charm of tending to the livestock and reading under the bed sheets, the drama of de-privatization efforts, and failed attempts at collectivism, as well as the bitter experiences of humiliation suffered at the hands of peers and the community.

It was kind of you to mention those who keep the memories alive through the internet, and I include myself among them. On a near-

daily basis, I receive selfless, touching proofs of remembrance via online communication, gestures that are so important to my loved ones and me.

It's good to have such a reliable, virtual Guardian Angel! It has been said that people who experienced clinical death, and have been to the other side, have extraordinary strength and are granted special abilities.

May the Good Lord give you the power to continue to create and to be successful.

All the best and may God bless you!

Best regards and with a grateful bow from Krakow's symbolic Lajkonik to the tune of the resounding hymn from the peak of St. Mary's Basilica Tower.

—Stefan Gala.

I read it and I was touched.

I am pleased to tell you that I finished reading Mr. Henry Czajewski's extraordinary life testament. The issues in the book are close to my heart because I know that it is not a work of his imagination but rather a poignant truth. The times were exactly as he depicted them. I believe his story because we lived through the same realities. I go forward with the unwavering certainty of many extraordinary and unique individuals, who unlike the Author have neither the courage, the ability, nor the motivation to give witness to these frightening times of our history. I am full of admiration for this Man; this is why I refer to Him in capital letters. I shed tears when reading certain parts of this book, and I was in awe of His enthusiasm, optimism, and sense of humor. What a wonderful piece of work! I am glad that I will be able to refer back to the text. What gives me the most joy is the fact that the enemies of Poland, of Poles and of our Faith, who continue to rear their beastly heads, will grind their teeth in fury as they read this book.

—B.F.

In the Shadow of My Guardian Angel is the title of my brother Henry's book. These are the memories of his childhood, youth, and adult years. These are also the experiences that he had to live through. They were often quite dramatic, often beyond the strength of a child or youth. His adult years were very stressful and adversely affected his health. These years were full of persecutions by Security Officials. After my brother returned from his nine-month visit to the United States, the communist regime began to regard him as the enemy of the People's Poland and began persecuting and torturing him. Various threats posed by the Communists led to my brother's emigration to the United States. There he had to face many difficulties and struggle with many obstacles. Nevertheless, he always trusted in his Guardian Angel, who was always by his side and surrounded him with His care. As he wrote this book, he always remained in His shadow. I wish my brother continued care of his health by his Guardian Angel and further literary success.

—Father Canon Major W.P. Romuald Czajewski

Preface

DOCUMENT OF COMMUNIST PERSECUTION

Before the year 1989, that is, before the fall of Communism in Poland, the Communist government ordered the destruction of any documents that could have implicated them in the persecution of people opposed to the Communist Party. The documents would have been proof of their ignominious actions. Therefore, they were taken away by the truckload from the archives and burned outside of the city limits. In this way, my documents were destroyed in Bialystok as well, where my persecution was most severe. Nevertheless, most copies of my documents were preserved at the Ministry of Interior in Warsaw, where the Security Office had to deliver them. Based on these documents, I was considered harmed by the communist regime, and I was granted aggrieved-victim status. In order to receive that status, one must have had irrefutable evidence, and not many individuals received this status. Here I would like to add that thanks to my informer from the Ministry of Interior in Warsaw, I avoided jail and many unfortunate situations, including death.

The following is an official document from the Polish government issued only to those citizens who were directly persecuted by Communist authorities:

Translator: Michael Gosiewski

BFDated: Warsaw, May 23, 2005.

CHAIRMAN

Of the Instytut Pamięci Narodowej (IPN)

Komisji Ścigania Zbrodni przeciwko

Narodowi Polskiemu

[National Memorial Institute (NMI)

for Crimes against the Polish Nation

Prosecuting Commission]

Leon Kieres, Ph.D.

BP III—550—108/04

Mr. Henryk Czajewski

DECISION No. 54/05.

Pursuant to Art. 138, Par. 1, item 1 and in connection with Art. 144 and Art. 127, Par. 3 of the Kodeks Postępowania Administracyjnego [Code of Administrative Procedure] Act of June 14, 1960 (Journal of Acts of 2000, No. 98, item 1071, with further amendments) and Art. 30 of Act 2 of December 18, 1998 regarding the National Memorial Institute for the Crimes against the Polish Nation Prosecuting Commission (Journal of Acts of 1998, No. 155, item 1016 with further amendments) and upon consideration given to the Petition for Reconsideration of Mr. Henryk Czajewski's case of November 24, 2004.

I hereby overrule the Decision No. 23/04 of September 14, 2004 regarding the denial of a certification with the content requested by Mr. Henryk Czajewski to him and I hereby certify that Mr. Henryk Czajewski is a victim within the scope of Art. 6 of Act 1 of December 18, 1998 related to the National Memorial Institute for Crimes Against the Polish Nation Prosecuting Commission (Journal of Laws of 1998, No. 155, item 1016 with further amendments).

SUBSTANTIATION

On September 15, 2003, Mr. Henryk Czajewski filed a Petition for Document Production/ Victim Status Inquiry. Oddziałowe Biuro Udostępniania i Archiwizacji Dokumentów w Gdansku [Departmental Office for the Documents Accessibility and Filling in Gdansk] conducted a search of documents related to Mr. Henryk Czajewski in the NMI resources in Gdansk, Warsaw and Bialystok.

As a result of the conducted archive query, only passport files and personal records of Mr. Henryk Czajewski were found in the MSW [Ministerstwo Spraw Wewnętrznych- Ministry of Internal Affairs— MIA] Archives—Office C.

Based on the results of the conducted archive query, the Head of the Departmental Office for Documents Accessibility and Filling in Gdansk issued a Certification No. 734/04 which stated that on the basis of accessible and existing documentation, Mr. Henryk Czajewski was not a victim within the scope of Art. 6 of the Act regarding the National Memorial Institute—Crimes against the Polish

Nation Prosecuting Commission (Journal of Acts of 1998, No. 155, item 1016 with further amendments), further referred to as the "Memorial Institute Act."

Upon receipt of this certification, on June 29, 2004, Mr. Henryk Czajewski sent a document to the National Memorial Institute appealing the decision displayed on the certification which he found unjust. With his request, Mr. Henryk Czajewski forwarded his biography in the form of a book.

The abovementioned request was considered a motion for issuance of a certification stating that Mr. Henryk Czajewski was a victim within the scope of Art. 6 of the Memorial Institute Act. However, since no facts changed from the time the first certificate was issued, the Head of the Departmental Office for Documents Accessibility in Gdansk issued a Decision denying issuance of a certification with the content as requested in its decision No. 23/04 issued on September 14, 2004.

The substantiation for the Decision No. 23/04 indicated that pursuant to Art. 218, Par. 1 of the Administrative Procedure Code, a public administrative organ is required to issue a certificate, confirming the facts or a legal status based on a research of evidence, records, and other information it has at its disposal. The substantiation also indicated that documents confirming the fact that the national security organs collected, on the basis of purposely gathered data, Mr. Henryk Czajewski's information, were not found in the archival resources of the National Memorial Institute.

Upon receipt of the Decision No. 23/04, dated June 24, 2004, Mr. Henryk Czajewski filed a Motion for Reconsideration of the Case. In the Motion for Reconsideration of the Case, Mr. Henryk Czajewski stated that the decision was in his opinion unjust and asked to be provided with substantiation given the fact one of the letters he had received stated the documents were destroyed. He indicated that in the book he attached to the request dated June 29, 2004, he described the persecution of his person by the socialist government and further indicated that if these facts could not be verified that would be regrettable. Mr. Henryk Czajewski also requested permission to access archived documentation.

In consideration of the Motion to Reconsider Case, a Chairman for the National Memorial Institute found the following:

Pursuant to Art. 6 of the Memorial Institute Act, a victim is an individual about whom national security organs purposely collected information in a confidential manner.

As a result of the conducted archive query in the case of Mr. Henryk Czajewski, a record was found in the MIA Office C files and passport files were found. The contents of these records indicate that Mr. Henryk Czajewski was researched by the national security organs on two occasions. The first time he was checked during the years 1968–69, in connection with a suspicion that during his temporary residency in the USA he was approached by counterintelligence organs. The research was concluded as no hostile activity was found. The second research took place in 1971 in connection with the fact that during his stay in the USA during the years 1967–68, he was questioned by the police about unknown topics and he spoke antagonistically about the Soviet Union and then current reality. This research was concluded with no hostile activity finding.

A thorough analysis of the case reveals that it falls under the language of Art. 6 of the Memorial Institute Act. Given what has been shown above, in the case of Mr. Henryk Czajewski, national security organs researched, e.g. gathered information based on the purposely collected data. However, the linguistic interpretation of the Act indicates too broad of a spectrum with respect to the understanding of the term information collection. In order to interpret Art. 6 in greater detail, we have to consider interpretation of the purpose, and so the objectives for the regulations contained in the Act must be considered. The objective of the Memorial Institute Act was related by the legislator in the preamble. In accordance with the contents of the preamble, the purpose of the NMI is: "to maintain the memory of magnitude of the victims, losses and damages suffered by the Polish Nation during the WWII years and after its conclusion, patriotic tradition of the Polish Nation's struggles with the occupation, Nazism and Communism, acts of citizens designed to reclaim independence of the Polish State and to the fight for freedom and human dignity, the obligation to prosecute for crimes against peace, humanity and for war crimes and also the duty of the State to compensate all of the State victims for their violated human rights." Taking into consideration the content of the records found at the MIA Office C and in the passport files, it has to be determined that in the case of Mr. Henryk Czajewski, the last purpose indicated in the preamble to the Act applies, namely "the duty of the State to compensate all of the State victims violated human rights." The content of the found documentation indicates that national security organs gathered information based on an incorrect suspicion of counterintelligence activity and that there was an instance of the police questioning without a cause. It is hard to assume that in a democratic country a citizen could have been scrutinized for no other reason than refusing to reveal the purpose for which police conducted a hearing. Therefore, in consideration of the reasons given above, the U.B.'s (Urząd Bezpieczeństwa) [Security Office's- SO] interest in Mr. Henryk Czajewski indicates that the Petitioner's case was a case in which human rights violation did occur. In consideration of the above mentioned, the Chairman for the Institute finds Mr. Henryk Czajewski is a victim within the scope of Art. 6 of the Memorial Institute Act.

Based on the abovementioned, the Decision of September 14, 2004, No. 23/04 regarding the denial of victim certification had to be overruled and the case had to be considered in substance, which in this case means issuance of a Certification confirming Mr. Henryk

Czajewski's victimization within the scope of Art. 6 of the Memorial Institute Act.

This Decision is final and no administrative appeal is allowed. This Decision can be appealed by petitioner at the Wojewodzki Sad Administracyjny w Warszawie [Regional Administrative Court in Warsaw] within 30 days of the receipt of this Decision. The complaint is filed through the Chairman's Office of the National Memorial Institute for Crimes Against the Polish Nation Prosecuting Commission at [street address] ul. Towarowa 28, 00–839 Warsaw.

Oblong seal: CHAIRMAN

Of the National Memorial Institute

Leon Kieres, Ph.D.

/-/ illegible signature

Grażyna Skutnik

Head of the Departmental

Office of Document Rendering and Filling System in Gdansk

[Street address] ul. Polanki 124

80–308 Gdansk

Introduction

On September 1, 1939, at four forty-five in the morning, the German warship, *Shleswig Holstein,* which docked in the Gdansk port with a supposed friendly visit, opened fire on the Polish military base, Westerplatte. With this attack began World War II, which was considered the bloodiest war in the history of man to this day. The attack on Poland was first and foremost made by Hitler with premeditation and a shrewdly designed plan. The German intelligence was well aware that the allies, England and France, had abandoned Poland, despite the military pact regarding mutual aid in case of aggression instigated by another nation.

Nevertheless, it was known that in case of the opposite situation, that is, an invasion first on France or England, Poland would certainly come to their relief and attack Germany from the other side.

These predictions turned out to be justified. Despite the fact that England and France officially declared war on Germany on paper, they never came with military aid to Poland, leaving it to the mercy of its looters.

The attack was concentrated on the western border. The armored divisions and the German air force left corpses and ashes on the lands of the Polish nation, which enjoyed only a twenty-year period of freedom from November 16, 1918, to September 1, 1939, after 123 years of slavery and having been erased from the maps of Europe. From October 24, 1795, to November 16, 1918, three countries, Austria, Prussia (later changed to Germany), and Russia, divided Poland among themselves, with our part of Poland under Russian control.

The heroism of the Polish soldier defending his beloved homeland was immense. Despite the attacks from land, sea, and air, Poland successfully resisted until September 17. It was then that Hitler's ally, an equally murderous Soviet Russia, stabbed Poland's defenders in the back from the east, forcing it to surrender. The occupants divided Poland among themselves, and, once again, the Polish nation ceased to exist until the end of the war on May 9, 1945. Unfortunately, this wasn't liberation but enslavement by our well-known occupier called the United Soviet Socialist Republics (Soviet Russia). The most painful fact was that the entire democratic world recognized the new Polish Communist government as legitimate, despite the human rights violations and political murders it had committed.

The establishment of the Independent Self-Governing Trade Union "Solidarnosc" in 1980 in Gdansk gave Poles hope for change. The spiritual father of the formation of this union was our countryman, Pope John Paul II, without whom neither "Solidarity" nor freedom would exist. Unfortunately, the road to freedom was still long and riddled with thorns. The year 1989 brought the freedom that Poland had so longed for.

I lived through this very difficult time. I wish to document my experiences and what I saw with my own eyes, so that my descendants may come to know about the efforts of the Polish nation, which loved freedom above everything and which fought on all the fronts of World War II so that the people of the world may live better lives.

My wife, my son, and I standing at the Westerplatte monument in Poland. Wester-platte is a peninsula in Gdansk located on the Baltic Sea where WWII began. From 1926 to 1939, it was the location of the Polish Military Transit Depot (WST) sanc-tioned within the territory Gdansk. The monument was erected, after WWII, in honor of those who died during the war.

Gdansk postcard

Memorable Childhood Moments

I dreamed, as each living person does, to be "the maker of my own destiny," but I think that I was not always able to have influence over it. Life took its own path regardless of my actions. The question I always ponder is do we really have the chance to choose our own most beautiful way?

It seems that each of us walks on a road already paved for us, whether it's cobblestone or colorful cement or black asphalt, which after each winter is left with cracks and potholes in disrepair. Despite this, we shouldn't give up but fight for our future until the end, so that the road conquered and the deeds done fill us with pride, instead of the feeling of slightly or entirely wasted time.

I arrived in this world as the fourth child of Jan and Zofia. I was born "in the bonnet." (If the placenta does not break during childbirth, the child is born with a cap that can be easily removed by a midwife.) Since the middle ages, this was seen as a sign of good fortune. The bonnet, by tradition, brings luck. But if it was the bonnet that helped me throughout my life, and to what extent, I will leave to the conclusion of my readers.

My birthplace is Budne, near the Military Fortress of Osowiec and a village by the same name. It is located in the center of Biebrzanski Park, named after the river flowing nearby. Biebrzanski Park is now under federal protection and is famous for its unique resources of flora and fauna.

World War II erupted when I was a one-year-old child, and it wasn't until the years after 1943 that my experiences were etched in

5

my memory, some so deeply that I cannot uproot them despite the passage of so many years. I cannot provide exact dates because I only remember facts and events, which, like a filmstrip, play in my mind. When I think back to those times, the recorded film is recreated with the same brightness and clarity.

The Osowiec fortress was a strategic military vantage point. It was here that the Czar began its construction. During this period, Poland was erased from the map of Europe for 123 years. This part of Poland, where my family lived, belonged to Russia and later to the Soviet Union. Marshall Pilsudski, the new leader of free Poland, finished the construction during the years 1920–25. The fortress was practically unconquerable due to the swampy terrain surrounding it that was to effectively protect it from ground armed force attacks. In those times, air forces were not taken into consideration. It was not until the World War II that air forces played a dominating role. These two forces complemented one another during World War II, and their destructive power was immense.

On September 17, 1939, the Polish Army abandoned the Osowiec fortress, and it was taken over by the Red Army, allied with the Hitler occupier at the time. The Soviets began the mass deportation of Polish patriots and people of wealth to Siberia. It was our turn. We were marked for deportation, when three days before the appointed date (June 22, 1941), the Wehrmacht, in an operation known as Barbarossa, began an invasion on its present ally, the USSR (Soviet Russia). This situation represented a two-sided coin because from being under the control of one occupant, we found ourselves under another. At least for the time being, we remained where we were.

Now, a different chapter of Polish history began. The Nazi terror rose up day by day. In 1941, Poland became the birthplace of the Holocaust. The German occupier began to build factories of death, concentration camps on Polish land. Mass executions and hangings were the daily order. Innocent hostages were murdered or publicly tortured. People were gathered up at the place of punishment especially for this purpose. The pacification of villages took place alongside the pacification of cities along the entire Polish territory. During the war, six million Polish citizens died at the hands of the two occupants. Thousands of cities and villages were leveled.

In August 1944, Soviet forces were already approaching the Biebrza River. Our house stood on the German side, but on the front line, which came to a standstill there for a few months. Air raids became permanent, and we were in their epicenter.

One night, when we were settled in for sleep, an airplane beamed a light on our house and surrounding areas so brightly that it blinded us. Our father, in order to disengage our attention from this, yelled loudly, "Run!" My elder siblings tore from their beds at once, while my mother picked me up, wrapping me in a blanket, and ran outside. My father pointed to the direction in which we should run. He put himself in the line of machine gunfire, so that we could escape along with our mother. Behind us, we heard the terrible noise of explosions as sand poured onto our heads.

The force of one of the blasts toppled us to the ground. In spite of herself, my mother let me fall from her arms. Just then, the lights went out, and we found ourselves in complete darkness. At first, my mother couldn't find me. Even though she called my name, I lay quietly since I was so scared. I couldn't make a noise. Finally, she found me, and hugging me close to her, she ran with my older siblings in the direction of our neighbor, who lived two kilometers away. Both of our families lived far away from our village.

By sheer luck, my mother stumbled upon a shelter dug in the middle of the field by the neighbor. We encountered his entire family there. They took us in with joy and tears in their eyes. Right away, we felt safe, although the shelter was nothing but a makeshift place. It didn't guarantee our total safety and only served to mask our whereabouts. We didn't hear any more shooting and explosions of dropped bombs, so we calmed down a bit. We were still worried about our father though. He found us when the sun was already high, and there was no end to our joy.

From what our father told us, it was by a miracle that he avoided death. The barn door, which he had opened to release the animals, saved his life. At that time, a bomb that fell from the plane exploded and tore apart a piece of the wall. The door flew off its hinges and pinned my father to the ground, thereby saving his life. He ran from the danger zone and hid in one of the craters from the bomb. He knew that there was little possibility that another one might fall in the same spot. We returned home with the hope that the next night would not bring any surprises and that we could sleep somewhat peacefully. But the raids on the Osowiec fortress became more frequent because the Soviet forces attempted to break the front line on the Biebrza River in order to force the Germans to flee from the territories in which we lived.

At dawn, we went to bed, tired by our experiences, and we fell asleep immediately. We weren't granted a peaceful sleep, however because a sudden knocking on our window made us jump to our feet. How great was my parents' astonishment to see a Soviet Russian soldier on the other side of the window! At first, my fearful parents didn't know what to do or how to act. Since Germans were all around, had we been caught with the Russian soldier in our house, we would all surely have been shot.

Despite this, a sense of humanity prevailed. My father opened the door in haste, and speaking in Russian, invited him inside. The soldier had lost his orientation during the night and didn't know where he was. When my parents told him that he was in the German zone, he panicked and begged my parents to save his life. My mother, taking advantage of the nightly darkness, took the poor fellow to the barn. There she hid him in a specially prepared hideout, telling him to keep completely quiet.

My parents lived in constant fear and prayed that an ordinary event wouldn't bring the Germans to search the barn. They hoped that soon the Soviets would push the Germans from the area. Their hope was in vain, and the front stood at the Biebrza River for almost six months. Meanwhile, my mother carried food to the barn three times a day, which she hid in a pail. In that way, she fed the soldier. In retrospect, I'm able to appreciate the courage of my parents who did not hesitate, even for a moment, to save someone's life while risking their own.

Ivan (in English, John, the same as my father's name), as the soldier called himself, told my parents what had happened during the offensive of Soviet soldiers that ill-fated night. Many Soviet soldiers perished while crossing the river, but both he and his friend were able to make it to the other side. Unfortunately, a round of fire from a machine gun fatally wounded his friend. The dark night saved Ivan's life as he roamed and accidentally found our house. He knocked on the door hoping to find help, and as it turned out, he wasn't disappointed.

One night my father, using his tried and true method "without a squeal," killed a pig, and it seemed like no one had turned him in. Sporadically, he even helped his neighbors do the same, simply because he knew how to do it. The farmers were given an order to raise pigs, but only for German army soldiers, not to feed their own families. The next day we were surprised to see two German soldiers walking our way. Not having enough time to hide anything, my mother took a sheet, wrapped it around the piece of meat, laid it on the furnace, sat me on it, and ordered, "Henry, sit on it and don't move!"

My parents' fear was beyond words because they had no idea for what purpose the German soldiers were coming. In any case, whether for harboring a Soviet soldier or for killing a pig, we could face the same punishment—execution or deportation to a death camp. My mother began to pray until her pleading to God for salvation was interrupted by a loud banging of the rifle butt on the door.

My father opened the door, and as soon as the soldiers stepped through the threshold, the search began. I sat calmly in my spot, and no one touched me. One of the soldiers opened the hatch door to the basement and descended the ladder. My father followed him. The German opened a barrel that contained the rest of the meat of the pig, which we killed the day before. The soldier reported to the one upstairs that there wasn't anything downstairs. The other one had already checked the pot and oven, where my mother had hidden the meat at the last moment, but he did not want our deaths on his conscience either, so he said that he hadn't found anything. They left the house, but we couldn't be certain that they wouldn't go to the barn. When my parents noticed that the Germans were headed toward Osowiec, they both fell to their knees to thank God for saving their lives once again. Perhaps the sight of four frightened children caused the soldiers to spare us our lives, or they simply had a conscience and were human in the full sense of the word.

As it turned out later, it was our own countryman who informed the occupier about the pig that my father killed. My parents never found out the reason for the behavior of this so-called human. They were not able to understand why anyone could have such hatred that they would give us up to a certain death!

Soon after this event, Soviet forces once again launched an attack on the Germans, this time holding the front line on our territory for a few weeks. This marked the end of Ivan's suffering. When my parents informed him that he could finally come out of hiding, there was no end to his joy. Both sides breathed a sigh of relief. Hunger struck us as well because the meat from the pig was long gone. It also struck the Soviet soldiers, for whom the food rations never arrived. My mother baked a few loaves of bread from the remains of flour and laid them on the table near the window. Because this was in the evening, soon everyone went to sleep. In the morning, my father noticed that there was only one loaf of bread! Frightened, he awakened my mother asking where she had hidden the missing loaves of bread. They could not find the answer, so the blame fell on Ivan. It was he who had to have stolen them. But how? The windows and doors were still closed.

Since Ivan sat in the nearby trenches, my parents invited him into the house and directly asked him why he would resort to stealing when he knew that if he asked, he would be given his appropriate share. He confessed and begged for forgiveness, but he was sure that if he had asked, he wouldn't have gotten more than half a loaf, and there were fourteen soldiers dying of hunger. He just wanted to keep them alive. All that was left was to forgive him.

The mystery of how Ivan took the bread was solved as well. He removed the glass from the window, but first, he had to scratch out the filling around the pane. Then he unscrewed the hinges very quietly, so as not to wake my parents who slept nearby. He slipped the loaves into a bag, replaced the windowpane, reinserted the screws, and happily returned to his colleagues. They emptied the bag in the blink of an eye, eagerly devouring the attained bread. My parents treated Ivan like a member of the family, so they soon forgot about the incident, even though, we, as a family, were hungry from then on since we had no flour left to bake more bread. The war brought its own circumstances, and one paid no attention to small incidents because, after all, it was a matter of survival, saving one's life while not causing harm to others.

German planes were seen returning more often badly beaten up by Soviet anti-aircraft artillery. One of the planes even fell near our house. It had a full load of bombs onboard, which it couldn't drop since it flew too close to the ground. Its own bombs would have killed the pilot in an attempt to drop them. Another German plane attempted to land somewhere nearby, intending to pick up the crew from the downed plane. Unfortunately, my brother and I were playing in that spot, and it seemed like the wheels of the plane were about to graze our heads. The force of the oncoming plane's gust was so strong that it toppled us over several times. The plane circled around and began to fly in our direction again. Terrified that it was us who they wanted to kill, we ran toward the house. Ivan ran out to meet us, grasped the backs of our heads with his palms, and began to calm us down by saying, "Nie bojsia malczyk!" (Don't be afraid, children).

I cannot recall Ivan's face in my mind. However, I still clearly hear his words ringing in my ears. Ivan promised my parents that when the war ended, he would absolutely visit us because the kind of help they gave him was unforgettable. He didn't keep his word, most likely because he perished on the way to Berlin. That is the destiny of a soldier, no matter on which side he is fighting.

The Germans refused to retreat. In their next attack, they pushed the Soviets to the other side of the Biebrza River once again, this time giving us only twenty-four hours to abandon our properties. Our buildings were located on a hill near the Osowiec fortress in a strategic point, in the point of view of the military. These buildings were in the way of artillery fire.

These were desperate moments for my parents because they were forced to abandon everything, their whole life's earnings, to its fate. They could not take their belongings with them, so my father buried only as many of them as would fit in a trunk. Before burying the trunk, he called all of us children to him and showed us the noble family crest in a gold-plated frame, so that we would not forget about it and be proud of our heritage. Later he wrapped it in foil and placed it at the very top of the trunk, which he locked shut with a padlock. I wasn't able to see him bury it or where it was hidden. I didn't understand what the crest meant, but I knew that it was important since my father pointed it out to us with such significance.

We left our home with our weeping mother leading her children. My father, with the usual serious look on his face, walked first carrying only the necessities, a bit of food and some clothing. They forged ahead, not knowing who would take in such destitute people with four kids into their home. The situation was unenviable.

When we arrived at the home of our distant cousins, my father entered alone. We patiently waited outside wondering, "Will they take us in or not?" Time seemed to creep along slowly. Then our cousin ran outside and invited us into the house. We saw joy in their eyes and that comforted us. We were happy to nestle up close to them.

Evening approached as all of the children played outside. Suddenly my older siblings noticed a glow in the sky. We saw our buildings burning and called to our father. My mother, shocked by the news, didn't want to watch.

My father walked up a hill and stood staring at the glow as if hypnotized by it. I ran to my father and looked into his eyes. For the first time, I saw big tears flowing from my dear father's eyes. I knew that these were tears of despair, but I could do nothing to help. I just stood at his side and looked at the glow, which took on a sinister shape and became very clear because the sun had long set. My father stood a long time, a very long time, until the glow disappeared from the horizon. Then he took me by the hand, and we both walked to my cousin's house, not saying a word to each other.

For the first night, we were able to sleep calmly, although not very comfortably since we were on the floor, but we felt safe. Our hosts made us feel comfortable and treated us like close family members. Unfortunately, the second night was quite unpleasant for us. The fog wrapped the entire area so densely that we could only see a step ahead. Suddenly, the neighbor ran over. Terrified, holding a wet handkerchief to his mouth and nose, he informed us that the Germans had released toxic gas. Our cousin immediately tore a new bed sheet to pieces, soaked it in water, and placed it over our mouths and noses as she told us to breathe only through it. She and others still remembered when during World War I, on the night of August 15, 1915, the Germans used toxic gas, killing many Russian soldiers at the Osowiec fortress and residents of nearby villages.

The decision was made to escape immediately from the place of danger, and once again, we took what we could. Each of us, like a flock of geese with my father in the lead, slowly walked away from the river and fortress toward the woods. Since we each clutched our belongings in one hand and held the handkerchiefs up to our mouths with the other, we walked slowly. We admired our father, who knew where he was going in such dense fog. He knew very well the topography of the area and flawlessly led the way forward where he intended. From time to time, my father would stop and survey the situation, listening for German language nearby. We did not want to fall into their hands because that would end badly.

The sun finally rose, and we could spot the first boughs of trees. The fog slowly subsided. When we reached a haystack, my father announced that this would now be our home. He started to tear apart the hay and make a larger opening inside. My mother threw aside the already torn hay. Then my parents invited us into the opening. We went inside like rats, one after the other, with me, the youngest, at the end of the group. It was dark, but our eyes quickly adjusted to the new environment. Exhausted, we fell on the hay like flies, in our clothes just as we had come. Due to lack of space, we lay huddled together as we immediately fell asleep.

We awoke around noon. My mother called us outside. We were surprised that breakfast was already prepared, spread out atop of a cloak. As usual, we prayed before each meal. This time, when we got to the words, "Give us this day our daily bread," we looked at each other because we noticed that, in fact, we had bread, but only this day. One slice was allotted to each of us, and it disappeared in the blink of an eye into our starved stomachs. Our father wasn't at breakfast, so we asked about him.

"He went to survey where and how he can get food for us," was the answer. He probably went hungry to leave us more food.

"Mom, what's going to happen if Dad doesn't find anything and doesn't bring back anything?"

"Don't worry. He promised that even if he was to dig up something from the ground, he would bring food back and won't leave us to our fate."

We trusted and believed in our parents because they had never disappointed us. This time, too, we hoped that we would not have to lie down to sleep too hungry. It had been a long time since we ate, and we became used to hunger, but it would have been better if we could be full for a few days in a row. Satiety became our childhood dream, and the prayer verse "our daily bread" became so significant that we prayed the words more loudly and emphasized them.

Evening was upon us, and we ran and played around the haystack, becoming hungrier. We longingly looked to see if, by chance, our father was coming, carrying something for us. We began to lose hope, and our mother called us to sleep when a figure appeared in the darkness, which we recognized as our father.

We yelled, "Dad's coming!" and noticed that he was carrying something on his back in a bag. We ran out to meet him, and we helped to carry the bag, hoping that we would not go to sleep hungry this time. We arrived at the haystack and threw ourselves on the bag like vultures. We took out its contents one at a time. Our parents didn't say anything, just waited until we emptied the bag. There wasn't much of it, but for us it was a fortune. We were so very happy. There was even milk in a bottle, a loaf of bread, lard in a jar, and potatoes. What a treat; what a celebration it was for us! Someone spread out a jacket on the ground, and we sat down right away looking to our mother to hand out the treats at last.

For a few days, as long as there was lard, bread, and water in the pond (standing water in the meadow, which after boiling was made potable), we were able to exist. It was a fight for our survival. The supply of lard and bread quickly ran out, and my parents had to find other resources. Father knew these areas, and just as he did the first time, he went to the nearest village to request a piece of bread, some potatoes, or a bottle of milk. Each time we were happy that we had something to eat. No one thought about tomorrow because tomorrow was far away, and it wasn't right to talk about it.

Finally, people from the nearby villages, running out of supplies themselves, gave less and less to us. More often than not, we were hungry rather than full. Full isn't the right word here because a slice of bread or a single potato for the entire day was not enough to be able to say that we were satiated. We even resorted to desperate measures. My father had no other choice but to go out at night where the potatoes grew and dig them out with his hands carefully so the owner of the field didn't notice. He had to steal in order to bring his four children something to eat.

The activities of the Russian artillery continued, and often bullets would explode by our haystack, fortunately not harming anyone. I remember the menacing whistle of the bullets flying over our heads. My father explained to us that if a bullet is making a constant whistling sound then that means it will keep flying through, and there is nothing to fear; but if it makes a clacking noise, that means it will drop somewhere nearby, and that is dangerous. We were in constant danger, whether it was from gunfire or bombs dropped from airplanes because the raids were becoming more frequent.

My family wasn't alone in this situation. The people that lived in neighboring haystacks lived through the same ordeals. We stayed there for over two months, and when fall came, and along with it the bothersome frosts, the situation was worse. I was even able to slide on the ice with my bare feet because my shoes had been long worn out.

One night there came an announcement from an airplane with its engine turned off for a moment (so as not to drown out words). The announcement, made in Polish, was that everyone should leave this area because soon the war was going to be over. After this night, one family even hung out their comforters to dry as they felt safer after this announcement. They didn't realize what danger they had put themselves and others in with their premature decision. An air raid followed, and the entire area was bombed, especially the white objects that looked like army tents. The comforters turned to feathers and covered a large part of the forest. By a miracle no one was killed; only a few people were wounded. The incident and a total lack of resources for further survival caused people to leave the forest in search of other shelter.

Each family had their own plan. My father, having consulted with a fellow distressed neighbor, that is, the resident of the next haystack, decided to take one of the beaten down and trodden paths toward the east. We hadn't even walked two kilometers when suddenly a German soldier jumped out from behind the bushes, pointed a gun at us, and in a stern voice yelled, "Halt!"

A second soldier, assisting the first one, stood nearby, and had a machine gun pointed at us. My father ordered us to stop and stay where we were because each move could be interpreted as an attempt to escape, which would mean certain death. The first soldier walked up to us and started a search. They were most likely looking for weapons. Then he told us to follow him while the other one, with his finger on the trigger, walked behind us. Finally, we reached a clearing in the middle of the woods, where we were ordered to sit on the ground. Only then were we able to spot the German army hidden in the forest.

It was the end of September 1944. We had left our hideout in the haystack early in the morning, and noon was nearly approaching. More and more people, who were captured just like us by the Germans, came to the clearing. One of the farmers even arrived in his wagon loaded with his possessions, his dog calmly walking behind. Near evening, the entire grassy clearing was bursting at the seams with so many people flushed out of the forest by this trap.

Hunger bothered us immensely, and only the cries of children younger than I indicated that they too were hungry. Neither my parents nor the others were able to help, and everyone became only a passive witness to what was happening. German soldiers constantly walked around keeping order, which wasn't disturbed at all because everyone sat calmly on the ground exhausted and hungry. One of the soldiers watching over us looked around, and then threw a pack of crackers to the children next to us. The toddlers greedily began to swallow them. At that moment, my stomach climbed to my throat. The hunger grew to the point that I contemplated walking up to them and asking for at least one cracker. *And what if they refuse to give it to me? Then I'll go and take it by force,* the thought overtook my mind. A moment later, a great shame came upon me that something like that could even cross my mind. I turned the other way so I wouldn't see what was happening with the crackers. I became overcome with sadness. Why hadn't the soldier noticed me?

A few minutes later, I saw him returning. I looked into his eyes, and he must have understood my pleading for mercy. He walked up to the truck, took something out, and headed in our direction again. He discretely glanced at me once again, and this time, he threw a pack of crackers to us. He was probably making sure that his commanders didn't notice what he was doing.

My father, bending to the ground, opened the packet. Beginning with me, he offered each of us some, not leaving anything for my mother and himself. When evening came, the Germans gathered only the young children. They arranged us in line. I stood as the last child behind my brother. They rationed out a slice of bread for each. They finally reached my brother. He got the last slice, and there was none left for me. The German told my brother in broken Polish to share his slice with me. I was sure that I would receive a piece. After all, he was my brother, and at the very least, he should act brotherly toward me and give me a little. The German waited until my brother broke off a piece and handed it to me.

"Gut, gut!" he said and walked away.

We returned to my parents. Each of us clutched their half slice of bread in their hand, but we had to share it further with the older siblings. We went to sleep hungry and directly on the ground. The night was a real nightmare. Prior to that, we at least had the hay to protect us from the cold. This time there wasn't even that. Nevertheless, no one complained. Only the cries of one of the children interrupted the nightly quiet.

The morning greeted us with a beautiful sunrise, and it foreshadowed a nice, sunny day. Soon the yelling of the German soldiers interrupted the morning calm, and everyone was ordered to their feet. The clearing was full of people. It was surprising that in one day and one night so many could be rounded up from the forest. An order to march followed. A couple of soldiers in the front and a few on the sides and in the back watched to see if there was any attempt at dissension. Among those walking, there was one already mentioned wagon with the driver and a dog slowly following behind it.

Suddenly, my sister saw a doll lying on the road. She ran up to it, picked it up, and hugged it. One of the children from the front of the march must have dropped it, not being able to carry it much longer. My sister was so happy and clutched that doll tightly in her arms the whole time. Unfortunately, a few kilometers further, she too had to let go of her find. In tears, she laid it back on the road. No one was able to help anyone else due to incredible exhaustion because the marchers barely held themselves up on their own, and there was no end of the road in sight.

The situation looked hopeless when finally there were orders to stop. Everyone fell to the ground where they stood. It was the second day that my parents had nothing to eat, and we children only had two army crackers and a bit of bread the previous day. What was one slice of bread for the four of us?

On one of the rest stops, one of the escorting soldiers approached the dog that accompanied us in this sad procession, probably intending to pet it, when it showed its teeth and menacingly growled at the stranger. What happened a second later stunned everyone! The soldier began to shoot at the dog, although there were plenty of people around. He shot a series of ammo from his machine gun as the dog instinctively ran behind a tree to try to save its life. The soldier did not stop but ran around the tree shooting until the dog fell dead.

Everyone stood still. We expected the worst to happen; either the owner of the dog would be executed or even several people. The angered German soldier was beyond the reach of the law and could open fire on innocent people. Fortunately, one of the officers approached him. After their short conversation, we were ordered to our feet again and forced to continue the march despite the short rest, if it could be called a rest at all.

As evening fell, the entire procession reached its destination, Grajewo, where a concentration camp was prepared for us. We saw a high fence, barbed wire, and a building in which the smell of chlorine didn't let us breathe normally. That's how densely it filled the air. The men were separated, and the children were left with their mothers. We didn't realize that we would only be able to see our father just once. Everyone, without exception, was ordered to strip naked. Rumor spread that we would now be killed, since taking all clothing off was known to precede an execution. The women started to pray loudly. Someone started singing a song to the Holy Mary, "Under your care…," and the entire room was filled with song and cries for help.

I was surprised to see my mother, my neighbor, and other women naked. I didn't understand that this was an order, and to the officer, its non-fulfillment meant death. A few hours later, we were told to put our clothes back on, and everyone breathed a sigh of relief because they hoped to see the next day. In the evening, they gave us our first meal—a bowl of soup per person. Whoever could get a piece of potato was lucky.

The second day at the concentration camp is remembered as a day of great sadness for us. In the morning, they ordered us to gather in the square. On the other side of the high gate made of barbed wire, we saw the men standing. When we walked closer, we could recognize our father among them. It turned out that they were chosen to be taken away for forced labor in Germany. These were our last moments with my father, and we couldn't even hug him because the evil barbed-wire fence came between us. Upon the orders to march away, we wept and lamented, since no one could predict what was to happen beyond the gate. My older sister began to choke and vomit with despair and cries. As my mother tried to help her, my father disappeared with the others behind the camp gate.

We were left with my mother "for better or worse," and the latter had already been with us for a few years. There was no end in sight. My father was taken away, and no one could predict where and what destiny was awaiting him. A menacing emptiness filled our hearts. Only questions remained. What will happen to our father? What will happen to us? What fate awaits us?

We were lucky that my uncle's fiancée, who lived in Grajewo, found out that we were in the camp and went to the camp commander. Because she knew German, she asked him to set us free while handing him a bribe. The commander accepted the bribe. He must have been satisfied with its amount because two weeks later he released us.

We were overjoyed but having left the camp, we were still left with the questions. Where were we to go, which way, and to whom?

My mother decided we would go to her sister Regina's, who lived in Swidry, about fifteen kilometers from Grajewo. We were free, and no one complained, despite our bleeding feet at the end of the walk. Our aunt came to welcome us with open arms. This lifted our spirits and eased our suffering. Our aunt's husband was also taken away for labor to Germany, and she was left behind with five children. That is how two lonely women and nine children came to live in a two-room house with a tiny kitchen. The other side of the house was seized by the Germans to serve as a shop for their craftsmen—a cobbler and a tailor.

There's always a blessing in disguise, as the famous saying goes. This time we were happy to be living next to German craftsmen. Having mercy on our fate and seeing our starved bodies, they offered us crackers, breadcrumbs, and sometimes even chocolate. We liked them very much, and we would play close to their door, especially during dinnertime. They would share with us what was left over from their meal.

There were surprises as well. My mother bought a cow from a German shepherd in exchange for a half liter of homemade vodka. The cow was immediately slaughtered, but no one reported us to the German authorities. At times, we would even eat meat without bread. It was amazing! We hadn't had such feasts since the beginning of the war, that is, in five years. Each of us could eat when we wanted and however much we wanted. This only lasted so long, and then once again, we were forced to tighten our belts.

My mother, to earn money for bread, found work digging potatoes. She left in the morning when we all were still asleep and returned in the evening. I missed her very much, and I withered away with longing. That is why one day I decided to shorten my waiting time, and I went to look for her myself. I walked straight ahead hoping that I would find her somewhere. Unfortunately, I was too far from home, and when I lost hope of finding her, I decided to head back. I turned around, but instead of houses, I saw the forest edge. I lost my sense of direction and started to run, but I wasn't sure if it was the right way back. Night fell, the road ended, and I ended up in the middle of a freshly plowed field. I stumbled several times, catching my foot against the balk. I was completely exhausted as night fell. I started to despair that I would never see my dear mom again. I was terrified because many times I had heard stories of wolves tearing people to shreds. I was left to mercy and the merciless whim of fate. I hid like a rabbit in a hollow under the balk. Exhausted, and despite the cold, I fell asleep.

After returning home, my mother couldn't find me anywhere. In a panic, she informed all the village residents who, without delay, set out to find me. Unfortunately, the night did not lend much hope of finding me. Nevertheless, they searched tirelessly until morning. Finally one of the searchers discovered me curled up, in tears and shivering with cold, but alive. He immediately covered me with his jacket, and to the delight of all of those seeking me, he carried me home to my rejoicing mother.

Finally, the End of the War!

The end of the war approached. In January 1945, the Soviet Russians had emancipated our terrains. One night someone knocked at our door. Our mother jumped up from bed to see who the intruder was at this time of night, disquieting our sleep. She couldn't believe her eyes when on the other side of the door she saw her husband. They fell into an embrace and loudly began asking each other questions. Everyone jumped to his or her feet to welcome such an unexpected guest. Because I slept a deep sleep, I wasn't woken up. In the morning when I got up from the bedding on the floor where I slept, I saw a man with a long beard and mustache, who came to me to hug and squeeze me. I retreated to the depth of the room. I felt resentment toward my mother for trying to convince me that this was my father. After all, my father didn't have a beard and moustache and looked completely different.

Pressed to the corner of the room, I stared at this strange man, and he never took his eyes off of me. Finally, he got up and left to go to the kitchen. After a while, he returned with a slice of bread with butter, the butter thicker than the bread. He approached me and asked that I not refuse but eat it, since he had carried the bread and butter on his own shoulders from Germany just for us. It was such a fine morsel that I couldn't refuse, so I took it without any qualms and began to eat. As I chewed, I became more and more convinced that this man must be my father because a stranger would never give me this much butter. I ate it greedily, and from that moment, I was sure that this was my father. During this entire time my father observed me, and when I swallowed the last bite, I didn't protest when he took me in his arms, brought me in, and held me close. At that moment, our close bond came alive again, and I was happy that I once again had a dad.

We were all happy, and the next night again promised to be sleepless since we had much to share with one another. Suddenly, someone again knocked on the door. This time my father opened the door. It became apparent that it was another prisoner of war returning from Germany who wanted to relay a message but directly to my aunt. Lament and weeping followed as the stranger brought news of her husband's death. He also described the terrible way my uncle was killed by German murderers. They threw him in a tied sack down a flight of stairs until he died.

Our happiness melted with the despair and sadness of our cousins. My aunt's children were the same age as us. We had a common language and the same point of view on many issues. That night, we were unable help them ease their cries and despair upon the loss of their father. My aunt did not break down but bravely rose to the new challenge that unexpectedly fell on her shoulders. She knew that she would now have to feed and raise the children on her own, and later life proved that she rose to the occasion splendidly.

My mother asked my father that they not return to Budne. She wanted to make her way to the recovered territories where houses and farms were ready to be settled (left behind by German settlers). Many farmers did this already and were happy with their decisions. Nevertheless, my father's decision was a determined negative. He vowed to himself that if he were to return alive, he would never set foot on recovered soil from Germany, despite those lands being returned to Poland.

My father had unpleasant experiences while performing labor in Germany. Two of his friends attempted to escape, failed, were caught, and later severely punished. All of the prisoners were ordered to stand at attention. A few men, among them my father, were selectively chosen and ordered to dig a ditch. They brought my father's two friends to the readied ditch, and one of the German soldiers shot them in the back of their heads. Not one of the soldiers checked if they were still alive. They ordered, however, that the bodies be buried. Everyone was warned that each attempt to escape would end in this way.

It was appalling. That is why my father didn't even want to return to those days in his memories, much less to permanently settle on these terrains. Many people, even from the neighboring villages, took advantage of the situation and settled in what were called the recovered territories. In reality, we had nothing to return to because our buildings were leveled, and the field was riddled with mines. No one, however, could have changed my father's mind about going back to Budne.

I would like to note that during this time, in the West, we recovered our ancestral lands from the time of the Piast dynasty (from the year 966), but we lost our Eastern territories that were annexed into the Soviet Republics, that is, Soviet Russia. Poles chased out from those areas were forced to settle on lands abandoned by the German population in the recovered territories.

The paradox of post-war Poland was that compared to the pre-war state, it had lost over seventy thousand-square kilometers of territory despite the fact that the Polish Army, to a great extent, contributed to the victory over Germany while fighting in the east and west of Europe.

The compliance of the United States and Great Britain in Yalta toward Stalin was astonishing and humiliating to both of these countries' leaders. It could easily be said that Poland was betrayed and sold to Soviet Russia. After this brief reflection, I return to the history of my family, which continued despite the war.

One day my mother's brother, Witold, came to visit us. My mother's parents, her three younger brothers, and her sister lived in the village of Modzele. When the horses were hitched, and Uncle Witold bid farewell to us, my oldest sister Anastazja decided to go with him to visit Grandma and Grandpa.

As they were nearing the village, they were stopped by the German armed police and ordered to get off the wagon. They were escorted to a point where the entire population of the village was gathered. There my uncle found out what had happened. The Germans heard gunfire. They surrounded the village assuming that Home Army partisans were hiding there.

A German officer (through an interpreter) demanded that whoever shot the gun step forward; otherwise, everyone would be shot. He gave everyone ten minutes to think. Either the culprit wasn't among those who were stopped or he became cowardly, since no one stepped forward. Time elapsed, and the officer raised his hand to give orders to shoot the hostages.

My sister always speaks of this moment with a bitter tone in her voice despite the years that have passed. She remembers the event clearly, although she was only fifteen years old at the time. Our uncle hugged her tightly to him just as the German officer raised his hand to order the execution of those innocent people. The terror was heightened at this moment since earlier the village had just been burned down. In the foreground of the fire and smoke, the raised hand of the German officer was truly the hand of an executioner. Just then, they all spotted a motorcyclist who appeared out of nowhere, like a ghost, and approached the German soldiers at full throttle. The execution was halted. The motorcyclist delivered a message to the officer. A moment later, a new decision was announced. This time the village head was to choose three people from the crowd to be shot before the eyes of the others. The village head, a young, handsome, well-educated man, shocked the executioners with his decision. He refused to point out anyone and asked that he be executed instead of the three that he was supposed to choose.

Unfortunately, he was placed on the other side. From the row of people among whom were women, children, and as I mentioned my sister, Anastazja, one of the German soldiers chose three adult men. They placed them next to the village head. One of them made an attempt to escape and came close to a nearby stream when a series of ammo from the machine gun reached him. He fell dead. A second one of the chosen men began to cry. The village head stood calmly looking up to the sky. A third one ripped his shirt, made the sign of the cross, and began to say, "I am innocent," when series of bullets from the gun interrupted his words. The rest were dismissed to return to their homes. This event took place two days before the emancipation of these lands. It was an irony of fate.

The war migrated, from east to west, and the German forces retreated along the entire length of the front. The Germans fiercely defended themselves and did not want to concede even a piece of the land. They placed mines in the fields behind them in order to stifle the maneuvers of the attacking Soviet and Polish forces and to ensure the greatest losses to their enemies. These Polish Army units of the Polish-Soviet forces were formed in 1944 and were composed of Polish citizens, the very citizens who were deported from former Poland to Siberia by Stalin. This deportation began in September 17, 1939, and ended when Hitler began the war with the Soviet Union in 1941. Because of German aggression against the Soviets, Sikorski, the Polish Prime Minister who moved with the Polish Government to London at the beginning of the war in 1939, struck a deal with Stalin to form Polish military units that fought alongside Soviet forces. Sikorski surely did that to help Poland become free after the war. Unfortunately, he was killed by unknown forces a short time after he signed the agreement with Stalin.

We expected emancipation at any moment, as the sound of artillery and machine guns came closer. We hid where we could; each basement was packed full of people. The time finally came when Poland's northeastern territories, where we presided, were liberated following a bloody battle. A general euphoria followed. It was believed that this time the Germans would leave the lands for the last time. The front moved closer to the west, and the way to Berlin became shorter by the day. A new spirit entered the people. They began to go about their daily responsibilities with enthusiasm.

One day because we had neither a horse nor a vehicle, our grandfather from our mother's side came to help us bring in the potatoes from the field. Unfortunately, on the way back from the field, he drove over an anti-tank mine. My grandpa had good and bad luck all rolled into one because the mine only exploded the back of the wagon.

Of course, nothing was left of the back part of the wagon, but the potatoes he was carrying saved his life because they shielded him from the shrapnel and flying debris from the destroyed wagon. My grandfather held onto the front part as the frightened horses pulled right into the front yard of the house and stopped there. What astonishment ensued when it turned out that aside from scratches, my grandpa had left the incident unscathed. It was probably not his time yet, and that is why he remained in this world. God probably had other plans for him.

The Nazi army retreated along the entire front line, and soon Modzele, my mother's parents' hometown, was liberated. We were invited to settle there, as it would be close to our family village of Budne. We graciously accepted the pleasant offer. There was plenty of room for all of us in our new home, even for our newborn sister, Barbara. I was happy that I was no longer the youngest of the siblings and that the spot was taken by my sister. Unfortunately, she wasn't meant to live long. Due to a lack of medical care and medication, she died within three months. When we returned from the funeral, my father carried her cradle out of the house, and it seemed to me that along with the cradle, he was taking out Barbara. For a long time, I could not get used to the fact that she wasn't there any longer and that she would never return.

A few weeks later, our village was also liberated. My parents went, of course, in a borrowed horse and wagon to find out about the chances of our return to Budne. They had many difficulties getting there, since all the bridges were blown up by retreating German forces. The first challenge they had was to traverse the canal. They were able to cross it despite the deep water. They became completely soaked since at points, the horse lost the ground under his feet, and the wagon became entirely submerged in water.

They arrived at the village of Osowiec. Further travel was impossible with the wagon. The area was riddled with signs that this terrain was mined. They continued farther on foot. My father walked slowly, carefully checking the terrain, while my mother followed him stepping in his footsteps. They finally reached a bunker in the ground, one very well masked and covered with a thick layer of sand. That was the legacy that the Germans left after destroying my parents' beautiful home and farm buildings. My father entered first, checking the entrance beforehand. He noticed something on the floor that appeared to be a chest covered in red velvet.

He told my mother to keep her distance from the bunker while he approached the trunk to see if there were any wires on the floor. Slowly and very carefully, he first checked the red fabric. He suspected that it might be a trap. He found a thin wire underneath the fabric. He gently broke it and took off the cover. Underneath was a plain trunk and in it a mine and detonator attached to that exact wire. If my father had taken off the cover, he would have detached the split pin from the detonator, and the mine would have ripped him to pieces.

It later turned out that another man from Osowiec died in a similar circumstance. There was a variety of innovative traps. It was mostly children, unaware of the danger, that died from them, and how many were seriously injured, no one knows for sure.

Adults were killed as well, whether it was from random mines or other types of games with weapons or explosives. That is how my cousin died, by throwing anti-tank grenades into the river. The grenades had wooden handles. Inside them was a string that set the detonator off when it was pulled. After pulling the string, at first one could hear a hissing sound, which meant that the grenade would go off any second. It was supposed to be thrown away immediately. One of the grenades failed to give off a hiss, so my cousin was convinced that it was a dud and didn't throw it away from himself. A friend, who was playing with him, ran behind a concrete barrier and saved his own life. The force of the explosion was so strong that it threw my cousin through the barrier and into the river. His friend pulled him out of the water, but what remained of him were shreds of a human. His hands were torn off, his eyes were burnt, and his whole body was mangled from the shrapnel.

His determined brother, in hopes of saving his life, put his body on a wagon and took him to a hospital in Szczuczyn, over twenty-five kilometers away, a significant distance for that mode of transportation. They took the shortest route through Modzele, where they came upon my father. The poor soul recognized my father's voice and asked, "Uncle, will I live?"

"Of course, son, you will most certainly live," replied my father.

In the hospital, after looking over the patient, the doctor went into the hallway and talked to the older brother. He told him that my cousin would have no chance of survival. Listening to the pleas to save this young man's life, the doctor only shook his head and asked that they pray that he have a quick death. He added that the boy's agony was a horrendous suffering because the hospital didn't have any pain medication. After a few hours of agony, my cousin passed away from this world.

The war was near its end. The front was already beyond Poland's borders. All that remained was the battle for Berlin. Life went on, and now we had to work hard to survive. My parents decided to return to their lands as soon as possible. The first order of things was to de-mine our fields and then our meadows. All of the sappers, the engineers in charge of disarming mines, were off to war, so civilians needed to be recruited for the perilous job. Trenches dotted the area, so my father decided to penetrate at least those that were near the bunker. He noticed something lying on the ground, and as he looked closer, he was surprised to see that it was a wristwatch. He didn't pick it up right away because it could have been a mine, a trap. He knelt down and checked to see if it was tied to anything. Only then did he pick it up. It turned out to be a gold watch.

My parents returned do Osowiec where they found a volunteer to de-mine our field and meadows in exchange for that gold watch. The man who agreed to de-mine our area had already done so for many other farmers and was a skilled expert in the functions of mines, as well as to how to safely discharge them. The following day, he took to the task and at such a pace that my father feared for the man's life. After he discharged each mine individually or found a dud, he placed it one atop of the other. When he finished the task, it formed a big pile.

Then he placed a dynamite stick underneath the pile, fastened it with a fuse that he lit, and ran with my father one hundred meters away and hid in a ditch. When the burning fuse reached the dynamite, there was an enormous explosion of the pile of mines and duds.

Although the village of Osowiec was two kilometers away from the site of the explosion, many homes lost their windows. The sapper didn't foresee the consequences of the operation. Fortunately, no one laid claim to any material losses, and that's how the matter ended.

The next day my father was able to begin plowing the field with a borrowed horse. However, he first prayed fervently that the merciful Lord have him in His care because there still could have been duds or a mine that the sapper had missed. Fortunately, the first day ended without surprises, and my happy father returned to rest. He was hopeful that the coming days would be as lucky. My parents settled into the aforementioned bunker, and despite the uncomfortable conditions and lack of necessities, they were happy to be on their own.

My siblings and I remained in Modzele because my parents had neither a bed nor sheets nor pots nor livestock. They had only the clothes on their backs, and those were far from new. Instead of actual shoes, they wore shoes made from pigskin with wooden soles. We wore those kinds of shoes as well. They rubbed against our feet and ankles until they bled. No one complained because that was the reality. Everyone had to adapt to it. Those who were still alive were happy to be alive, and each secured their daily bread in their own way, not thinking about what they would eat tomorrow. Sorrel and other wild plants constituted normal food. One time my mother gathered an entire basket of berries and took it to Goniadz, about five kilometers away, where she sold them in the market. With her earnings, she bought a pair of pots. This was a good start because she could make soup out of sorrel or mushrooms.

September approached, and my mother's brother was assigned to Osowiec from Grajewo to teach and serve as the principal of the newly formed primary school. With the donations from an American charity called UNRA, my uncle received a cow that he gave to my parents for raising, ensuring milk for both himself and us. My parents brought my older siblings Romuald, Anastazja, and Henryka, who had to go to school, to their bunker. They left me in Modzele with my grandparents and Uncle Witold, who took over the farm from his aging parents, my grandparents.

In the meantime, kind people gave my parents a few sheep, a couple of piglets, a bit of wheat to sow, and a few sacks of potatoes for the winter. The conditions were difficult as winter approached. There was a makeshift furnace in the middle of the bunker, on which my mother cooked for the family and the livestock. This furnace served as a heater as well.

I missed my parents and siblings so much that more often than not, I would shed tears into my pillow as I lay down to sleep. I didn't complain to my uncle about my fate, but one night he heard my weeping and came to see what had happened. I told him the truth, and my uncle tried to convince me that they had nothing to eat there; meanwhile, with him I could have everything I asked for. I asked, or rather begged, that he take me to my mother and father and told him not to worry because I would rather suffer hunger than be away from my family. My uncle turned away and wept. A moment later, he told me that the next morning he would take me to my parents in Budne. To my delight, that's exactly what happened. My parents not only didn't oppose this idea but also were happy with the turn of events. Now the family was complete.

Modzele was about twenty kilometers away from Budne, so my uncle needed to spend the night in order to return to his village the next morning. I was afraid that in the morning something would change, and I would have to go back, but fortunately, no one even mentioned it. When my uncle's wagon disappeared around the bend, I was so happy that I jumped for joy. My uncle returned home, my parents were busy with their own matters, my brother and sisters went to school, and I had a lot of time to explore the area.

Trenches and artillery and tank bases remained everywhere. To my delight, I even found a tank. I had never sat in a tank before, and now this one was my own tank. Nearby I discovered an airplane that was shot down by anti-aircraft gunfire. Aside from a hole in its wing, it didn't have any major damage. What wonders I was able to see and touch in the pilot's cabin; it took my breath away. I imagined that I was a pilot and soared to the skies. It wasn't hard to find ammunition in the trunks, sometimes even still oiled. I hid it where I could and buried it to have it ready just in case I needed it for use.

My father destroyed whatever he found, but of course, he couldn't get to all of it. Meanwhile, I had a lot of time and imagination, and besides, I had to prepare for World War III, which was loudly predicted as starting with America's invasion of Russia. I couldn't imagine not personally participating in defending my country as a soldier.

I also found a great deal of weapons of all sorts—dynamite, anti-tank grenades with wooden handles, and basic ones, which looked like an ostrich egg with a pin and latch. I began to test the weapons and left only the good, ready-to-use ones hidden in places only I knew of. In this way, I hid two rifles that made excellent target shooters, as well as a hand grenade. My neighborhood friends and I would gather all of the duds and throw them into a bonfire. We relished the sight of an exploding mine or artillery bullet. Nothing remained of the fire as a result of the explosion, and a giant cloud of smoke and powder rose above the site. The sight filled us with pride that we were capable of putting on such a beautiful fireworks show. We often had shooting matches. As for the grenade, we took turns carrying it around, a week at a time, so that none of us would feel disadvantaged. Sometimes, for fun, while holding the grenade in our hand, we would pull the pin out and then replace it. We did it, of course, while holding the latch on the grenade, otherwise it would have exploded. Then the grenade returned to the pocket.

One day when it was my turn to carry the grenade, I saw our neighbor, the mother of my grenade playmates, running in the direction of our house. I was playing in the yard when she burst into our house in a big hurry. Only my mother was home. A moment later, they both ran outside and my mother called me to her. She saw my overstuffed pant pocket and asked what I had there.

"A grenade," I answered, as if it were a common children's toy.

"Show it to me," insisted my mother.

I was convinced that she only wanted to see it and that she would return it to me. I took the grenade out of my pocket and handed it to my mother, so she could look at it. I was disappointed when my mother began to lecture me about the dangers of being near a grenade in case of an explosion. I was aware of the dangers, but I didn't realize that a grenade could explode in the least predictable circumstances. My knowledge of operating one would not have been much help.

It was only by chance it was revealed that I was in possession of a grenade. When the neighboring brothers started a fight about whose turn it was to carry the grenade, they turned to their mother to referee the squabble. She asked about the details, and thanks to this, was able to retrieve the grenade. It quite possibly saved our lives. No one asked about the rifles, so they remained in our hands. I buried some of the ammunition near the house, and the rest, for daily use, I kept in a special hiding place underneath the house.

The shooting exercises took place according to a set schedule after classes finished at the school. My parents heard the shots and knew that I was in possession of a weapon. Since I was able to cover my tracks well, there was no way they could find out where I stored it. Nevertheless, they came up with a wonderful idea about how to take it from me. They invited a policeman, whom they knew, to come and persuade to me return the dangerous "toy." I was surprised when late one evening a policeman entered our home, and with a menacing look, came right up to me, passing by my parents.

"Where do you have the rifle?" he asked directly.

There was a silence. I counted on my parents to come to my defense. I lifted my gaze to my father, then my mother, and then back to my father, and to my surprise, I saw no reaction. On the contrary, they acted normally, as if this didn't concern their son at all.

Did they stop loving me or something? I thought.

The policeman stood right next to me. Staring me down from above, he announced, "If you don't bring me the rifle immediately, then get your jacket, and I'll take you to jail. It's cold outside."

I glanced at my parents again to see what impact this had on them, and to my disappointment, I saw complete disinterest on their part. I didn't understand why the change in my loving parents. They were letting me go to jail and didn't even try to defend me. In order to keep from going to jail, I had to give up my rifle; there was pain in my heart.

I ran to fetch it, even though the night was dark. My fear of going to jail prevailed over all of the midnight monsters put together. I brought back the weapon and handed it to the officer. I was afraid of what would happen if he asked for the other rifle. No one expected me to have two rifles, so luckily, one remained in my hiding spot.

One day, my brother informed me that he and a friend were going to disable a landmine. It was in our neighbor's field near our home. I was only allowed to watch from afar. I stood atop a nearby hill and observed to see exactly how "the specialists" did it. They didn't walk; instead, they moved their legs very slowly along the tall hay where they were supposed to find a thin wire, which was connected to a pin of the detonator. If it was pulled out, it would explode on the spot. Fortunately, they noticed the wire, reached the mine, and discharged the detonator. Then they gave it to me because their attempt to detonate it had failed. They were convinced it was a dud. I carried it in my pocket for a few days, and at dinner one day, I pulled the pin out just for fun. There was a flash of light and a loud explosion, but no one was harmed.

My Guardian Angel watched over me. My favorite daily prayer to Him kept me safe and sound even though all kinds of incidents happened, both sad and disturbing.

During my third grade at primary school, my mother's younger sister came to take care of me while my parents were away sorting out important matters. Being a novice altar boy at the time, I served at Holy Mass every day in the Osowiec Church. The church had bells without ringers, so I decided to fix them on my own time. For this, I needed lead, which could be found in some of the rifle bullets. All I had to do was put one of the bullets into the furnace to melt away material that I needed to repair the broken bells. I knew exactly which ones were made of lead and which ones shouldn't be put into the fire as they were explosive and dangerous. The explosive bullets had a different colored tip and were a different shape than the lead ones.

To this day, I don't know how I possibly could have made that mistake. I put the wrong bullet into the furnace. Quite by accident, the bullet exploded just as my aunt walked by the open furnace door. The blazing bullet pierced her hand, and she nearly fainted in pain. I stood there paralyzed and transfixed with fear, not knowing what to do. Fortunately, my aunt knew what to do. She immediately pulled the red-hot bullet out with a knife and placed a wet rag on the burning wound.

I quickly ran to fetch water from the well, and cold compresses eased her pain as she slowly regained her full senses. I stood by her, and in my mind, I begged her for forgiveness. How surprised I was when my aunt took me in her arms. She hugged me and told me that everything would be all right and that it wasn't my fault because I didn't do it intentionally. Accidents do happen for everyone. Good Grief! Despite the sadness, I was happy that my aunt forgave the dreadful deed.

To my relief, her hand healed quickly, and everyone soon forgot about the unfortunate incident. I, on the other hand, did not forget, and from that moment on, I never put anything in the furnace at home anymore. Instead, I would make bonfires in the open field, far from the buildings, where I could do my experimenting.

Primary School

My life changed diametrically when I began my studies on September 1, 1946, at the Osowiec Primary School. I went to school on foot, and when weather permitted and it wasn't too cold, I was often barefoot. I preferred to walk barefoot because the shoes with wooden soles rubbed against my heels and ankles, at times making them bleed. We wrapped rags around our feet, but even those didn't help. No one even dreamed of socks at that time.

My first months in the Osowiec School didn't fill me with optimism. Students from outside of the Osowiec terrain were called names by the native residents, and so I was picked on, only because I had come from another village. I was nicknamed "czajka" (as in lapwing, the bird), most likely because of my last name. I liked the beautiful bird, which reigned in our territories, but I hated the nickname.

Bullies often threatened to give me a whipping after school, and I had to run home from a pack of Osowiec boys who were chasing me. One could only imagine how petrified I was when my strength began to fail me, and they closed in on me. It seemed like the three kilometers between school and home would never end. I ran from them and took shortcuts through wet and muddy meadows. Even though I traversed water and mud, my way was still shorter. Breathing hard and feeling barely alive, I burst into the house all covered in mud, but happy that I was able to escape.

I didn't complain to my parents because my honor forbade it. I didn't know why others were left alone, and I continued to be the object of interest to the Osowiec boys. I defended myself as best as I could, but unfortunately, I sometimes got a big whooping. It wasn't until a couple of months later that I found out the reason for their behavior. My uncle was the teacher and principal at the school that I attended. My uncle as a teacher was very demanding. The students didn't like it, and that is why they called me names.

Unfortunately, my uncle did not spare even me, and he called on me during every class. I resented that even my own family member didn't let me be. What kind of uncle was he when he harassed me in this way? The Osowiec boys noticed that I didn't have it easy. He was even stricter when he dealt with me, so they finally left me alone. After a while, some of my former tormentors became my friends.

The Biebrza River, which ran not too far from our house, overflowed its banks each spring and autumn and flooded the nearby fields and meadows. At times, the flood was so tremendous that the only way to reach the school was by boat. In the winter, however, the river would freeze over. All of the children would merrily play on the ice. Whoever had ice skates really had a chance to show off. I was one of those lucky ones who owned ice skates. I would fasten them to the wooden soles of my shoes, which in this rare case proved to be indispensable. The skates, attached to these soles, stayed on perfectly and never fell off. When I arrived at school on these ice skates, my friends were quite envious of me. As if this weren't enough, my uncle, the teacher, gave me a brand new pair of skis as a gift. At that moment, I changed my mind about him.

There was a shortage of teachers after the war because most members of the Polish Intelligence were murdered by the Germans or by the Soviet occupiers. As a result, each teacher would teach several subjects.

I began to understand that my uncle called on me so that I could learn more. I wasn't entirely convinced, however, since I had to devote a lot of time to studying, instead of enjoying myself ice skating or skiing. During my entire seven-year primary school education, he only let me off the hook one time. He didn't call on me on the day that we had stayed up until four in the morning constructing a pigeon cage together.

Nevertheless, Sunday belonged to me. My favorite activity during the wintertime was skiing on the hill, which was very close to my house. One day I represented my school in the district skiing tournament in Grajewo. I didn't win a medal, but I was very happy because following the tournament, a hot meal awaited all of the contestants. My joy was short-lived though because I soon had to return the skis to my uncle's wife. My aunt demanded them back just a few minutes before the train departed from Grajewo to Osowiec. I was already on the train when I noticed through the window that she was looking for me, but I didn't suspect that it was about the skis. How mortified I was when my friend, Kazik, the other skiing representative of our school, skied from the Osowiec train station, while I walked home beside him on foot. I never owned another pair of skis again in my life. However, my father did make a sled for me to ride on the snow and slide down snowy hills, but that was a different kind of fun.

I used the sled over ice as well. As I stood on the rear end of the sled, I pushed myself along with a stick that had a sharp nail at the end. I could quickly move along the endless sheet of ice that surrounded our house in a couple of kilometers radius. Our house stood on a sandy mound, but sometimes, during a big flood, the water nearly reached our front door and, in the winter, turned to ice. It was a great place to play for the children.

One freezing cold day, I decided to take a ride on the sled toward the Biebrza River. The ice was thick, so I didn't worry that it would break beneath me. I sped along on my sled, pushing myself off with my stick. Despite the fog that surrounded me, I wasn't worried about getting lost, since I knew each nook of that area well. I didn't notice the spot in the ice where the water hadn't frozen, even though it was the middle of winter. Even if I had noticed it in time, it would have been too late to stop or maneuver the sled in another direction. I plunged into the water full force. Since I was a good swimmer, I was able to keep my head above water. However, my first attempts to get out of the trap proved unsuccessful. The ice around the unfrozen water was thin, and it cracked when I attempted to lift myself onto its edge. I desperately looked around, searching for rescue, but the fog was so dense that I could only see a few steps ahead. Finally, I found a thick layer of ice, but I didn't know how to get onto its surface. A few attempts were not successful. Each time my hands slipped off the ice and only left nail marks on it. Fog surrounded me. I couldn't see anything around me. I was too far from home, so calling for help would have been useless.

I knew that it was up to me to escape the trap. My thoughts raced as I tried to quickly think of something to save myself. Otherwise, I knew I would soon die. Finally, inspiration came as if from heaven. I had to support myself from the top with my hands and try to throw my body onto the sheet of ice. I tried the method. I lifted myself as high as I could, and I threw myself face-first. Unfortunately, the first attempt did not work, but I concluded that this was the only way to save my own life. The water was deep because when I plunged back

into it, I couldn't reach the bottom with my feet. I tried again and surprisingly, success! I now lay on the ice. I didn't know how thick the
ice really was, so I carefully twisted around to see the location of my
sled. Unfortunately, it was underneath the ice. I didn't want to give up
my sled, so I tried to retrieve it. I felt my hands get a hold of it, but I
leaned too far, and I fell into the water again. Knowing how to get the
sled and myself out of the abyss, I threw the sled out onto the ice, and
then pulled myself up and fell on my face. I was successful with the
first try, and once again, I lay on top of the ice.

It was impossible to ride on the sled, since I immediately became
icy once out of the water. I felt very cold. The surface of my pants and
jacket became hard. I walked further, pulling the sled behind me. I
tried to run, but was unable, since the frozen clothes only allowed
limited movement. Slowly, I was losing hope that I would reach home
before I became a pillar of ice. The water dripping down my jacket
began to freeze and turned into icicles at the bottom. I looked like a
Christmas tree. I constantly rubbed my ears, nose, and face to protect
myself against frostbite.

I finally reached the top of the hill, not by climbing, but rather
crawling along its side and saw my house. It was close, at arm's
reach, two hundred meters away, but how hard it was to walk that distance. I arrived home, having turned into a pillar of ice. I was afraid to
go inside and show myself to my mother in such a state. It was just
my luck that my mother was on the porch. When she heard a strange
rustling sound, she went outside to see what it could be. She didn't
expect such a sight; she stood terrified and became speechless. She
quickly took control, took me by the arm, and pulled me inside the
house. She removed my jacket and shoes. My pants wouldn't come
off for anything. They were like steel. My mother poured water over
the pants and then pulled them off forcefully. Once I was fully
unclothed, she rubbed a rag dipped in cold water over my body. I felt
that I was warming up. After this water treatment, which I didn't
understand, she threw me under a down blanket and covered me up to
my ears. It was just then that I felt an incredible relief to my body and
soul.

Meanwhile, my father had gone into the forest to gather wood.
When he returned home that evening, he saw me doing homework at
the table as if nothing had happened. It turned out my mother's remedies with cold water were so effective that I didn't even catch cold
after this adventure.

I survived, but who could have given me the idea that I was able to get out of such a predicament alive? That evening, as usual, before slumber, I began my prayer with "Angel of God, my guardian dear…"

One day, I accidentally overheard my parents' conversation. My father revealed to my mother that he had a German gun, similar to the one he had before the war. At that time, he had a gun license, so legally he was able to store it in the house, but since these were communist times, he hid it in the barn. I was curious to see what the gun looked like, so I decided to search for it. The barn was large and finding an object that size wouldn't be an easy task. I climbed the beams up to the top to peer into a crevice that connected the roof with the wall of the barn. I squeezed my head into it, and just then, my foot slipped off the beam. I hung from my twisted head, and I started to choke. Once again, I was left to the mercy of fate. My parents were far from home, somewhere in the field. The thought passed my mind this would be the end of me. I couldn't see since my head was trapped in the opening. Blindly, I tried to feel something to hold onto. I was close to losing consciousness and saw darkness before my eyes, when I was able to grab hold of an object, and then suddenly fell to the ground, holding onto a beam. How lucky I was that the beam wasn't fastened well and had detached itself under my weight! Unfortunately, a long nail caught against my arm below my elbow and tore it deeply. Blood gushed out as if from a fountain. I took my shirt off quickly, wrapped it around my arm, and ran to my parents. My mother, as usual, took the matter into her own hands and stopped the bleeding. She healed my wound with her home-method remedies. She pressed some leaves to it and soaked it in something, but I wasn't taken to the doctor. A few weeks later, all that was left was a large scar, which reminds me of the accident to this day.

Today, a reflection arises in my mind that I know someone watched over me so that I could live. Every misfortune is a blessing in disguise, as my mother used to say, and that's what happened in my case. From that day on, I lost interest in weapons, ammunition, dynamite, and other explosives, and became interested in books. Reading, especially fictional novels, consumed all of my spare time. In my imagination, I was taken with the characters to other continents, and in this way, I visited different corners of the world.

As I took the cows out to graze, I forgot that I had to keep watch over them. A newly begun book would absorb me to such a degree that often I wouldn't know where the cows were located. It wasn't until my neighbor's voice calling, "Jan, your cows are in my wheat!" brought me back from my daze, and I ran to chase them away from there. My father's replies to the neighbor's complaints were most amusing. "Stop nagging, Franek, Henry's looking after them."

Then I felt guilty, but unfortunately, the situation repeated itself regularly. My father, knowing that I was a poor cattle herder, fenced barbed wire around a portion of the meadow, and there the cows were able to graze without being watched over.

Responsibilities at school and chores around the house consumed most of my time, so I had less of it for playtime. Raking the hay and stacking the wheat or other grain were my normal chores. From time to time, I herded the cows along the roads where more clover grew, which the cows liked best. This tired me terribly because than I wasn't able to do what I liked, which was to read books. Nevertheless, for that I accidentally found a solution.

One day, an insect that looked like a bumblebee began to buzz around one of the cows. It lifted its tail and started running for the barn, and the other cows followed suit. One day, after a few hours of observing the cows graze, and becoming bored, I began to pretend I was a buzzing bumblebee. I didn't have to wait long for the effects. This time, all of the cows, as if under orders, lifted their tails, and I ran after them buzzing until they made it to the barn. I was pleased with myself that I found a way to get out of herding the cows for so long.

I herded them for shorter and shorter periods of time, and each time my method was foolproof. Yet one day my father questioned me as to why the bumblebee kept attacking the cows so early in the morning, when this hadn't happened before. "Henry, by any chance, are you the bumblebee?" he asked.

"Dad, I'm not a bumblebee," I answered. "I'm just pretending to buzz like one. It's not my fault that the cows run away."

The next day my father sent my brother, who was five years older, along with me to herd the cows. He was automatically my boss, and I had to obey all his orders. He was deep in his reading himself. Just like me when I was by myself, he didn't pay attention to what was going on around him. He depended on me to take care of everything.

This time, besides the cows, our horses were grazing. I tried to shoo a horse away from harm's way, but I got too close to him. It unexpectedly kicked me right in the chest. I lost consciousness. I lay on my back with no signs of life. I don't know how long this lasted, but after a while, as if in a dream, I heard my brother calling, "Henry, don't die! Don't die; I'm begging you! Oh God, save him!"

His prayers were heard, and I awoke in a daze. I couldn't move, but my brain began to function. I asked my brother what had happened. I felt a sharp pain around my heart and then lost consciousness again. I don't know how long that lasted. Later, from my brother's account to my parents, I found out that he begged God to spare my life. This could only have happened through the intercession of my Guardian Angel, who never abandoned me, and I relied on him always and everywhere. The area around my heart and my heart itself ached for a long time, but there came a day when the pain subsided and everything returned to normal.

To our great delight, our parents built a small wooden house, and we were finally able to leave the German bunker. Even I, the youngest and smallest of the family, had to bend down when entering the bunker. Otherwise, I would hit my head on the beam that held the threshold up. My mother often cursed her fate because she frequently hit her head on the miserable beam as she left the bunker.

Our house was tiny, and it literally looked like it came straight out of a fairytale about dwarves. In it, we only had a small kitchen and one somewhat larger room. It couldn't compare to our pre-war spacious house that had many rooms, including a ballroom where parties were held. But something is better than nothing, the saying goes. My parents, and we along with them, were thrilled that we could finally stop coming and going like rats from a burrow and could come and go through a normal door.

We didn't have a stove for cooking yet, so my parents built a makeshift stove outside of the house, which served to prepare meals for us, as well as for the livestock. In a twist of fate, the stove was built exactly on the spot where I had buried a few boxes of bullets earlier, in case World War III erupted, which I believed was about to occur at any moment. I had many such boxes, but of course, grass covered them, and I couldn't remember exactly where they were.

The first day passed without surprises. All of the dishes were prepared, and we were able to eat dinner in our new home normally. The next day my mother prepared and placed the pots accordingly. My sister, who was two years older, and I were to keep the fire going by adding wood. We were to watch over the cooking food. Slowly, I added wood to the fire that was located literally on the sand right above the buried boxes of bullets that I had forgotten about. The fire heated up the bullets until they started to explode, but luckily for us, they began to explode one at a time.

As children of war, without unnecessary words, we both dove into a nearby ditch, where we lay waiting the next order of events. Following the individual explosions, we heard a series of shots that sounded like a machine gun. Then there was an earthshaking explosion, and a pile of ash and sand flew into the air. We waited a moment to see what else would happen, but nothing did. Only silence remained. I glanced at my sister, who was covered in ash and yellow sand. I looked identical to her. We were afraid to poke our heads out of the ditch, so, just in case, we crawled along its bottom, away from the site of the explosion. My terrified parents ran from the fields to see just a torn hole where their stove once stood. They panicked and started to call us loudly, although they were already convinced that the explosion blew us to pieces, not even a trace of us. When they saw us coming out of the ditch fifty meters from the site of the explosion, they yelled in relief, "You're alive!"

Well, Guardian Angel, once again you gave a sign of yourself. My father was convinced that the stove was accidentally built atop of a dud, and he never inquired about the details. I didn't insist on explaining the cause of the accident, and that's how it ended. I never confessed to it because I was embarrassed that I didn't remember where I had hidden the ammunition and a few sticks of dynamite, which actually caused such a large explosion.

I hid a few sticks of dynamite underneath the house as well. When I saw the danger it put us all in when the explosion occurred, I immediately moved the dynamite, hid it behind Leszczowa Hill, about two hundred meters away from our house, and detonated it in a bonfire. Once again, a cloud of fire and ash rose up in the air, but I was able to enjoy the beautiful sight from a distance because this time there wasn't a stove or pots on it.

This was my last wartime exhibition. War and weapons were no longer of interest to me, and, as I mentioned earlier, I begun to read stories and books. Along with the heroes of the books, I experienced their adventures. Nothing could pry me away from a book I had begun to read. Unfortunately, during the evening I had difficulties. While reading beside the flickering gas lamp, the letters flickered before my eyes as well. That is why I asked my parents for a flashlight, which could only be bought on special occasion in a store in Grajewo, a town about twenty-five kilometers away.

My parents went to the market once a month to sell their goods and buy household necessities. Each month, I awaited their return and watched to see when the familiar wagon would appear, and I would finally get my coveted flashlight. Unfortunately, months passed, and I still didn't have a flashlight. Until one day, to my great joy my father pulled out a brand new one from his pocket and ceremoniously handed it to me. At night, so no one would rush me to go to sleep, I hid under my bed sheets and read. Unfortunately, the battery quickly wore out, and I had to wait another few months for a replacement. This time, I saved the battery and didn't use it as much. The fact that I owned a flashlight filled me with pride.

It is strange that even now, I catch myself looking at flashlights in various stores, although I own several of many kinds and don't need any more. I must subconsciously be programmed with longing for something that I had waited for in my childhood.

Me in front of Bunker Rock.

The Mysteries of the Osowiec Fortress

I listened to my father tell stories many times of the Osowiec bunkers and their unsolved mysteries. I became so intrigued by the bunkers that one day, after class, my friend Kazik and I set out to research the matter. We began at the first fort.

It turned out not to be as easy as it seemed. After only one step into the bunker, we were unable to see anything. We decided to explore the bunkers multiple times and returned the next day carrying a piece of plastic from the window of an airplane. We had retrieved it from an airplane that lay shot down near our homes. The plastic burned slowly, making it a perfectly good torch for our exploration.

The next day we yearned to penetrate as many bunkers as we could. In order to do so, we brought supplies. With a few pieces of plastic and some matches, we reported to fort number one again. At its entrance, we lit one of the plastic "torches" and entered. The wide hallway captivated us. The wall was covered in ceramic tiles! Seeing it for the first time in our lives, we thought it looked magnificent.

There were interesting views, but we had to carefully look down and make sure that no surprises lurked on the ground in the shape of mines or duds. Although we didn't notice suspicious shapes, we knew that anything was possible.

As we walked further, we began to feel an increasingly strong draft that made our flames sway back and forth after each step. Our desire to see further drove us forward. Just then, we almost fell into a well. It was unmarked in any way, and its opening was even with the ground.

During a moment of carelessness, we could have said good-bye to this world forever.

The flame flickered dangerously low as a stronger draft streamed from the well. We were able to see only a few feet around us, to the edge of the flickering light and not beyond it. In the distance lay total darkness. This reminded us that we were far away from the entrance. We noticed that metal bars were mounted along the wall of the well that would allow us to descend it. We were faced with the choices of continuing to walk, turn around and go back, or climb down the well.

Our curiosity got the best of us, and we took the risk of descending along the bars. I began to go down along the metal bars first, but since it was so dark, after a few meters, I was unable to see in front of me. Kazik and I had to climb down together, taking turns holding the light.

Our first attempt was successful, and we slowly made our way down. We passed the flame from one to another. The bottom was not yet visible when a sudden breeze blew out our only source of light. Complete darkness fell. It became unpleasant. Now we were in trouble! We had no other choice. We had to head back. It was easier said than done. We knew that the hardest part would be climbing out of the well, since the handles were not located at the entrance to the well above, only on the wall. The possibility of falling down the well was great. What kind of danger lurked? It was better not to think about it. There was no other alternative. We talked loudly the entire time, and only the echo reminded us of our location. The echo, in the midst of utter darkness, took on a life of its own, and it seemed like someone was laughing or mocking us. Helping one another, we climbed out onto the ground. We crawled away from the entrance of the well and raised ourselves up to our feet. We made it out of the well, but what about getting out of the bunker? So as not to stumble onto another well, we began to head back.

The draft did not permit us to light another flame. After a few attempts, we decided not to waste the matches that were like gold at the time. Our parents would splinter them into two, or even four pieces, so they would last longer. Touching the walls, we slowly moved forward. We were at the mercy of fate, and we could only count on luck now. It was a road through agony, and just as it seemed that we would never leave the abyss, we spotted a redeeming square of light in the distance.

A great joy filled our hearts. We did not outwardly show it because neither of us wanted to admit to having a moment of weakness. The square of light became larger as we neared the exit. Finally, there was a curved passage, and behind it, we saw the field. We were saved, and we rejoiced!

On the way back home, we did not talk to each other much, since each of us silently planned our next outing to the bunkers. The bunkers entirely fascinated us! After the first forced exit, our desire to explore them further returned like a boomerang. As we parted ways, we planned our return. Supplies for the next trip would include more matches and an improved lighting system. We thought of ways to prevent the draft from blowing out the flame from our plastic torch.

Kazik and I put our ideas to work. After a few days of preparation, our imaginations took to the skies, and we once again returned to the mysterious and infinitely interesting place. After reaching the entrance to the bunker, we took the same route, which was familiar, at least until we reached the well. The supply of matches and plastic in our pockets gave us the illusion of safety, even if we were to come upon unexpected surprises. The flame shield we constructed was proving effective. Once again, we started to climb down the well lower and lower with our tried method. We reached its bottom and thought that it was the end of our journey. How great was our amazement, when in the light of the torch, we spotted another corridor!

We decided to take the corridor into the unknown because our curiosity pushed us forward. We were aware that on the way there could be traps or mines, which we would not notice, and this could be our last journey. Our imaginations took over and pushed us further and further. We stumbled upon another well. Convinced that there would be another corridor at its bottom, we climbed down. After lighting the third torch in a row, we continued. The last corridor turned into a hall in which there were two exits. We chose one of them. Amazed at how the walls and floor were tiled and everything was very neat, we made our way forward. We got a bit anxious that our journey was prolonged and began to wonder what would happen if we didn't find an exit soon.

At that point, we had only one piece of plastic left, and once that burned out, we would be in trouble. We walked on as if an unseen force pushed us forward. Finally, a small white square appeared, and we felt certain that we would soon return safe and sound from our new adventure. The square became bigger, and finally, it took on its actual dimensions. We were able to exit. We looked around eagerly, not sure which side of the fort we had exited. We climbed to the top of the bunker and then were able to recognize the area. We were shocked to see that we journeyed the entire length of the fort and came out the other end!

We returned to the bunkers many times thereafter and enjoyed new discoveries each time. Changing the route of our journey with each entrance, we exited on various sides of the fort.

My best friend, Kazik, and me in Poland, 1956.

Fun Roles in the School Theater

By nature, I was a dreamer and always exhibited a sense of humor, which is why the teacher, who knew my likes and dislikes, entrusted me with the most humorous roles in the school plays. At school, we held all kinds of contests and won prizes, which we pre-purchased for one another after drawing cards of last names. As luck would have it, one time I drew my own name and had to buy a present for myself. I told my mother about it, expecting her to treat me, her son, to something special. Nothing of that sort happened. My mom simply made some flour pancakes and wrapped them in paper. When I carried the prize to school, I was reluctant to show anyone what was inside because I didn't want to be the laughingstock of the entire school.

On the day of the drawing, everyone got prizes, but mine somehow got lost. The teacher became worried because she really didn't know what had happened to it. It was a few days later that she found it and ceremoniously presented the prize to me. Everyone expected me to show off my prize, since I wasn't expected to know what was inside the bundle, but I wasn't too thrilled to do it.

At the end of classes, on my way home, my hunger reminded me of the pancakes. I pulled them out of my backpack, sat down by the roadside stream, and began to eat them with an appetite. In that moment, I was reminded of my mother and how such a present became notably useful, since I didn't return hungry from school.

By the stream, I was able to watch the many species of fish, eagerly swimming up to the banks, lured by the pancake crumbs I fed them. In that spot, the water reached only to my knees because it stretched widely across the white sandy bottom. This stream originated in a deep lake, in which we would often take a swim after a long day of classes at school. That is how we entertained ourselves in summer until late autumn.

Despite walking home from school alone, I decided to swim to the other side of the lake to dive from a steep bank into the water. Unfortunately, the dive proved ill fated for me, since I had no idea that further down at the bottom lay a large rock. As fate would have it, I hit my head right on it. I saw stars before my eyes and lost consciousness. I do not know how I came to the surface of the water. After I surfaced, I awoke from the momentary lull. I was able to swim to the shore. As I reached the bank, I began to feel a strong headache. I vomited the excess water that I had swallowed when I had become momentarily unconscious. With my hand, I felt a rather large bump on my head and blood streamed down my face. Just then, I connected the entire string of events and how I made the irrational decision to swim alone. It could have ended tragically for me because I couldn't count on any help in that case. Before I fell asleep that evening, I didn't forget about my favorite prayer, and this time I knew whom to thank for my survival.

When I was eleven years old, in 1949, I was enrolled in the third grade of primary school. I began first grade a year late as schools were closed during the war. The children who finished primary school after the war took two grades in one year to make up for the lost time.

In November of that year, I went with my parents to my maternal family's village of Modzele to visit my ailing grandfather. On the way back from our visit, while we were driving through the forest, my father spotted a long, dried-up branch. Content with bringing something back with which he could light a fire in the stove, he laid it on the wagon. A few hours later, we arrived at a temporary bridge that stretched across the canal, as the old bridge had been blown up at the beginning of the war. There we saw two men, who were covering holes with boards to ensure safe passage across the narrow bridge that had no side railings.

The horse, as if sensing that something was amiss, snorted and slowly started to shuffle his hooves. When it stepped onto one of the newly placed sections of wood, its leg twisted and its hoof fell into the gap. The horse lost its balance and caused the wagon to fall. I was launched from the wagon as if from a catapult and fell down twenty meters into the canal. It happened so suddenly that it seemed like a dream. I automatically started to move my arms and reached the surface of the water. I knew that it was not a dream anymore, since I spotted my father on the bank of the canal trying to take off his high officer's boots. He jumped up when he saw me at the surface and yelled in my direction, "Henry, can you make it?"

I wanted to yell "help," but I swallowed so much water that I choked and couldn't utter a word. I vomited instead. I felt a bit relieved, but I still couldn't breathe. I was glad I could swim because the water-soaked winter jacket pulled me down. My shoes were two sizes too big so there was room for my feet to grow into them. Stubbornly, they refused to fall off and stifled my moves. My father, seeing that I was swimming, focused on saving my mother. It wasn't until then that I realized that my mother had fallen into the water as well, and she couldn't swim. I was finally aware that I was on my own because my father wasn't able to save us both. A moment later, I filled my lungs with air, and I began to breathe, but the wet winter clothing and shoes didn't let me move freely. Despite this, I tried to paddle with my arms. I inched my way toward the shore.

My mother sank to the bottom like a rock. But water usually throws a drowning person up to the surface before it finally sucks them in forever. When my mother rose to the surface, my father handed her the saved dried branch, which was supposed to serve as a starter to light a fire. My mother took hold of it and didn't let go until she was hauled to the bank. Near the bridge's concrete wall, the two men lowered my father by his feet, so he could give my mother a hand. Soon they were both pulled out to the side of the canal. Just then, I lost sight of them and decided that I needed to change the direction of my swimming, so I could reach the grassy bank. My strength began to fail me, but an incredible force held up my spirits, and I believed that I would reach the shore.

Once more, I mustered my strength, and only through sheer willpower was able to reach my goal. I was at the brink of exhaustion. The water was deep, even near the banks, so to rest a bit, I grasped a root showing itself from the surface. My father ran down to check what was happening with me, and when he noticed that I was near the bank, he turned around and ran back.

I wanted to see what was happening with my mother as soon as possible. I tried to pull myself out of the abyss, and gripping onto the root, I pulled myself up. The root snapped, and I fell back into the water. This time my dive was under control, and I floated back up to the surface without a problem. I had perfected my diving skills jumping from a high bank into the Biebrza River almost every day. I even bet my friends on who was able to hold their breath underwater the longest. This time, my diving and swimming skills saved the lives of both my mother and I, since my father was only able to rescue one of us.

I knew that in this particular part of the canal, I would have no chance to get out. The nearly vertical bank, although grassy, proved to be an impossible escape. I decided to swim to a less steep embankment to a bush growing right on the water. Its protruding branch helped me reach the top, though with great difficulty. I climbed on my knees up to the top of the embankment. I dragged myself to the spot where my mother lay on the ground.

I breathed a sigh of relief when I saw that my mother was alive, and her eyes were open. She turned to me, and in a quiet voice she said, "Henry, the entire time I thought of you drowning in that canal. I begged God that he would save you and that I would be willing to sacrifice my life for yours. The Lord heard my prayers and spared my life too!"

I became sad since I didn't think of sparing my mother's life in exchange for mine. I didn't admit to it and harbored deep feelings in my heart about it. Although still a child, I realized that nothing would replace a mother's love. My mom reached her hand out to me. I knelt by her, and she pulled me toward her. We remained embraced for a long while. I felt such great relief at that moment. My father and the two strangers laid my mother onto the wagon. Soaked and cold, but happy, we headed toward home.

Upon our arrival home, as we changed into dry clothes, my father described what had happened. The wagon toppled over, but he held onto the ladder, and thanks to this, kept from falling off. The horse was able to pull the fallen wagon from the bridge back onto the road. It was nearly miraculous that the horse did not fall into the canal along with the wagon. If that would have happened, none of us would have stood a chance of survival.

My parents wondered for a long time about the two men who helped, but they never came to know the men's identities. Most of all, they regretted that they had forgotten to thank them for their help. My mother tried to comfort my father with the thought that the good Lord would repay them for saving our lives.

Was it a coincidence that they were there at exactly the time and the place where they were most needed? Who, then, stood over us, and who helped to rescue us from imminent death?

"Angel of God, my guardian dear…" as usual before I fell asleep, I began my daily prayer.

My father and brother-in-law, Anthony. A short time later, my father passed away, and the dog in the picture howled day and night, stopped eating, and died after two weeks.

Life in Post-War Poland

We settled into our tiny house, and the stove for heating and cooking, after my unfortunate blowing up of the temporary one, was quickly built. As wintertime approached, the cold became bothersome. As long as the stove was lit, it was relatively warm. The cold was especially noticeable during the nighttime. Only our noses were visible from beneath the down comforters because protruding a hand or an arm out from under the covers could have resulted in frostbite. The drinking water froze inside the bucket, and to drink it, we had to first break the ice. On the windows, the layers of frost were so thick that we took turns blowing on it to see what was happening outside.

My parents got up each morning to light the stove in order to heat the house a bit before we got ready for school. My father and mother teased each other every morning about who would be the first to get out of bed and light the fire. It looked silly because my father would usually lose and had to get up first. We traveled to school on foot, often through knee-deep snow. No one complained because we were accustomed to the weather conditions. At times, our noses became a little frostbitten, but after rubbing them with snow, they returned to normal.

Soon my eldest sister, Anastazja, and brother, Romuald, left home to go to school in Elk. I remained behind with my sister Henryka, and we took over their responsibilities. My parents worked hard to support two children who were away from home. There was room and board to be paid and clothes and food to be bought. Every Saturday my brother and sister came home to replenish their supplies, and each Sunday my father would take them to the train station with two suitcases of food to last them until the next visit.

It was 1950, the time of the harshest Communist terror. Due to my father's noble heritage and my mother's great Hetman Gosiewski lineage, the Communists decided to humiliate my family at great length and ensure that my father went to jail. They had many methods of realizing their plan. The easiest was to levy a tax so high that my parents were unable to pay it. This method was chosen and utilized because they recognized it to be the most effective way to bring down my parents. My father was perceived to be a "kulak" (in Russian and Soviet history, a wealthy or prosperous peasant, financially capable of employing hired labor, leasing land and providing mortgages) and with that, automatically the enemy of the people's Poland because he owned an above-average amount of land. My father descended from a noble family and himself was an aristocrat, which bothered the Communists, mostly because they knew that those sorts of people hated the Communist regime the most. (Currently, our name is included in the "Great Crest Reference of Polish Lineages" on page 354, authored by Andrzej Kulikowski, published in 2005).

As a child, I remember one of the scenarios of "de-kulaking" the enemies of communism. Two trucks pulled up to our house. The evicting officials knew that my father was not home at the time, he was in Grajewo, where they had come from, and they immediately began to take from the house whatever they could lay their hands on. I will never forget my mother's cries, raising her hands to the sky as if searching for mercy. My mother ran to the neighbors, borrowed money from them, and in that way, saved our possessions from being confiscated. Unfortunately, what was already loaded onto the trucks was never returned to us.

I began to hate those people who were supposed to be the saviors of our country, but who instead were its oppressors. I was still a boy, but I was brought up during the war, and I understood very well the meaning of Communism and the Soviet Union (Soviet Russia). I decided at that moment to avenge my mother's tears. A few years later, however, it turned out that it would not be as easy as it seemed.

The time following Stalin's death became a temporary "thaw." Yet later another type of repression followed that proved more refined. There were various measures taken to force farmers to surrender their lands to the government and join the communal production facilities, which were called kolkhozes. Not many of them gave in, and thanks to that, a comprehensive collectivization of peasants' land never took place in Poland.

At that time, my brother, Romuald, having finished the ninth grade in the Elk High School, decided to join the Lower Seminary in Frombork. When he announced his decision to my parents, he expected support and joy on their part. Nothing of the sort happened, and this was for two significant reasons.

First, my parents weren't sure that Romuald really did have a calling to the priesthood, although they wished for it with all their hearts. My father decided to tell us the history of his father, our grandfather, who passed away in the spring of 1938. Our grandfather's parents decided that their son would become a priest. Without asking his opinion, they sent him to the seminary. This was a tremendous mistake. Grandfather didn't have a calling to priesthood, and he soon abandoned his studies at the seminary.

My parents didn't want history to repeat itself and categorically opposed sending Romuald to the Lower Seminary. They suggested that he finish high school, and after that, if he was certain that his calling was to be a priest, then they would do everything to guide his studies. He could then enroll in a seminary, but in the Higher Seminary.

The second reason for their refusal was the great cost they would incur. Completing his studies at the seminary would be an enormous expense. In order to pay the first year's tuition, they would have to sell one or even two cows. Milk was the basis of our family's support, and my parents weren't willing to take that risk until Romuald was entirely certain.

My brother reconciled himself to his fate and returned to the high school in Elk to continue his education. It seemed that everything had returned to normal when in the spring of the following year, an unexpected event occurred that determined his future career in the most unexpected of ways.

Yearly and during springtime, the Biebrza River overflows its bed and floods the nearby meadows, leaving only the higher grounds above the water. The cows were let out of the barn to forage for food. At times, they even swam to the knolls above the water in order to reach the fresh grass. By evening, they returned to the barn by themselves. This time, despite the impending dawn, the cows had not yet returned, and my father became worried. He got a boat and went to see what happened. When he reached the site, he couldn't believe his eyes. He thought it was perhaps just a dream. Unfortunately, it wasn't a dream, but a tragic reality. All of the cows lay dead. When my father returned home bearing the news, my mother began to panic. She started to roam around not knowing what to do or say. I got scared seeing my mother in this state.

Finally, she fell to her knees. I feared that she might have fainted. Then I heard my mother's cries and her calling, "Dear God, it is our fault, forgive us this sin."

"Jan," she turned to my father, "we didn't let Romuald enter the seminary because we refused to sell just one cow, even though we had five of them and two calves. It's a sign from heaven that we made the wrong decision by not letting him go. Now we have to take on the new calling, and I think that with God's help, we can manage."

"Jan," she turned to my father again, "do you remember what your father said when Romuald was born?"

"Yes, I remember well," replied my father. "He called us all to the crib and leaning over it he said, 'Remember, take care of him. He will grow up to be a great man.'"

"Now I'm certain," stated my mother, "that his grandfather's prediction will come true, and Romuald will become a priest in order to serve people and God. Your father never became a priest because he didn't have a calling, but he probably asked in heaven for this calling for his grandson."

I was shocked to hear this unexpected but very determinate decision. That same year, after summer vacation, my brother began his studies at the Lower Seminary in Frombork. Unfortunately, the next year, during vacation, the Office of Security closed down all Lower Seminaries in Poland. My brother finished his final grade in Olsztyn High School, and there he entered the Higher Seminary. His dream came true.

Since my mother mentioned my grandfather, a person who intrigued me to such a degree, one day I asked her to tell me more about him.

"You see, child," she turned to me, "I'm not sure where to begin, since you had heard a bit about him already, but it's an endless topic. I met your grandfather when I became your father's fiancée. In those times, usually an acquaintance, called a matchmaker, would introduce a girl to a boy. If they liked each other, then a few months later the wedding would take place. I'm talking about young people who lived far from one another, like we did."

"What year was this, Mom?" I asked, and then I heard the whole story.

"We met in 1928, and the following February, we got married. There was a lot of snow. It was the winter of the century, and temperatures would fall to 40 degrees below 0 Celsius. Our best man had frostbitten ears. Your father was a twin. Besides that, he had two brothers and a sister. Your father's mother died at a very young age. She was forty years old, and I never knew her. However, your grandfather was a man with a wonderful heart. The very fact that he was able to raise five children without their mother was proof enough.

"After our wedding, the two elder brothers left permanently for the United States, Chicago to be exact. Those were hard times; the great depression took place at that time. One of the brothers soon married and got a job as a model in one of Chicago's largest stores. Among three hundred auditioning, he was chosen by a committee because he was one of the most handsome men. He and his wife were doing well and soon bought a house, then later a car. They were the first ones on their block to have such a luxury."

"The other brother didn't have such luck, as he lived in poverty. He wasn't an exception, since millions of Americans lived on government aid at the time. We helped the brothers pay for their trip to America and to purchase their part ownership of Grandfather's estate. Fortunately, Grandfather's estate prospered well, and we were not affected much by our payments."

"Nevertheless, soon his twin brother and the sister decided to immigrate to South America, to Argentina. This time it became a problem because getting the cash in such a short time was not an easy task. We had to rise to the challenge, and after their departure, we were left with only your grandfather."

"We were young, full of energy and hope for the future. What I enjoyed most were Saturday night parties that were popular at the time. Those were beautiful times, which I remember fondly. There were roasted pigs, all kinds of cakes, homemade beer, wine for the ladies, and something stronger for the men."

"Grandfather was the life of the party. He could entertain everyone because he had a wonderful talent for it. He attended every officer's ball at the Osowiec Fortress. There he entertained not only the officers, but guests from Warsaw as well. Generals and their wives, politicians, even ministers attended these parties. Each time a carriage would arrive pulled by two white horses to pick up Grandfather, a coachman would open the carriage door for him. Since he was an educated man, he read a lot and possessed a wide range of knowledge. He was respected and well known, not only in our area, but as news spread, far beyond it. That is why nearly every evening, and especially on Saturdays and Sundays, the house was full of people.

"He not only spoke of what he had read, but he also answered many, often strange, questions. One would often conclude that 'We are human and nothing that is human is alien to us.' Most of the questions were about the future of man and the world. Everyone was most intrigued with this topic. He recited entire Bible verses by memory and knew quite well the predictions of Cybil and Nostradamus, as well as Poland's history and world history. He never repeated a story once told, unless someone asked him to."

"He advised his sons and daughters against immigrating to the United States. In his visions, he didn't see a future there. He repeated to each of them, 'Remember that these prophecies will sooner or later come true, perhaps not in your lifetimes, but surely in your children's and grandchildren's times. Americans will be punished for possessing the greatest amount of material things and because they expose their bodies without shame. New York will disappear from the face of the Earth. Florida will be flooded. Huge earthquakes will consume California, and it, too, will end up under water. Remember that America will not perish because of war, but from cataclysmic events which plague it. People will try to flee in panic across the ocean to Europe, but not many will save their lives. I predict a bright future for Poland. It will flow with milk and honey because Poland was, is, and will be the stronghold of Christianity, faithful to the nation and God. Besides this, Mary, the mother of our Lord Jesus Christ, was entrusted as the Queen of Poland by our king, Jan Kazimierz. She will protect us from global misfortune, which will plague this world. '"

I listened to these stories with my mouth gaping, and I couldn't believe how wise my grandfather was. I wished that I had inherited at least some of his wisdom and vigor. I regretted that I was born "a bit too late," and I wasn't given the opportunity to meet him and remember at least a few episodes from his life. Unfortunately, my grandfather died three months before I was born.

"Mom, what happened to Dad's sister and brothers who went abroad? They were my aunt and uncles, so they're close relatives," I asked.

"Son," my mother replied, "I'm sorry to say this, but life in a foreign land wasn't easy. Of course, as I had mentioned, all turned out well with the eldest one. He had a wonderful, loving wife, and soon they had a daughter, Dolores. Unfortunately, he was barely forty years old when he passed away. Although your aunt was a young widow, she never remarried. She decided that, on her own, she would raise their daughter, whom she loved more than anything.

"The other uncle's life didn't turn out as he had hoped. He wasn't wealthy, and he couldn't dream of landing a job during the recession. He mostly lived on welfare, and only worked side jobs from time to time. You may find what happened to him hard to imagine. One day he started experiencing a painful headache. He tolerated it and didn't bother going to the doctor because he didn't think it was anything serious. Unfortunately, three days later he was no longer living. He was forty-one years old. We received the news of your uncle's death from your aunt a few years later at the beginning of 1946. He had passed away in Chicago during the war, but the post office in Poland didn't resume operation until the end of 1945. Your father, Henry, was very depressed a long time after receiving the devastating news."

"Mom, what happened with dad's twin who lived in Argentina? I only recall a letter from abroad, and when Father began to read it, he dropped it on the floor in disbelief," I said.

Mother answered, "Yes, that was a real shock because we expected his visit to Poland, and instead, a letter came informing us of his sudden death. His sister, who had left for Argentina along with him, was the one who notified us. Your father and his twin brother were the youngest of the siblings. It was 1948, so he was forty years old when he passed away. Henry, you can't even imagine how devastated and depressed your father was. Your father couldn't read the letter any further. It fell from his hands, and I picked it up to finish reading it. I scanned over it and couldn't believe my eyes at what was written in the rest of the letter. I didn't know what to do, but I had to finish reading what it said. Your father was very shocked that all three of his brothers had passed away in such a short time.

"Our aunt from Chicago helped us a lot right after the war. She sent us gifts with clothing and food, and ingeniously hid dollars in the packages. She indicated in her letters that we should not burn the packaging, and then we knew that money was hidden there. Over time, we collected a whole $50. At that time it was a significant sum, but we saved it in case of emergency, instead of buying necessities for the farm."

My mother's story was so interesting that, with mouth wide open, I waited to hear the rest. I was all ears. Finally Mom continued her story.

"One day, when your father was away from home, I changed that straw in the mattress on which we slept because it was too packed. I was very happy that I could manage it without anyone's help. When he entered the house, your father noticed the change because the bed was high with new straw in the mattress. He asked me where I had thrown out the old straw. I quickly answered that I threw it into the pig-pen."

"It turned out that the dollars were there, which we had so carefully saved. We both ran to the pigpen, but the pigs had already gotten to them, and there was nothing, but tiny shreds left. Father decided that everything was lost because we couldn't change the course of events or destiny. That must have been how it was supposed to be."

"Mom, tell me more about Dad's parents. Yours are still living, but I didn't know Dad's parents," I said. "Well, you know a bit about Grandpa, but I didn't know Grandma myself because she died at a young age. Grandpa was twenty years older than Grandma, and despite that, he outlived his wife," Mother replied.

Then a question came to mind, "Why did three of her sons pass away at the exact same age as her? Was it a coincidence or some higher power?" No one can comprehend God's judgments, and simple man is only a passive witness.

Noble Family Crest

Affairs of the Osowiec Parish

My father was a member of the church board. The board meetings were held once a month and touched upon various issues regarding church activities. At one of the meetings, the members expressed their concern about how only a small number of boys were interested in serving at Holy Mass. They searched for a reason for such a matter. They finally came to the conclusion that, in a majority of the cases, the parents were to blame. When my father returned home from the meeting, he relayed the board's conclusion to my mother. A heated discussion ensued between my parents regarding the matter. Overhearing their arguments, I decided that during the next religion class, I would ask the priest if I could become schooled and serve Holy Mass. The priest was overjoyed and expressed his agreement without reservation. After returning home from school that day, I informed my parents about my decision. My mother was very happy with my resolution. The following Monday, she bought white fabric, and a tailor made a surplice for me within that same week. I was very proud, when, for the first time, I stood along with the other altar boys, so close to the altar and the priest, who was celebrating the Holy Mass. I had to be watchful not to miss anything. Although I was the one who repaired the bells, which had already served the church for a couple of years, only the older altar boys were allowed to use them. I was one of the youngest and didn't have permission to use them. Soon enough, to my surprise, the priest asked me to serve Holy Mass each morning. How astonished I was when on the first day it turned out that I was the only server who came to church. I was very nervous about whether or not I could handle this new challenge. Father Urban, our pastor, consoled me by offering his help in case I made a mistake.

I gained experience, and just after a week, I was satisfied that I was able to do my job without help. From that moment on, I was able to personally use the bells, the same bells that had caused me such difficulty to fix. Sporadically, another altar boy would help and serve with me, but for most masses, I served alone. I enjoyed this new responsibility to such a degree that I would wake up at six o'clock each morning, and after morning preparations (which consisted of a quick washing of my face with cold water), I would run to the church as if I had wings.

Father Urban awaited my arrival not in the church, but outdoors on a hilltop, until I ran to him. I had a two-kilometer path to conquer. He had no problems monitoring me since he was able to see at any moment my entire journey from where he stood. I greeted him with the words, "May the Christ Lord be blessed," and he answered, "Forever and ever." Then we would walk together to the church.

One day I was taken aback, upset even, when the priest tried to slip some money into my shirt pocket. I immediately returned it to him and stated that I came to church each day not for money, but to serve God. The priest was quite surprised by my comeback, and after thinking it over, he tried to convince me that the money was supposed to be a reward, not a payment. Despite this, I did not accept the money, not even as a reward.

I had a surplus of life energy, and I was constantly searching for novel games. Once I flipped myself backwards over the metal bar while holding on with my hands. The metal bar was used to dry laundry and was hung quite high. It was great, but only to a point. I am not sure how it happened, but suddenly, my hands slipped from the bar, and I fell to the ground hitting the back of my head and neck on the ground. I lost consciousness for a moment. I woke up with a sharp pain in my neck and chest. I tried to stand, but the piercing pain kept me down. I lay on my back and noticed that I had trouble breathing. I wasn't able to take a deep breath. I felt as if something might have been torn inside my chest because each attempt at taking air into my lungs was excruciating. Although I was able to move my head, my neck hurt mercilessly, and I hoped it wasn't damaged.

No one was home at the time, so I was on my own. I lay calmly and from time to time, I tried different ways to get up off the ground. I rolled from side to side until I was able to crawl to a pole, and holding onto it, I propped myself up to my feet. I was relieved that I was able to stand up on my own. I was able to breathe but could to take in only a bit of air. Moving my head was very hard, and I had to turn my entire body to look around and see what was going on to my side and back.

I did not admit to my parents that this event happened because I did not want to worry them. Luckily, they didn't notice a thing, although it could have been suspicious that suddenly I was doing everything very slowly.

A few days later, I was able to move my head, although it still hurt a little, but breathing was still a challenge. Short breaths were exhausting and efforts to breathe normally caused me unbearable pain. I felt that perhaps it could be a broken or displaced a rib, which wasn't letting me take a deep breath. I walked around with pain in my lungs without telling anyone about it. It wasn't until a week later that everything returned to normal. That sharp pain didn't even let me sneeze. But one time I could not keep from sneezing, and I let out such a big one, that I heard a creak inside my chest. Just then, I took a deep breath, and strangely, the chest pain immediately subsided. I attempted another deep breath and felt only a mild discomfort. I jumped with joy, happy that I accidentally cured myself. I was back to living normally. From then on, I was able to run freely instead of, as for the past week, walking slowly like a turtle with its legs tied.

The school year was quickly over, and my cousin from Swidry visited us for the summer. We knew each other well because my cousin's home was our first stop after leaving the concentration camp in Grajewo. She was younger than I was, so I was the one who dictated where and what we would play. We would make up different ways to play and had a lot of fun together. Our summer vacation was ending, and it was time to take my cousin home. My parents were surprised at her request to stay with us permanently.

They agreed without qualms, but first we had to get my aunt's permission and enroll her in school. My parents got my aunt's permission, my uncle admitted her to the local school without any problems, and my cousin stayed with us as a part of the family.

One day I came up with an idea to slide down the board that connected the roof of our house with the annex. My cousin was afraid of such treacherous games, but for me it was something new and exciting. The first few attempts were successful, and it seemed like there would be no end to the game. As I slid down the board the next time, I hit my leg against the ground but unfortunately that the leg couldn't bear the impact and cracked across the top of my ankle. The bone was exposed. I felt a sharp pain and couldn't get up. Besides my cousin, no one else was there. I called in a pleading tone for her to come and help me because my foot was broken. Indeed, she came up to me, but thought that I was joking, so she wanted to leave. It wasn't until I grabbed her hand that she realized I was in trouble. She noticed the beads of sweat forming on my forehead and hands. Although she was still a child, she understood the gravity of the situation, but she was helpless and didn't know what to do. I realized this, so I only asked her to notify the neighbors. Yet the closest neighbor lived over one and a half kilometers away.

I saw the fear in her eyes; she didn't want to leave me alone. I begged her not to delay and get help right away. Immediately she got up from her knees, and I saw her running until she disappeared behind the hill. Time dragged on as the pain intensified with each passing minute. It seemed like an eternity before I finally spotted my neighbor running in my direction.

My neighbor lifted me onto her back to take me into the house and put me in my bed. She was a petite woman, so my broken leg dragged on the ground. There was no other way, so I clenched my teeth to keep from screaming out in pain. I noticed that my foot was twisting the other way. The worst was yet to come because as we crossed the eight-inch-high threshold, my leg caught against it. The neighbor didn't know what was happening behind her and kept pulling me. I didn't protest, but even if I had wanted to, the pain rendered me speechless.

Finally, the neighbor carried me to my bed and laid me on it diagonally. Now she had to lift my legs, so I could rest them on the bed. The ordeal started all over again. She managed quickly and began to treat my broken leg. She put a wet towel on it, which helped me a lot because it eased the pain a bit. She took care of me for a few hours until my parents returned from the Goniadz market.

I did not expect anyone to come to my rescue because in those days, there were no telephones or ambulances, and the nearest hospital was in Grajewo, about twenty-five kilometers away. There were two possibilities of getting there, by horse and wagon or by train, as the bus did not run in that direction yet. The train arrival time was still a few hours away, so my parents used the time to prepare me for the journey. They put my leg in a brace, laid me onto the wagon, and took me to the train station in Osowiec. My mother returned home while my father carried me in his arms onto the train, and in the same way, he carried me to the Grajewo hospital.

There we waited in the hospital a few hours. Late that night it was finally my turn, and I was taken into the operating room. The horror repeated itself as if everything started all over again. Medical anesthetics were not available. Everything was performed "live." As they took off my pants, no one seemed to mind that I was dying of pain. There didn't seem to be any other resolution. They put the hospital gown on me.

I didn't know that the worst was yet to come. The doctor came and began by setting my leg in its proper position. They tied me to the bed, and two nurses held me by the hands. The pain I felt then was more excruciating than the pain I felt when I broke the leg. The doctor pulled the leg and rotated it, so the bones would set in place. At first, I could still hear the creaking of my bones rubbing together. After that, I can't recall anything else because I fainted from the pain. I awoke to see the nurses bandaging my leg and putting a cast on it.

After the procedure, I was taken to a room where a few other people lay. An elderly man in the neighboring bed surrounded me with heartfelt care. Thanks to his intervention, I did not fall out of bed upon falling asleep for a moment after the entire day's ordeal. He chatted with me and consoled me as best as he could. It was due to his efforts that I was able to gather physical, and most of all, mental strength. I missed my parents. My longing intensified when I saw visitors coming to see the other patients, but no one came to see me.

Finally, a few days later, on Sunday, I spotted my father through the window walking toward the hospital. As much as I clenched my teeth and bit my tongue, I couldn't stop myself and cried aloud. When my father entered the room, I lost control of my emotions, and my sobbing shook my whole body. When my father took me in his arms, I suddenly felt safe and full of hope for the future. At that moment, I wished in my thoughts that my father's train would never arrive to take him back home. Unfortunately, the few hours passed like seconds. Visitation time ended. My father got up to say good-bye. I wanted to prove to him that I was a man, that crying was "a girl thing," so I clenched my teeth again, but tears streamed down my face despite my determination.

Two weeks later, I came home, but I wore the cast for another six weeks. My leg was in a brace above my knee, and I couldn't even walk with crutches, so I was sentenced to remain in bed. The itchy skin under my cast was extremely bothersome. I tried to scratch myself by inserting a stick under the cast. I wasn't aware that I was injuring myself until I saw how awful the wounds appeared when my cast was removed. When I returned to school, I had to make up for the backlog of class work I missed, but that wasn't much of a problem.

My father drove me to school until my leg was completely healed. Soon, everything returned to normal, and I further enjoyed life.

A few months later, my school organized a field trip to Bialystok. Aside from our frequent trips to Grajewo, I had never been to a big city before. St. Roch's Church, which towered on a hilltop, delighted me the most. It was visible all the way from the train station. What beautiful architecture, with the towers reaching the sky. The buildings seemed so tall, they took my breath away. I looked up, so I wouldn't miss anything, and more than once, I bumped my head into someone's belly. It was comical!

When we returned from our trip, I proposed to my friend Kazik that we should dress as city slickers. In Bialystok, we were impressed by the men in hats. The next day we put our idea to work. The only thing we didn't think of was that we didn't have any shoes. Children younger than sixth grade didn't wear shoes in summer to play or to school. Shoes were worn only to church due to lack of availability after World War II. That didn't bother us. Proud and straight as arrows, we made our way to school wearing our hats but barefoot.

All of Osowiec had much to gossip about for the next few months. People playfully bowed low and greeted us with the words:

"Good day, hatters without shoes!"

What could I say? We became the victims of our own joke.

Czajewski Family, 1956. I'm in the back on the left.

High School

The year 1953 came upon us, and it was time to part with my elementary school in Osowiec. I filed documents for admission to the Pedagogical School in Elk. One of the members on the board of admissions, impressed with my answers, asked me an additional question about current events in the press. He was probably not expecting a boy from the countryside to read newspapers. I surprised the board when I began to name newspaper titles and the topics they touched on. Among them, I described in detail the infamous, at the time, Rosenberg Affair, in which that married couple was charged in the United States with divulging secret atomic bomb information to the Soviets. All the board members looked at me in disbelief, and the Polish literature teacher gave me the highest possible mark, a five plus. I passed all my subjects with very good grades. There was also a physical fitness test and a one-hundred-meter dash, in which I placed first. In addition, each candidate had to show good hearing and singing skills. I was to sing a song I freely chose. Without giving it much thought, I began singing a religious patriotic song in a loud voice, "God, who throughout the ages..."

Confusion ensued. The board members lowered their heads. The infuriated teacher yelled, "Enough! Stop!"

It was 1953, Stalin times, when the terror of communism flew to rage. It was no wonder that the teacher reacted this way to my words of God and to the freedom of Poland. I decided, however, to finish at least the first verse of the song, so I continued further, "...Surrounded Poland with your splendor and glory. We take to your altars, our prayers, bless our free nation...!"

Following these words was the silence of a funeral. Not one of the board members spoke. The teacher was so vexed that her hands shook, and using big letters, she wrote down the lowest possible mark on my report, a two so big that it took over the top and bottom square in the grade book. The grade book consisted of graph paper. A two was the lowest mark.

I thought that I had no chance of acceptance, and I decided to leave the school grounds. As I neared the exit door, someone caught up with me and announced that the principal wanted to speak with me. I was sure I was in for a big scolding, nonetheless, I entered the appointed room. I was very nervous and in low spirits, but as soon as the door closed behind me, I regained my confidence. Inside I noticed a person sitting behind a desk acutely observing me. Because I had nothing to offer, I kept quiet. The director continued his observation and didn't lower his gaze from me. This lasted a while. Finally, he looked in the grade book, and without further hesitation simply said, "I am admitting you to my school."

I was barely able to blurt out a "thank you very much," and left astonished at such an incredible decision. It wasn't until I was in the hallway that I began to understand that he was a good man and a Communist only insofar as his position required it. At the time, many Poles humiliated themselves in that way.

As it turned out, I did not go to that school because I could not see myself in the role of a teacher. In August, I passed the entrance exam to Grajewo High School, and there I was admitted. I lived with my uncle, my former teacher. After three months, I transferred to the high school in Elk, and I lived with my oldest sister, Anastazja. Anastazja was extraordinarily family-oriented and helpful. She largely assisted all of her younger siblings to finish high school. Although she lived with her husband, Anthony, in a tiny room, the three of us were able to pass through this difficult time with good fortune and reach our goals. I reached my goal when I received the diploma of maturity on June 7, 1957, from Elk High School.

In my first year of high school, I missed my parents so much that I took the train to my parent's home each Saturday. To shorten my way, I would jump off the speeding train. I somersaulted down the embankment several times, which was a breakneck feat, but that was my youthful nature. My beloved dog, Rex, would await my arrival by the bridge from which I once fell into the canal surrounding the Osowiec Fortress. Rex would lay on the ground, and as I crossed the bridge, he would get up quickly and with all his strength jump on me, toppling me over. He would lick my face and hands as he let out incredible squeals and barks. Then we would run together. Rex would bark, run circles around me, and try to topple me over again for the two kilometers that separated us from the house. There, I felt happy.

At first, I had a very hard time getting accustomed to city life. I had to face many obstacles and humiliation before I came to know the new customs. The post-war poverty was the greatest source of these troubles. My parents could not afford to meet all of our needs. When they bought us clothes or shoes, those items were meant to last us for the next two years. My friends ridiculed me because of the way I dressed.

One day, I arrived in Elk wearing a brand new jacket that my parents bought for me in the Goniadz market. They complemented me that it fit me like a glove. I was pleased that I finally had something solid. I didn't take pride in the new purchase for long because the next day my friends called after me, "Hey, Papa, where'd you get that jacket?" Then I realized the jacket did not fit me like a glove after all, but I didn't blame my parents. I continued to admire them for their ability to give my siblings and me an education, which was a truly heroic feat. After all, each week I brought back one or two suitcases of food to Elk, which lasted me the entire week. One year, my parents were able to support four children outside of the house—three in Elk, and one son in the seminary in Frombork.

Nevertheless, during my second year in high school, I felt like a real city boy. My friends were mostly from the city, so I picked up similar qualities and habits from them. I was also known for my anti-communist views, and this added to my popularity.

One day I arrived at school early, when no one was there yet. I intended to take down Rokossowski's portrait, which hung in my classroom. The Communists claimed that he was the son of a Polish paver, but I knew the truth about his background. He was a Soviet General sent from Moscow, who became the Polish Marshall and Minister of Defense. After I ripped down the portrait, it turned out that underneath it was the likeness of the former Minister Zymirski, wearing an elegant sash across his shoulder. A friend, who came in a moment later, helped me finish the task. The new portrait looked impressive. I peered out the door and spotted my teacher walking toward the classroom with a group of students. Rokossowski's picture was still lying on the table. I yelled to my friend, and he immediately crumpled up the evidence and put it in his pocket because there wasn't another choice. During class, the teacher sat with his back to the portrait and didn't know the reason why everyone was laughing. He asked one of the students what was going on, and the student pointed at the picture. The teacher immediately became upset and stormed out of the room.

A moment later, he returned with the school principal, who looked at the portrait and stated, "I am giving you three minutes to think about it. Whoever did this must confess." I was afraid that my friend would give in, but no such thing happened. "Please stand," ordered the principal. He then called students up individually by their last name and asked them, "Did you do this?" Of course, everyone denied it.

It was my turn. "Czajewski, did you do this?"

"No, sir," I answered with confidence. When he posed the question to my partner in crime, I noticed his overstuffed pocket. I thought that this would be the end of us; the principal would surely notice it, and we would be caught. My friend denied it as well. I let out a sigh of relief when the director told him to sit. I thought we were out of the woods. To my surprise, the principal made everyone stand a second time, and this time he began very firmly posed the same question to us one by one. Once again, no one confessed and the principal, threatening that he would find out anyway, left the classroom.

The high school was buzzing about the incident for a while. Everyone wondered whether or not they would catch the one who did this. We kept the secret between the two of us, and thanks to this, we weren't suspended from school.

There was a period of four years when on the school grounds, before the start of class, all of the students had to sing the International Hymn. My friends who were standing close to me heard that I was singing something completely different. It caused a few smirks and commotion around me. It was a serious matter, tantamount to insubordination if someone was found mocking communist education. It was reported to the director, and after a couple of days, he called me in for questioning. He threatened that I would be suspended from school if I did not comply and continued to "sew sinister propaganda." I explained that I didn't remember the words to the song, and I must have made a mistake. I was harshly reprimanded, and I had to hear that it was unacceptable that a citizen of the People's Republic of Poland behave that way.

Whenever I found myself in these situations, I was reminded of the "de-kulaking" scene and my mother's weeping. The more I thought about this, the more I wanted to rebel against communist violence and the repression of Poles.

The next day I was approached by one of my classmates, a leader of the Socialist Youth Organization, who invited me to join the society. I began to laugh at the idea and firmly refused. Nevertheless, he did not give up, and a few days later, he demanded to talk with me. This time he used a threat saying, "Forget about passing your final exams if you don't join the organization."

I suspected that the principal was forcing him to convince me to join this awful organization. I wasn't in the mood to argue with him further, so after saying, "get lost," I walked away. I knew that many people did fine, even taking their final exams, so I would manage too.

On the day Stalin died, the principal called everyone to the auditorium and turned on the radio. When the speaker in a solemn voice started saying, "Our beloved Generalissimo, Joseph Stalin, is dead," the principal shed tears. When I returned to class, I turned to the leader of the Youth Organization and joked, "You'd better watch out! Now you're the one not going to pass the final exams."

After Stalin's death, there was a temporary "thaw," and the principal was fired. He probably foresaw this course of events already and had reason to cry. The thaw didn't last long and another tightening of the screws occurred a year later. During this short period, we lived with the hope that we would be liberated again. The history teacher finally began to tell the truth and opened our eyes to matters that were unknown and misunderstood by us until then.

The Socialist Youth Organization changed its name to the Polish Youth Organization, but its leader remained the same. The ideology did not change but became much more subtle.

The school year ended, and I decided to terminate my education there. My father tried to convince me to stay on the farm and become my own boss. I was swayed by the idea of being my own boss, and, of course, by the fact that the entire farm would be mine. My oldest sister married and lived permanently in Elk. My brother Romuald was studying to be a priest, so he would work at a parish one day. My sister Henryka was in her third year in a high school for kindergarten teachers and probably was not planning on returning to the farm either. I was my father's last hope, the son that would inherit this estate, so I did not want to disappoint him.

Right after returning from school, I went to mow the hay with my father. He handed me a sickle and put a whetstone in my pocket. I walked behind him with confidence in my step, thinking that I would show my father that I would be a good farmer. We started to cut the hay, but I only made it halfway. I tried to sharpen the scythe instead of sharpening the blade. I made it so blunt that it slid over the hay. I asked my father to show me the right way of sharpening. I started up again and the sickle cut as it should, but only until the next sharpening. My father finished cutting his area and started another. Meanwhile, I was still in the middle of my first try. I knew I wouldn't be able to catch up to him, and I didn't want to embarrass myself on the second attempt. I tried as hard as I could, but my strength failed me to the point that he caught up to me and pressured me from behind. On and on it went until dinner. Father cut two areas, while I cut one, as he easily caught up to me every time.

When my mother called us to the house for dinner, I no longer walked with a sure step but barely dragged behind my father. After dinner, my father sent me to tend to the cows. He didn't want to hassle me anymore. This time I herded them honestly, so that a bumblebee wouldn't send them running for the barn. I remembered that, as a young boy, I pretended to be a bumblebee, and I started to laugh to myself. This time, I would shoo the bee away because I would rather tend to the cows than cut hay.

The second day of hay cutting was just like the first. Once again, I only made it until noon. We went through the same routine until my father cut six hectares of hay by himself. I wondered what would happen, if one day, I were to cut the entire meadow myself. Most likely new hay would have grown before I could cut the first. Eight days later, we had to rake the hay and pile it into mounds. This was easier because Mom and Henryka helped. The most difficult job was carrying the mounds to one spot to make haystacks. The task required a lot of strength, but my parents did it with great skill.

Now I came to experience what work on the farm really was. I realized that it was a difficult way to make a living, so I decided that it would be easier if I got an education. I changed my mind about farming and decided to return to school. My father still had hope that I would become a farmer. He didn't know about the decision I had made.

After summer vacation, I started back to school. I came back to my parent's home each Saturday as usual. In time, however, I was less and less homesick. I was becoming used to city conditions. During one of the Saturdays, when I came home from school to see my parents, my father asked me to bring the dug potatoes from the field. I had a bit of trouble harnessing the horse to the wagon, but somehow I managed. I tied the reins around a stake, and knowing that the horse would make it to the yard on its own, I sat with my back to the front and began reading a book. Soon it became dark, and I was forced to stop reading. Then I noticed that the horse was missing and the harness was on the ground. Just then, I saw my father's shadow appear from the darkness leading the horse. He showed me the right way to put on the harness, and we returned home. After this incident, my father no longer tried to convince me to stay on the farm. He probably concluded that I was attracted to learning more than to work on the farm, and he left me to my whims.

In high school, I was interested in sports and was involved in many of them. My favorites were the one-hundred-meter dash and the long jump. I was also a good marksman. Because I always placed first in intramural sports, I was chosen to represent the school in the provincial and district competitions. Unfortunately, I didn't have much success during the Bialystok Province matches, and I had to settle for third place in the one-hundred-meter dash with a time of 11.6 seconds. For those times, it was a very good score, and I was proud when I was awarded a diploma. In the shooting competition, I was the best, but that was to be expected, as I had practiced shooting even as a kindergartener. Even the local press wrote about my feats, which lifted my spirits.

In high school, I had two good friends—one of them was the one with whom I took down Rokossowski's portrait. I went with them to the movie theater, for walks in the park, or to the lake. We had similar interests, which brought us together. We could always count on each other.

One beautiful, Saturday afternoon, we sat on a bench just near the lake observing the passersby. Just then, four slightly older, drunk boys passed us. First, they started to laugh at my friend who was a bit chubby. Then they surrounded us, and one of them suddenly pulled a bottle out of his pocket and aimed to hit my friend on the head. Because my friend was extraordinarily quick, in a second he had twisted the opponent's arm, tore the bottle from his hand, and hit him on the head with all his might. The bottle shattered into pieces, spilling red wine all over him. He looked like he was covered in blood. He stood there in a daze, unable to fight back, but the others jumped on us like lions. One of them got a hold of me and was prepared to strike. I had experience fighting the Osowiec boys in primary school, so I defended myself successfully and fought back with such strength that the one who held me spun around and fell beside the lake. I grabbed him by the shoulders and wanted to throw him into the water, just for fun, but he bit my finger in the meantime. Then I punched him in the jaw and at that moment, my friend yelled, "Let's go!" I scanned the "battleground" where they all lay. We ran away, but I had to go to the hospital, since my finger looked bad and wouldn't stop bleeding.

The next day in the evening, a Polish army captain, whom I tutored in math, paid us a visit, and began to tell us about the amazing sight he had seen the day before at the lake. "It was a real battle; I couldn't take my eyes off it," he commented.

My sister looked down at my finger and asked, "You weren't there by any chance, were you?" When I confirmed her suspicion, she took it as a joke. That day the officer had stood with several onlookers on the bridge, too far away to recognize me. The fighting was a necessary defense; we had no other choice. Nevertheless, I couldn't forgive my friend for smashing the bottle in revenge, so I stopped associating with him. After we ran away, the others were arrested. It turned out they were just a bunch of bullies. The press later reported the incident. We were lucky that it ended the way it did.

My oldest sister, Anastazja, who helped me the most in my youth.

The Difficulties of Exit Exams

The Polish high school exit exams are, and have always been, an important experience. Repeatedly the question would subconsciously appear, *Would I or would I not pass?* Finally, the written part of the exam was upon me, and with it, much emotion. A couple of days later, the list of candidates who passed the oral portion was displayed for the students to see. I went to see if I was on it. I glanced at the entire list. I did not see my name. I read the list again, but the result was the same. I broke down completely and turned to leave, when my friend pointed at the list and said, "Look, your name appears on the list, but mine doesn't." This time I calmly helped my friend look for his name. Unfortunately, we didn't find it. My friend became depressed, and not even my empathy consoled him much. He comforted himself with the thought that there were several others who hadn't passed the written exam either.

I passed the exam and graduated without any obstacles. I didn't hesitate to write to my brother about it. I relayed the news of my success, thrilled that the whole world was open before me. My brother's reply surprised me. He wrote back stating that real world problems were just about to begin, and how I solved them would be the real test of maturity.

Nevertheless, his words did not dampen my enthusiasm. At the senior dance, wearing a new watch on my wrist, a gift from my parents for graduation, I had a great time. I was the second one in my class to own a watch, and that counted for a lot. Before exit exams, I tutored a classmate in math. He was the first one who had a watch. I wasn't exactly envious of him, but I knew that someday, I would like to own such a trinket. Now I was proud that my parents recognized my hard work and gave me such a wonderful gift.

After the exit exams, I applied for admission to the Institute of Technology in Warsaw. I passed the exams but was not admitted as only limited spots were available. The reason for this was that children of Communist parents were given priority. This surprised me greatly.

During summer vacation, I helped my parents in the fields, and later Anastazja arranged a job for me in the Elk power plant where she worked. I moved in with my sister once again, and we walked to work on the same road together. I liked working in the office, and I had no problems performing all of the administrative tasks well. Soon, my work was rewarded with a stamp allowing me to purchase a bicycle. This was a great luxury at the time, since they weren't sold on the free market. I decided that it would be a gift for my parents.

A time later, I crossed paths with a former leader of the Polish Youth Organization, who asked me to forget his past behavior. What has passed is past, I thought. At times, we met for a cup of coffee at a cafe. We never discussed the past. It would have been uncomfortable for both of us. One day, as we returned home after coffee, a group of boys stopped us, and without any reason, began to assault my friend. Of course, even though there were six of them and only two of us, I didn't back away but came to his defense. The fight was uneven and initially doomed to fail, but I couldn't leave my friend to his own fate. I was surprised as to why just two of them jumped on me, but four beat my friend. Then, they stopped hitting me altogether and only pressed me against the wall and held back my hands. It was then that I saw how badly they were torturing my friend. I tried to escape and come to his aid, but I was punched in the jaw again and pressed harder to the wall. Suddenly, one of the onlookers yelled "Police!" and the boys started to disperse.

I saw the one who started the fight and took him by the collar. The policemen surrounded us and without asking any questions, took us to the Police Station. I was arrested and accused of the beatings. My main witness was left bleeding on the street, and I was defenseless. I was very upset that I wasn't even allowed to notify my sister, who lived across the street. A few hours passed, and I didn't know what would happen to me. The guy whom I held by the collar joked that I would do time just like him. I wasn't overjoyed with the idea. Through a small window in the door, I could see people entering the police station. Just then, I saw my friend, who received the beating, with his mother, so I started to punch the door with all my strength to draw attention to me. Fortunately, he noticed me as well. He had just left the hospital, where he had been treated for his injuries. At the police station, he was filing a report regarding the incident. He came close and asked, "Henry, what are you doing here?"

"Doing my time," I answered calmly.

"That's incredible," he replied and ran to the police chief.

A moment later, a policeman came to open the door and set me free. I saw that my friend was in poor condition. Although he was bandaged in the hospital, it was impossible to hide signs of the beating. The reason for the attack was never determined and deemed nothing more than a hooligan prank. I personally had a different view of the situation. Most likely, someone was taking revenge on him for being the former head of the Polish Youth Organization, and I regarded this as a purely political stunt. Otherwise, I should have been more badly hurt than he was, but that didn't happen. I did not rule out other reason for the attack, however.

It was February 2, 1958, an important and memorable moment for our family. It was on this day that my brother was ordained to be a priest in the Olsztyn Cathedral by the hands of Bishop Tomasz Wilczynski. I was touched to see the deacons. They lay on the floor of the sanctuary waiting for the moment of consecration. During the singing of the Litany of the Saints, all of the deacons were given one last opportunity to decide that they wanted to become priests. At that time, the family members and acquaintances gathered in the church to pray for the future priests, that the Holy Spirit may guide them in the right direction. It is an extraordinarily special moment, not only for the deacons themselves, but for their families as well.

At a ceremony a year earlier, one of the deacons had stood up and left for the sacristy because he had changed his mind. The deacon's mother fainted when she saw what happened. It was a dramatic moment, and it was difficult for her to come to terms with her son's decision. After that, no one dropped out and all were ordained as priests. When the moment arrived for Romuald's ordination, I saw tears in my mother's eyes, but they were tears of joy. The moment was so moving that it is difficult to describe what was taking place in our hearts at that time.

After the conclusion of the ceremony, all of the newly ordained priests and their families made their way to their hometowns, where they celebrated their first mass. A week later, on Sunday, my brother Romuald's mass took place in Osowiec. The celebration was even more moving, since the church was full of parishioners as my brother led his first Holy Mass. My mother smiled through her tears as she looked proudly on her son, the priest. I know that when she sang, "Gloria in Excelsis Deo" (Glory be to the Lord), she thanked God for giving her son this unique gift of priesthood.

For this occasion, my father summoned a twenty-four-piece orchestra from Grajewo. It made a great impression on everyone, as the music seemed to ascend to the heavens. When the trumpeter performed a solo, it seemed as if the archangel was announcing spectacular news! After Holy Mass, a reception for all of the invited guests took place. There was no end in sight to the embraces and congratulations! The orchestra started to play its concert again, and the music awakened a spiritual state in everyone. This moment remains in my memory forever.

After a weeklong rest, my brother was nominated to become a curate at the St. Wojciech Parish in Elblag. He left the family home to devote himself to priestly duties.

The Biography of Father Canon
Major Romuald Czajewski

This biography is a part of the book entitled, *The Osowiec Parish Its Social and Natural Environment,* authored by Father Jaroslaw Sokolowski, published in 2000 by Episteme 5.

I was born on February 28, 1933, in the village of Budne. My father's name was Jan. My mother, Zofia, of the Gosiewski family, was from the Modzele Village. My father died on April 6, 1963, at age fifty-four. My mother is ninety-one years old.

I spent part of my childhood in the village of Budne. Later, because of mass integration of land in the village, my family moved to a colony. We were granted a plot of land to build a house in the colony.

In 1939, World War II erupted. On September 2, 1939, the Luftwaffe staged an air raid on the fortress in Osowiec. The bombers roared over our homes. Although I was only six years old at the time, the memories of those moments will remain with me forever.

The dire years of German occupation began. Polish schools were shut down, and I could not continue my education. I remember turning the pages of the children's magazine, *Plomyk* (Glimmer), and curiously looking at the pictures, since I could not read yet.

The nightmare of the occupation continued. In 1944, the German troops drove us out of our home, so we escaped to the forest. When the Soviet forces reached the Biebrza River, we thought that the war would be over in a matter of days. Unfortunately, it lasted another six months. We suffered great hunger in the forest, which served as our shelter. We were compelled to find other ways to survive.

When we left the woods, we came upon German troops, the other front line. We were captured, and on the second day, taken to the concentration camp in Grajewo. We spent a couple of weeks there. The food in the camp was dreadful. A potato found floating in a bowl of soup was a treat. My father was transferred away from the camp to perform forced labor near Elk (Lyck).

We left the camp thanks to the intervention of my Uncle Henryk's fiancée. She spoke German well and negotiated our release with the camp commander, who let us go with a bribe. We then stayed with my mother's sister in the village of Swidry.

Following the end of military operations in 1945, we returned to our family home in Budne. Everything was completely destroyed. We settled into the basement, which the German troops had converted into a bunker. The house and the buildings around it were either taken apart or burned down. Rodents and famine were all that was left of our lands. My father struggled to rebuild our home.

At age twelve, I began my studies at the elementary school. During each summer vacation, I was able to finish an entire grade. I attended Osowiec School until sixth grade, and then completed seventh grade, my last year, in Grajewo. I completed elementary school in four years.

I began high school in Grajewo. I finished tenth grade at the Lower Salesian Seminary in Frombork. During our summer vacation, the Security Office closed down our seminary. In 1952, I completed the eleventh and final grade in Olsztyn.

After graduating, I entered the Hosianum Higher Seminary in Olsztyn. The seminary rector, Father Dr. Jozef Kapot, from the Kielce Diocese, was a wonderful professor and mentor. Despite the difficulties that Stalinism rendered our country, conditions in our seminary were quite good.

With the Lord's help, I passed our exams, and on February 2, 1958, I was ordained by Bishop Tomasz Wilczynski as a priest. After a week of rest, I reported to my parish at the Warmie Diocese.

I was appointed to serve as the vicar for St. Wojciech's Parish in Elblag. It was a difficult job. As a young priest, I taught religion class in two schools, forty-two hours of class in all. In order to be able to get from one school to the other between classes, I had to spend my first pay on a bicycle. When I returned from the schools, I still had administrative matters to take care of, so, oftentimes, I ate lunch and dinner together as one meal. No one complained that they were too busy; we had learned the value of hard work during our seminary years.

After a year in Elblag, the bishop transferred me to St. John the Baptist Parish in Pisz. There I worked as catechist in the villages' schools and in Pisz High School. I also had responsibilities at the local hospital.

In 1960, I was nominated to the position of vicar at Our Mother of Mercy Parish in Ruciane-Nida, headed by Father Major Ludwik Bialek. I worked there for three years. The large parish had an extensive jurisdiction with many catechetical points because religion class was banned in the schools. I would get to the places where I had taught on my Junak motorcycle.

The nomination to vicar in Stare Juchy came from the bishop himself, instructing me to form a parish in Grabnik. When the Security Office found out that a new parish was in the works, they launched an attack on me in order to remove me from Grabnik.

The next day, a Secret Police agent came to see me, threatening to arrest me if I didn't leave Grabnik and move to Stare Juchy. Somehow, I managed to overcome the situation even though I remained in Grabnik, and I worked there for eight years. I was able to accomplish a great deal in the church and even bought a house, where I was able to live and work in better conditions.

In 1971, Bishop Jozef Drzazga transferred me to Holy Heart of Jesus Parish in Orzysz, where I have been working for twenty-nine years as a pastor.

In 1990, I began a ministry in the army quarters. My first assignment with the army was in the penal unit (Orzysz was known throughout Poland for this unit).

Since 1992, I have been an army chaplain, ranking as major, in the fourth Suwalska Brigade of the Armored Cavalry in Orzysz. Thanks to God's grace, I have been a priest for forty-nine years, and I thank the Lord, our Eternal Minister, for my calling to priesthood and for being able to serve others as part of Christ's community.

My wife, brother, and me in our home.

My brother and me in 1998.

My College Years

The next years of my life were closely linked to a tri-city area, which includes the three cities of Gdansk, Gdynia, and Sopot. After I took the entrance exams at the Institute of Technology in Gdansk, I began to explore. I chose to begin with Gdansk, since this was where I was going to study for the next five years. The city had enchanted me from first glance. I didn't fail to travel along the coast. It was my first visit to the Baltic Sea, and the water and beaches charmed me completely. I yearned to stay there, but it was up to the school dean to decide if I was to be admitted to the ranks of my student brothers. My exams went well, but I was afraid that history would repeat itself from the prior year, when due to lack of space for enrollment, I was left out in the cold. This time luck was on my side, and I was admitted without any problem. Unfortunately, I was denied a scholarship because of my "kulak" (affluent) background. Luckily, however, I was able to live in the dormitory for not too excessive of a price. Six students had to fit in one small room and sleep on bunk beds. Once again, I had to adjust to a new environment. This time the adjustment didn't take long. After all, we were grown men, and a short conversation was enough to become acquainted and be on good terms.

It was much more difficult becoming accustomed to a new method of teaching. We had more freedom, and the student could make his or her own decisions regarding many situations. The lectures were not mandatory, and self-discipline was very necessary. The lecture halls and classrooms were located in various buildings, so it took some coordination of time to get to each lecture on time. I quickly became used to the new living conditions, and I was sure that I would be able to manage.

Finding meals proved a challenge. I would receive care packages containing provisions from my parents, but I always shared the contents with my roommates. Everyone was grateful for my generosity and shared whatever they had with me as well. It was a friendly gesture, and we managed somehow. Nevertheless, there were always exceptions.

In our room, one of our fellow roommates did not share any of the provisions he received from home, even though he often threw away his spoiled and expired food. Another one of his negative attributes was talking in his sleep. Some friends in our room were so bothered by this that they carried him in his bed out of the room and into the bathroom down the hall. He slept in such a deep sleep that he didn't even know where he was spending the night. In the morning, the students who came into the bathroom poured a bucket of water over him to wake him up. This happened often, especially when he refused to share his food with us. He was carried out systematically throughout the entire school year. I felt a bit sorry for him, but unity had to be maintained, and I didn't veto it. What was worse was that no one helped him carry parts of his bed back to the room. Although it was difficult, he did it by himself. I couldn't understand why he preferred to sleep in the bathroom rather than share his food with us.

I often took advantage of free leftovers from the school's cafeteria. A line of famished students stood with plates and spoons in hand waiting to attack when the door opened for that particular shift. They all barged into the cafeteria, and whoever reached the pots first had the greatest chance to get to their food of choice. Even cutlets were put out for the taking. Unfortunately, there weren't many, so only those who stood in line for two hours or more got a chance to get a goody. Everything disappeared in a flash. Comical scenes took place, especially on Saturdays, when pots of beet salad were left out. The students wore white dress shirts for a party, and their sleeves turned red. Ten to fifteen hands would reach into the pot at once. It was no wonder that each student would make the other one drop from his spoon what the other was pulling upwards. Then we started this strange type of hunt all over again.

During the same period, my brother Romuald served as the vicar for the Elblag Parish. I visited him often, even twice a month. The eighty kilometers from my dormitory in Gdansk to Elblag was not too great of a distance and taking the train was convenient. My brother, even though he was poor himself, supported me financially. I never had to contribute payment for my train ticket, and he even gave me money for a poppy-seed bread roll. The pastor of the church was an honest canon priest. I was very fond of him because he never failed to invite me for dinner. During one of our discussions, he gave me the idea that I should not waste time at the Institute of Technology but enter the seminary instead. I was forced to explain to the canon priest that, although priesthood is a great thing, I didn't feel like I had the calling to it.

"It's a shame," he stated. "You would make a good priest and preacher."

My favorite part of the Elblag Church was the choir, from where I could get a wonderful view of the entire church. It was there that I met a girl who belonged to the church choir. Soon from a platonic acquaintance, she became a good friend of mine, but the friendship didn't last long because I wasn't ready to take on a serious relationship.

One Sunday afternoon, another girl came to the presbytery. Knowing that I was a student at the Institute of Technology, she wanted to find out about her chances of being admitted there. I couldn't give her an answer that day because I was in a hurry to catch a train back to Gdansk. Since summer vacation was approaching, I gave her my new address where I was staying during the break. I asked her to contact me by mail, and I assured her that I would answer any questions without delay.

I intended to spend my summer vacation working in the Gdansk shipyards, so I could save some money for books, for part of my room, and for board. I got the job thanks to patronage, and I reported to the shipyard right away. I was assigned to a unit that hired students from various universities. Our job was to restore Polish-made, Soviet Russia-purchased ships, which had already undergone their maiden voyages. I was awestruck when the supervisor took us on a tour around the ship. Our job was to clean it. The new unit was completely devastated. All of its loose parts were missing. The ship was incredibly filthy. I asked my boss who paid the costs of the repair. It turned out to be the shipyard (he meant Poland) because the ships were under warranty, and following each trial voyage, it would return to port to undergo any minor repairs. These, however, were not small adjustments, but a complete overhaul. Settling of accounts was also disadvantageous to Poland. The equipment and machinery that were installed on Soviet Russian ships were bought by Poland with foreign currency (dollars) in the West, but Soviet Russia paid Poland for the completed ships in rubles. As a result, Poland had little to gain, and most of the time came out at a loss.

That is what Polish trade with the Soviet Union looked like; those were our political relations. Poland's subjugation to the Soviet Union manifested itself not only in the political sphere but also in trade. The job was, to put it gently, very unpleasant, but for those days and student conditions, paid well and amounted to 100 zloty for eight hours of work. For 250 zloty a month, I rented a small, walk-through room from a young couple. It was not private, but the rent was low. I hoped to save some money during the three-month-long student break.

One particular Wednesday, I received a postcard from Elblag from the choir girl informing me she would come and visit me on Saturday. She asked that I pick her up from the train station. I was surprised. I thought our contact was cut off forever. It was too late to reply to her by mail, and at that time, only a few party honchos had telephones.

Friday I received a second postcard from Elblag. This time, it was from the girl who asked me for advice on attending the Institute of Technology. She, too, wrote to inform me that she would come on Saturday by train. I was overwhelmed by too many emotions, so I turned to my landlady for advice. I presented my dilemma to her. I was even prepared to run away from home, but she put my worries to rest with one statement, "Whatever you do, you'll regret it anyway. Bring both of them to the house for dinner that night, and, on Sunday, invite one of your male friends to come along with the three of you."

Saturday I went to the train station with dread, and although I don't usually lose my sense of humor, I was in no mood for joking around this time. The choir girl was the first one I spotted. I greeted her and explained that another friend of mine just arrived on the same train. When the other girl arrived, I introduced them. They acted cordially toward each other, so this calmed me down. We took a trolley home, and there we were in for a surprise. The landlady prepared a real party for us. After a delicious dinner and a bottle of wine, our tongues became untied, and everyone was content.

The next day we met with my friend, who worked as a sailor on a tour boat called, *Water Maiden*. The ship toured between Gdansk and the Hel Peninsula. He arranged for an all-day excursion on the boat, free of charge. After boarding the ship, my friend had to leave us to tend to his duties. We floated down the Motlawa River toward the Gdansk Bay. It was thrilling to see Gdansk from this perspective for the first time. I noticed that the girls were delighted as well. When we sailed out into the Baltic Sea, my friend joined us since the responsibility of navigating the ship didn't belong to him. The ship's orchestra started to play the waltz. My friend asked one of the girls to dance. After a short excursion to Hel Peninsula, we returned to the *Water Maiden*. The boat toured all day, and we enjoyed ourselves as we did in the olden days. After the last tour, we walked the girls to the train station. I was a bit surprised that my friend gushed as he bid farewell to the girl he had just met (the one who was interested in studying at the Institute of Technology).

As it later turned out, the day was a happy one for my friend because their friendship led them to the altar two years later. To this day, I ask myself, *Was it a coincidence or a stroke of fate?* That is the question.

I thought that this would be the end of my friendship with the girl from the choir. I became convinced that our paths would forever part. I was wrong. A few years later, our paths crossed again, but in entirely different and not so pleasant circumstances.

The next day, after work, I directed myself to the flower shop. I bought a beautiful bouquet of flowers and graciously gave them to my landlady to thank her for her help in getting me out of that difficult situation.

I took advantage of each spare moment to go the movie theater and see a good film. It was a habit I picked up in high school. I loved to watch circus performances also. When the circus came to Gdansk, I decided to go to their show. Before I bought a ticket, though, I turned my attention to a posting on one of the circus wagons. The sign announced The Talking Head Will Tell You the Truth. Unfortunately, the price of this truth was equal to the price of the circus ticket. These were two separate shows. At first, I couldn't make a decision on which to choose because I only had enough money for one ticket. Then I overheard a conversation about the amazing experiences to be had with the "talking head," so I decided to choose that show.

Six people were let into the show at a time. The séances lasted about fifteen minutes. The line of people moved along, and finally, it was my turn. I stepped into the circus wagon with the others. We stood along the railing, behind which was a curtain and nothing else. Suddenly, the curtain lifted, and I saw a live head sitting atop a long neck in the middle of the table. Shaken by the sight, I quickly glanced to my sides to see if anyone was running away. If anyone were to move, I would probably have been the first one to take the closed door of the wagon with me as I ran. A moment later, I calmed down and began to stare at the head, searching for the answer on how they were able to construct a head without a body. Then the door behind the table opened, and a man entered the room announcing, "Talking head, say hello to everyone!"

Its long eyelashes lifted and behind them pair of large beautiful blue eyes looked at us. The eyes and the light blond hair seemed wonderfully alluring. I discretely looked from side to side a second time to see if I could spot the reaction of my companions to the spectacle. Everyone stood gaping at the talking head, as if in a trance.

"Good day, everyone!" The talking head greeted us.

Amazing! I couldn't wait to see what would happen next. First, she scanned all of us with her beautiful blue eyes, and then she fixed her gaze on each one of us. For a long moment, she piercingly stared into each of our eyes. I remember this gaze because it seemed as if she had peered deep into my soul. Then, one by one, she foretold our futures. Her words weren't choreographed. Each of us heard something different. When she came to me, she stared into my eyes and said, "I see a stormy life full of surprises and turmoil. I see love of a woman, emigration abroad, and a lot of money."

Of course, what else could she have said? I thought.

Leaving the circus wagon, I regretted having spent my last zloty and not having found anything out. However, the man standing next to me seemed very pleased with her prediction. He grabbed my arm and excitedly started to analyze the words that I had just heard. "Mister, how could she have known that I just applied for a passport, and it was denied?" He repeated a few other details, which appeared to be true. I listened to his conclusions, but I still wasn't satisfied because my fortune seemed far from coming true. I didn't have a girlfriend, so love was nowhere in sight. The only time I had been abroad was through the characters in the books I had read, and an actual trip abroad was something I couldn't even dream of. Lots of money? I wasn't sure what money she was referring to because I barely had enough to buy a ticket to the talking head show, not to mention the circus. I hung my head low and headed home, not knowing that her fortune would come true exactly as she had foretold it.

Working in the Gdansk Shipyard

After two weeks, my job at the shipyard was complete because the ship had been renovated, cleaned, and given back to the Soviet owners for their use. Luckily, the owner of the apartment where I rented a room offered me a job at his company. The company was located on the shipyard grounds and specialized in installing cranes and gantries. I gladly accepted the proposition, even though it required working at great heights and was dangerous. I didn't have a fear of heights, and I wasn't afraid to take risks either.

On my second day, I was already assigned to a unit for training. After a few days of apprenticeship, I was sent on a trip to Zamech in Elblag. The company manufactured propellers for ships, and our job was to mount gantries in the newly built warehouse there. I worked alongside two other assembly technicians, and our schedules depended solely upon us. We worked a few extra hours during the week, and in exchange, took a Saturday off to relax, visit the city, and explore the surrounding area.

Because the job required high qualifications, the pay was commensurately high. In addition, the company paid for room, board, and commuting costs when one was required to travel. They called this "the delegation." Each of us tried as best as we could to eat as inexpensively as we could and save a bit of money. We usually ate breakfast at the Milk Bar Diner and dinner in the hotel restaurant. We ate our lunch in the company cafeteria. That was our weekday schedule. Our weekends differed significantly from workdays, since we tried to take private trips, either individually or as a group.

Although I worked in Elblag, I did not associate with the two girls whose visit I had unexpectedly hosted in Gdansk. I tried to be loyal to my resolution not to become permanently involved with any girl until I finished my studies. My brother was transferred to Pisz, so I no longer attended the church at which he previously worked, where the girls lived and had attended mass. Instead, I attended the one near our hotel.

I enjoyed taking boat trips along Vistula Bay. That is how I got to Tolkmick, Krynica Morska, and Frombork. Frombork particularly interested me, since it is the city of our great Polish astronomer, Nicholas Copernicus. I visited the bell tower and the planetarium, then Copernicus' Tower and the former apartment in which he lived. I also visited the gothic Cathedral of the Ascension of Our Lady, where Copernicus is said to be buried in the undergrounds. I took a train to Malbork to visit the castle complex, residence of the great Teutonic Knights. The castle is surrounded by fortified walls and gates and is one of the largest medieval strongholds in Europe. Spending time surrounded by nature and traveling inspired me; it gave me the strength and encouragement to realize my goals.

I was young and fascinated with life, so I took every opportunity to go to a fine restaurant or coffee shop and observe how people from a higher society lived their lives. One day I went with a friend to one of the most exclusive restaurants in Elblag. Some sort of reception was taking place at the time, and we were unable to be seated. My friend, who was originally from the Kaszuby region, had the idea that we should pretend to be Germans from the other side of the iron curtain (Western Germany). The waiters were eager to serve such guests, counting on generous tips. My friend turned to the waiter, asking him in German for quick service, as we were flying back to Hamburg in a few hours. A split second later, an empty table was found. The waiter recommended the best and most expensive dishes the restaurant had to offer. We felt like real gentlemen from the "rotten West," and without a moment of hesitation, we accepted the recommended dishes as well as two shots of cognac. The alcohol immediately acted on our empty stomachs, and my friend ordered another round. Although, pretending to be German I repeated "ya, ya," (yes, yes), I was really thinking "no, no," because I feared that "us Germans" wouldn't have enough money to pay the bill. The dinner turned out to be wonderful, but it seemed that the bill had a few zeros too many. It wouldn't have been proper to inspect the bill closer, so without hesitating, we paid the owed amount, adding a generous tip for the waiter. Pleased with our exploit, we took a taxi to the hotel.

In the morning, we counted our money and went to church to pray that we might survive until the first of the following month as salaries were paid out on the first day of each month. Nevertheless, we were drawn to the restaurant and decided to go there again, but this time because of our thin wallets, we took a trolley there. This time the restaurant was empty; only a few diners occupied the tables. We took a seat at the table in the middle of the room, and surprisingly, the same waiter ran up to us who had served us the previous day. This time, speaking Polish, we ordered two hamburgers, the cheapest dishes on the menu. The waiter laughed and said, "Oh, so you gentlemen arrived back from Hamburg already?"

A moment later, the waiters and kitchen staff came out to admire the "exotic" Germans. We waved to them and laughed along with them at our good sense of humor.

Then, I became curious about my friend's identity, and I asked him if he considered himself a Pole or a German. His answer startled me. "Before the war, when our lands were German, we considered ourselves Poles, and fought for Poland. But now I consider myself German because I hate the nasty Soviet Communists," he said. He wasn't afraid to reveal this to me because he knew my view on the topic very well, and we discussed it many times. He had a tough Kaszub nature, which impressed me.

Another time, the three of us were having dinner, and our "Kaszub," as we called him, bet us that he could eat an entire glass beer mug except for the handle. Of course, we figured he was joking, and the bet was on. We watched with horror as the Kaszub bit off a piece of the mug, having drunk the beer, and began crushing it with his teeth. We were completely dumbfounded when we saw him swallowing it and getting ready to take another bite out of the jagged mug. We couldn't utter a word, since what he did was beyond all rationale, and what we saw was surreal to us. He crushed another bite of glass and swallowed again. He looked at us and waited for our reaction. He didn't take a third bite because we stopped him for fear that his feat would end badly.

As we paid him his winnings, the Kaszub laughed and suggested that he would eat the worst part of the mug, the handle, but that would cost more because the handle was tough to bite through! Of course, we didn't accept his bet because we had enough of what we had seen already. Then the Kaszub admitted that the handle eating bet was just a joke because as he told us before, he could eat the mug except for the handle. He explained that this wasn't as awful as it looked because saliva softens the glass so it can't injure the stomach. We just wondered why he didn't cut his mouth, but we decided that we didn't want to discuss it any further.

Soon both of my co-workers were transferred to another job, and Mr. Jozef joined me. He was a forty-year-old bachelor (unmarried men were usually chosen as part of a delegation, so as not to separate families). He was a head-to-toe gentleman. I came to like him a lot because from the first day on the job together, we understood each other without words. What's more, he was an extraordinary expert, and I valued this virtue in him. I learned a lot at his side—above all, a good work ethic, which proved fruitful throughout my life. We always spoke formally with one another, via "Mr." and that's how it remained until the end of our working together.

One day, I was performing a duty on the gantry, and I had to move a steel line to another place. As I moved the line, I didn't notice that its other end, hanging outside of the gantry, was coming into contact with the high voltage electrical lines. Sparks started to fly at the highest point of the gantry, and it looked like a fireworks display! After this accident, the electricians especially were astonished at why I wasn't electrocuted and how I survived. It was decided that the rubber-soled shoes I was wearing probably saved my life. I thought otherwise, and I quietly thanked my Guardian Angel.

Soon after this accident, there was another one. It affected not only me and Mr. Jozef but all of the people working in that area of the company. While the oxygen burner was in use, an explosion occurred, and the fire, tearing apart the hoses, flashed toward the tank. I was on the gantry at the time, and I could only survey the danger of the situation from the top. I had no chance of escape. Fortunately, Mr. Józef was on the ground, and it took him only a few jumps to get to the tanks and turn off the valves before the fire reached them. There were spare tanks next to it, so one could only image what would have happened if all of them had exploded. Half of the warehouse would have been blown to pieces. We took a break from work and went into the city to recover from the "What if…?"

I headed toward the movie theater to relax. Mr. Jozef went to the restaurant for a beer; even though he usually avoided alcoholic drinks. I left to go to the movies, and saw a comedy. I then returned to my hotel room. I got comfortable in bed and started to turn the pages of an interesting book I was reading. A few hours later, I heard a knock on the door. Already at the door, Mr. Jozef began to apologize for bothering me, but he had come about an urgent matter. He just returned from a restaurant where he met two charming girls. He arranged a date with both of them at our hotel restaurant for the next day, hoping that I would join them. He assured me that he knew women, and that I wouldn't be disappointed. I wasn't interested in his proposition, but he finally convinced me to give in.

Our delegation pay had arrived from Gdansk, so we were able to permit ourselves a small expense. We went down to the restaurant at the appointed time, and he cheerfully introduced me to the new acquaintances. I had to admit, he did have good taste, and his description of them was fairly accurate.

Mr. Jozef was in his element. He ordered whatever we asked for, and because he was naturally cordial, the girls were pleased. I was somewhat uneasy with the way they spoke and with their overconfidence. I began to observe them, and at a certain point, I noticed one of them winking to the other. Just then, I realized whom we were dealing with. Then they excused themselves to go to the bathroom. I took advantage of the moment to explain to Mr. Jozef that these girls were "girls for money." With every effort I made to dissuade him, he argued that he had twice the life experience. Then I understood that further discussion was pointless. The ladies came out of the bathroom very cheerful, but my older friend's mood soured for the moment, so I had to take charge of the situation. Because I always had a good sense of humor, I had no trouble carrying on the rest of the conversation. At the same time, I tried to find out as much as I could about them, hoping that my older friend would finally open his eyes. Soon I realized that my hopes were pointless. I decided to leave the table, regretting that I agreed to the date in the first place. I excused myself to go to the bathroom, and then I discretely left the restaurant. I hoped that Mr. Jozef would manage somehow. I didn't go back to my hotel room because I knew they would try to look for me there. Instead, I headed to the park across the street.

I wondered if abandoning my friend was the right thing to do. I justified it by thinking that he didn't need my protection and since he wouldn't be insulted, I would pay him back for my half of the bill. I relaxed and joined the people walking through the park. I wandered aimlessly until the locale closed. At exactly midnight, the lights began to go off, and I decided to return to my room. I went straight to bed and fell into a deep sleep. In the morning, I went to Mr. Jozef's room to apologize for my undiplomatic behavior. I was surprised that despite knocking several times on the door, no one answered. When I found out at the reception desk that he didn't spend the night in the hotel at all, I became very worried.

I took a trolley to our milk bar hoping to see him there. It proved to be a disappointment, so after breakfast I planned to go to the warehouse, although I was sure he wouldn't be there either. I exited onto the street and made my way toward the trolley stop. I was startled to see Mr. Jozef on the other side of the street. He noticed me as well and started to motion wildly with his hands, calling me to him. Happy that he was finally found, I ran across the street. He didn't let me speak but started showing me his open wallet. I wasn't sure what he was trying to say. Finally, he began with a question, "Mr. Henry, do you have your money?"

"Of course I do," I answered.

"Thank God, I'm saved," he replied. "The 20 zloty I showed you in my wallet is all that is left of yesterday's delegation pay," he said.

"Well, where is the rest of the 10,000 that you had gotten yesterday?" I probed to find out more. Then he began to explain in detail what had happened.

"We tried looking for you everywhere, but you seemed to have disappeared. The girls invited me over to their apartment, so we took a taxi to the appointed address. I only remember that they took out a bottle of vodka, and I drank maybe two shots of it. Then they stripped naked and nonchalantly told me that if I caught one of them, she would be mine. Of course, I started chasing them around the large apartment, but suddenly, I blacked out. In the morning, I woke up on the sofa with a throbbing headache. My first thought was, *Do I have my wallet?* I was so happy when I felt it in my pocket. Just to be sure, I checked its contents. I couldn't believe my eyes; I saw only the 20 zloty I just showed you! When I realized what had happened, I sobered up straight away and even forgot about the headache.

"The girls were already sitting at the table and cheerfully drinking coffee. This time I lost my temper and demanded my money back, threatening that if they didn't do it, I would call the police. I probably amused them with the threat because they began to mock me. Then one of them yelled, 'You pauper, you didn't have a penny to your name. Give us the money back for the half-liter of vodka we offered you last night, or we'll call the police!' I quickly left the apartment and walked back here because I wasn't sure if the 20 zloty they left in my wallet would be enough for a taxi. Now you know why my first question was about your money."

I consoled Mr. Jozef by telling him that I would lend him as much as he needed until his next payday. He was impressed by my perceptiveness, and he changed his mind about insisting that he surpassed me in life experience. Until the end of our job in Zamech, we didn't have another amorous adventure, but that was only because we avoided girls like the plague.

In mid-September of 1959, we finished mounting the gantry and reported its completion to the supervisors. The inspection commission pointed out a few flaws, which we repaired within a day. Those were my last days of working for the company because on October 1st, I was to begin my second year at the Institute of Technology. Mr. Jozef took a train back to Gdansk. I was on my own for those few days and needed to wait for the truck, which was my responsibility in its transport of the company's tools and equipment that were used for the assembly process.

The next day the truck arrived at noon, and the worker began to load. In the meantime, I went to the General Mechanic's Department to take care of the formalities and paperwork necessary to transport the equipment. With the specification sheet in hand, I went to see how the loading was coming along. It took longer because there was plenty of work. The job was finally finished and the driver, loader, and I drove the truck up to the gate. The company guard came out of his office and told the driver to take the truck out to the parking lot. He began carefully inspecting all of the units on the specification sheet. We were forced to unload everything and then load the truck again after the inspection. The irritated loader said something to the guard, who immediately found a mistake, and decided that we were transporting too much electrical cable. I began to convince the guard that this cable was specific to the gantries, and that we had exactly the amount indicated on the document. I proposed that he measure it to determine whether we had too much, or perhaps, not enough of it. It was obvious that I just upset him further, and without saying a word, he threw the biggest cable off the truck, and then went to his office.

A half an hour later, a police jeep arrived. The officer walked up to us and asked us who was responsible for the vehicle and the load. I got out of the truck and went with the policeman to the guard's office. There I was notified that I was under arrest for attempting to steal electrical cable. Once more, I tried to explain to the policeman that the thick-as-an-arm cable would be of no use to anyone, and furthermore, Zamech didn't use this type of cable, so it didn't belong to the company. I wasn't able to prove it because it was late, and all of the offices were already closed. The policeman told us that he would have to arrest all of us until we were able to clear up the matter. It was Saturday, and since it was an arrest case, we would have to stay in jail until Monday.

I started to plead for the release of the loader and driver. I asked if they would be able to go back to our base in Gdansk. By now, the disputed cable was strewn on the ground, but the rest was correct according to the specification sheet. This time I was able to convince the policeman, and he let them leave the gate. I was relieved that at least they wouldn't have to suffer the consequences of the guard's mistake, especially since neither of them was guilty. The vehicle, along with the driver and loader, was being leased from another company who had nothing to do with it. The policeman took me outside and put me in the back seat of his jeep. It was already getting dark when we sped along the streets of Elblag to the local Civic Police Station. I forgot to take my jacket from the truck and felt the cold run through my body as the wind blew my hair in all directions.

I was convinced that, after questioning, I would be released. No such thing happened, and what's worse, they didn't even check my identification. The policemen confiscated my personal belongings and led me down the steps to the basement level. At the end of a long hallway, they opened one of many metal doors and forcefully pushed me inside a cell.

It was the second arrest of my life. The first time was in Elk, where I was held only in the interrogation room, but here I was in an actual jail cell. The long creaking of the door and the loud thud as it closed made a great impression on me. I felt totally helpless. I would have been lost in my emotional distress, if it hadn't been for three pairs of curious eyes staring at me. Startled, I quickly controlled my emotions. I was comforted by the fact that I was not alone and would have companions in my suffering. I greeted them and sat on a bunk made of boards that they indicated I could use. At twenty-one years old, I was the youngest one among them. Seeing that I was troubled and helpless, my cellmates offered to help. Each of them first took turns telling me the reason for their detention and then shared interesting stories about their lives. Their stories began to interest me, so I calmed down after a while seeing that they were very relaxed.

One of them was detained for the illegal trade of paintings. He was a door-to-door salesman and went from house to house offering his products. I had to admit that he had a great talent for speaking. He described his story so vividly that we were all ears. We intently listened to his adventures at work, as well as incredibly fantastic love stories. I listened to his musings with a bit of apprehension; some of his stories sounded too far-fetched. Perhaps he was just trying to take us away from this brutal reality and wanted to add some psychological balance. He probably realized his goal, but in my case, not entirely. I was inconsolable, and late into the night, my mind was plagued with dark scenarios about my near future.

In the morning, the door opened every hour, and someone was called by his last name. Soon I was left alone because not one cellmate came back after the interrogations. Hours passed, and no one came for me. The previous day I had eaten only breakfast, planning to have dinner after leaving Zamech. The tiny window high up in the basement wall let in less and less light as dusk fell. I concluded that it had already been twenty-four hours since my arrest. One would be held in jail for a day before being taken to prison. My anxiety about what would happen next reached its peak. I paced back and forth in the cell, my steps becoming more nervous. I had to do something to call attention to myself.

I started banging at the dirty metal door, hoping that someone would notice me. When no one responded, I became more distressed. I had no other choice but to keep up the procedure and await any answer. When I lost all hope of regaining my freedom, I heard the creek of the door latch, and the silhouette of a policeman appeared at the door.

"Your name, citizen?" he asked. After obtaining the information, he closed the door again and left. Now I could only wait patiently for what was to happen next. Time passed very slowly.

Finally, another officer appeared, and after mispronouncing my name, he ordered me to come with him. I didn't correct his mistake because I was afraid the explanation would cost me a few more days in the cell. I followed the policeman obediently, and only when we got to the interrogation room did I give him the correct pronunciation of my name. After signing the report, they returned my belongings and ordered me to appear at the office of Zamech's General Mechanic at eight o'clock Monday to hand in documents confirming my report. "You are free to go, citizen," the civic police officer said dryly.

I left the building with incredible feelings of joy. I was finally able to see the starry sky and go wherever I pleased. Because I hadn't eaten anything since Saturday morning, I first went to a restaurant and then to the hotel to relax after the awful ordeal. I concluded that I was forgotten, and I had unlawfully spent over twenty-four hours in jail. I knew that in the People's Republic of Poland, people had no voice. The rule was to be quiet or not exist at all.

In the morning, as the police ordered, I reported to Zamech. The permits were controlled by the same guard who reported the "crime" to the police on Saturday. He lowered his head as I walked past him. He issued me the entry permit on Saturday, so according to the law, I could no longer enter the company grounds. I waited for his decision. He finally lifted his head, and his eyes gave away his humiliation. He wasn't able to utter a word, and he only motioned for me to enter. Saturday's insolence and confidence were now lost somewhere.

The General Mechanic's Department prepared the necessary documents. All of the workers were taken aback by the guard's behavior. The policeman, who waited for my arrival at the office, looked over the documents and turned to me saying, "You're free to go."

I was upset by the arrogance of the regime's representative, so I asked, "Is that all?" He didn't understand what I was referring to, so I explained that I was waiting for an apology.

"Let's go already," the words barely left his mouth.

As I left the company grounds, I thanked the guard and asked that, in the future, he follow his sense of reason, if he had one at all, rather than his emotions. I took the next train to Gdansk to settle financial matters with the company. A week later, I had to begin a new year at the Institute of Technology, but after my adventures, I decided that I deserved a few days of relaxation.

My Trips around Poland

I was surprised with the dean's rejection of my application for a room in the school dormitory, so I moved in with a friend in Gdansk who happened to be looking for a roommate. The costs of room and board were much higher this way. Struggling to manage, I had to make up the difference by tutoring mathematics.

Our landlady, an elderly woman, was very fond of us. She made good wine, and she treated us to some occasionally. When she left the city, she entrusted us with her entire fortune. She had two vessels of wine, which were still in the fermenting phase and not yet ready to bottle. Despite this, two weeks later, my friend and I tried the wine from one of the vessels. It was so good that, once in a while, we permitted ourselves a glass. After six weeks of her absence, half of the vessel was already empty. Before she came back, I added water so she wouldn't notice the loss.

When the landlady returned, the first thing she did was to bottle the wine, beginning with the vessel that was untouched. First, she tried some herself and then offered some to us. It was very good, and we praised her product. When she tried some wine from the other vessel, she was unpleasantly surprised by the different taste. She poured some for us to judge. With all seriousness, I remarked that someone must have added water to the wine because there could be no other reason for the difference in taste. The landlady began laughing and decided that our punishment would be to drink the entire vessel of watered-down wine. We begged her to let us pay our penalty over time because we would burst at the seams if we drank so much water at once, the water, which by some unexplainable accident, didn't turn to wine. I added that we must live too far away from Cana of Galilee, which is why one vessel turned to wine and the other one didn't. She had a good sense of humor, so she dismissed the matter.

The school year was nearing its end, and I was planning on working during summer break, when I unexpectedly received two letters. One was from my brother with an offer to go with him, along with two of his friends, on a motorcycle trip around Poland. The other letter came from my oldest sister, Anastazja. She wrote that she had moved from Elk to a newly built home in Bialystok. She insisted that I move into her home while I finished my studies in the Higher Engineering College of Bialystok. (Later the name was changed to the Institute of Technology). My sister was very family-oriented, and knowing my difficult financial situation, she still wanted to help me. We became very close when I lived with her before, five years prior. My brother-in-law was never opposed to my sister's decisions; I appreciated that about him. Now two years had passed, and we barely saw one another. I took this under consideration, but first, I decided to take my brother up on his enticing offer.

I replied to his letter right away, and informed him when my last exam would be, after which I would be available. I proposed that we begin the trip in Gdansk. Soon I received a reply that all of the companions on our journey agreed to the date and to my proposal to start the trip from the coast.

On July 2, 1960, on three motorcycles, we began our journey around the "world," our name for this trip around Poland with great exaggeration. My brother traded in his Polish WFM motorcycle for a Junak, a motorcycle of the highest class in those times, which was made in Poland on an English license. I was grateful to my brother for taking me on this trip at his own expense. I served as the guide around the adjoining tri-cities of Gdansk, Sopot, and Gdynia.

By afternoon, we were already on our way. We planned to spend the night in Kolobrzeg. We had no regrets; it was a beautiful tourist area. Following a nightly walk along the Baltic Sea and dinner, we managed to get accommodations. I was delighted and touched. Before I fell asleep, I wondered if my childhood dreams were starting to come true. I felt as if I was becoming one of the heroes from the books I read.

The next day we arrived at Auschwitz-Birkenau. I saw this place of Polish martyrdom and that of many other nations for the first time. The museum of this former Nazi concentration camp left a big and lasting impression on me. One room had a display of hundreds of pairs of shoes of children who were killed in the concentration camp.

It reminded me of a time when I was a child, when two German soldiers took pity on our family and didn't report us for hiding meat in our cellar. They pretended that they did not see it. If the authorities had found out, we would have been killed, and it could have been our shoes in that display case, along with the others.

At each larger destination, I bought an emblem and attached it to my garrison cap (we were not required to wear helmets yet). We were almost halfway through our trip and already there wasn't enough empty space on my cap to attach more. I was thrilled that I was able to be in so many interesting places. I didn't assume that most of the curious places and most beautiful sights were still to come.

Our first goal was to make it to the top of Giewont Peak, which had a visible metal cross towering the top. Although our guide, Father Turek, my brother's friend, took on a quick pace from the start, we managed to keep up with him. He was born close to the mountains and was quite used to its terrain. Soon the trail became steeper, and it was hard to catch up to our guide. He would stop from time to time to wait patiently for us as we slowly made our way to the destination. As we neared the summit, and the cross atop, we gained new strength as if a magnet drew us upward. We finally reached the top. As we touched the cross, we could not feel the efforts of our climb any longer. The view extending all around us was unforgettable. Nothing could take away the wonderful feeling of accomplishment in that moment. I felt as if I stood on top of the world; it was 1,894 meters above sea level. I wanted to stay there longer, but our guide hurried us along because he knew what was ahead. On one side of the Giewont is a precipice. Out of curiosity, I peered down. I wondered how long it would take me to reach the bottom if I fell. The very thought sent chills down my spine.

From there our untiring guide took us up the mountain trail to Kasprowy Wierch. Its summit was even higher at 1,985 meters above sea level. There we rested at the local restaurant. The meal and coffee gave us strength to continue the trek. I proposed that we take the cable car down the mountain, but Father Turek convinced us that it would only be a short walk down Kasprowy Wierch. Later I came to regret that walk because as it turned out, it was easier to climb to the top than to descend the mountain. At least it seemed like it to me. By now, we were completely exhausted. Only our guide, Father Turek, experienced in these kinds of expeditions, felt great. Later that evening we reached his house, where we fell like logs onto our beds and into a blissful sleep.

In the morning, I wanted to get out of bed and put my legs on the floor. I noticed that I had difficulty doing this. My legs took on a life of their own, and I couldn't take a single step. I decided then that I was a true highlander but from the plains after all. To take a step, I had to lift my legs with my arms. At breakfast, I told my friends of my sorry state, hoping for some sympathy, but to my disappointment, everyone burst out laughing. We took a day of rest, and on the next day, we went to see Morskie Oko. This lake lies at 1,393 meters above sea level. We got as close as we could on our motorcycles and then walked the rest of the way. The guidebooks don't exaggerate when they say that it is the most beautiful lake in the Polish Tatry Mountains. At the same time, it is the largest one in the range. When we reached its banks, I could not believe that water could be so clean and clear. We saw the famous health resort in Szczawnica and then turned back on the road towards Warsaw.

We passed through Krakow, so we wouldn't miss the chance to visit at least part of this former Polish capital and the largest castle complex in the country. We hoped that one day we would return and see the city more thoroughly because each nook of the city was a monument in itself.

The sun was setting when we departed beautiful Krakow. The next city on our itinerary was nearby Wieliczka, with its unique and world-renowned salt mines. It turns out that it's a very old mine with documents mentioning that it dates back to the year 1044. We descended 135 meters, admiring along the way the mine's enormous drifts, underground lakes, and chapels sculpted from salt. We left the mine in awe of the artistic imagination and the great effort put into showing the site's beauty.

At noon, we left Wieliczka with the intent to arrive in Warsaw as soon as possible. I switched with my brother along the way and was supposed to drive through Warsaw to our next destination. We got into Warsaw and passed through the center of the city when it began to rain. Suddenly, I noticed that the car in front of me began to "dance" on the road. The motorcycle trailing him flipped over, and I saw sparks flying from the vehicle in spite of the wet road. Immediately, I began to brake lightly, trying not to hit any of those vehicles. I tried controlling my reduction in speed by braking intermittently. Unfortunately, the road was constructed with basalt pavers, which had become so slippery that even my subtle breaking didn't stop our fall. Subconsciously I held on to the motorcycle handle, while the heavy motorcycle pulled me across the road and swerved like a snake along the slippery length of the street. I heard some squeaks and grinding, but I didn't know what was going on. Finally, I stopped and saw my brother running in my direction.

I was surprised that the motorcycle carried me so far. Just then, I realized the situation we were in. At least five motorcycles and a couple of cars lay across the road. I stood in surprise that almost nothing happened to me. Of course, I had small scratches, but they were nothing compared to this massive accident. My brother wasn't injured because he fell off the bike in the beginning, and fortunately, no one hit him from behind. My leather jacket saved my left hand from being crushed, but only shreds were left of the sleeve. Angel of God, my guardian—I shrugged it off.

Unfortunately, the motorcycle was damaged, and we could not continue. The handlebar was cracked, and the clutch and reflector had broken off. My brother stayed with the motorcycle, while I took a trolley to buy the necessary parts in a store. The trolley passengers were fascinated with my garrison cap decorated with city emblems. One person even congratulated me on the number of cities and towns I had visited. After sunset, we finished repairing the damaged parts and headed down the road again. It was well after midnight when we reached my brother's presbytery in Ruciane-Nida, and we went right to bed. That night I couldn't fall asleep because I could not stop thinking about the unfortunate last day of our motorcycle trip around Poland.

My brother had nearly two weeks of summer vacation left, so he decided to take a kayaking trip. Once again, he asked me to take part in the excursion. I was ready for such adventures at the drop of a hat. I thought that I had a good brother who wasn't concerned about the expenses but took a poor student along on each trip. Because we didn't have much time, we were ready to leave right away. We rented a kayak and were joined by another kayaker, my brother's friend from the neighboring parish. The three of us loaded two kayaks with equipment and tents and set off to encounter another adventure. This time, it was a sporting event and we were ready to use some muscle. I had been on a boat several times as a boy, but a kayak was a new challenge in my life. A few hours later, I was already rowing like a veteran kayaker, or at least I thought so.

The first day was the most difficult. We didn't get very far. We sped across the waves of the lake and admired the beautiful scenery far from the banks. After a few days, we passed Niegocin Lake and reached Gizycko. I was sent to get food at the next stop. I kayaked to the other side, but unfortunately, the store was already closed. As a student, I was used to going hungry for a while, so the lack of food didn't bother me this time either. Since I couldn't buy supplies, I decided it wouldn't matter when I would return, so I went to the movies.

When I returned after the movie, my companions came out to help me carry the supplies for which they had sent me. I could feel that trouble would brew, so I yelled that I hadn't brought anything back and began to run away. They started chasing me, but of course, I was the 100-meter race champion, so I left them trailing far behind. I waited a while and then returned to camp to explain what had happened. I was forgiven, but they couldn't understand why I was away for so long. Then I told them the story of the hungry student. "Well, he went to the best restaurant in town and sat at a table with a couple in love. He ordered the same thing they did, and the waiter was convinced that they all came in together. After the meal, the student left the restaurant, and the couple was forced to pay the bill. Now you know why I took so long." I made them laugh with my joke and abated some frustration, but it wasn't until the next morning that we finally filled our stomachs.

The kayaking and earlier motorcycle trip inspired my imagination even more. I felt closer to the beauty of nature, and I began to appreciate the breadth and scope of human effort put into building and creating the masterpieces and architecture that I had the opportunity to admire.

Moving to Bialystok

My brother returned to work after the vacation break. Meanwhile, I still had two months of free time left. I decided to visit my sister and brother-in-law in their new home in Bialystok. I borrowed my brother's motorcycle and went to visit them to see about the possibility of moving there. My sister and brother-in-law graciously accepted me into their home. Our deep family bond, which had lain dormant during those last two years, came alive again. I decided to take them up on their offer and move to Bialystok.

All that was left was to take care of a few formalities in the Evening Higher Engineering College. That didn't pose a problem. The dean was pleased that I decided to transfer from such a renowned school to a local one. I fulfilled all of the requirements and brought my grade reports, along with an agreement from the Institute of Technology. I also needed to find a job before I began my studies.

I had the personality of a traveler, and this helped me decide to move. I liked my room at my sister's house, where I was to live. I would enjoy complete privacy, as opposed to Gdansk, where I rented rooms that were walk-through. I returned the Junak motorcycle to my brother and took the train to Gdansk, where I made all of the arrangements to move. I spent a week illegally sleeping in the dormitory, where I paid the receptionist 5 zloty per night. When I had everything in order, I bid farewell to Gdansk. Sadness overcame me as I watched the final buildings of my beloved city pass by through the open train window.

A surprise awaited me in Elblag, where I had a stopover. Because the train to Olsztyn was delayed, I went up to the officer on duty to ask how long I had to wait for its arrival. I was taken aback by the station manager's rude behavior. I noticed that he was completely drunk. I left the office convinced that something bad would happen as long as he remained on the job. Suddenly, I felt a hand on my shoulder and heard, "Citizen, please come with me."

I looked back and saw a man with the characteristic expression of an ORMO officer (Voluntary Reserve of the Civic Police). He led me outside of the station and threatened to arrest me if I so much as uttered a word about the station manager. He explained that the police knew me well, and I could find myself behind bars again. I was angry, not at the possibility of being arrested again, but at the audaciousness of some cop. I waved my hand in the air and exclaimed in a tone of conviction, "Please take the drunken station manager off of his post immediately. I will give you half an hour and I hope that during this time, a tragedy does not occur. I can be arrested later."

I walked away from him with a confident gait. I was surprised that he didn't try to stop me because I had expected the worst. Inside the train station, I disappeared into the crowd of people waiting for their train, uncertain if they would let me depart. Twenty minutes later, I noticed a different face in a red cap (the station manager wore a red cap). Once I boarded the train, I composed myself. I concluded that I was probably being watched, since I was on my way to visit my brother's rectory. The church where he served as a priest, along with other churches throughout Poland, was under surveillance and under great pressure. I couldn't believe how such lawlessness could prevail in Poland. A sense of revolt against the Communists grew inside of me.

After an overnight train ride, which passed through Elk and my family home in Osowiec, I arrived in Bialystok. I hoped that my life would be easier if I were closer to my parents and under my sister's care.

I was hired to work at the Bialystok Contracting Company as a Senior Inspector in the Head Mechanic's Department. My official responsibilities included inspecting construction machines for their operational safety and hygienic field of work. During the inspections, I had the opportunity to get acquainted not only with the maintenance of the construction equipment but with building management as well.

The job typically didn't place any specific restrictions on how to deal with workers. Variations guided me in this human environment, pleasant ones and unpleasant ones, sometimes even comical ones. One of the building supervisors called me saying that he needed a replacement for his broken cement mixer. Giving approval for delivery of a working mixer, I drove to the site to check the cause of the damage myself. On site, with all seriousness, I suggested to the operator that surely the equipment malfunctioned because he had oiled the ball bearings too much, and they probably locked up. He quickly, and without thinking, replied, "Sir, director, I swear to God...I never oil them."

He recovered from his brief disorientation, and upon realizing his mistake, turned bright red. After a while, he asked, "Sir, you really got me. What will happen now? Please don't punish me too severely. I swear that from this moment, I'll service each machine correctly, and I will never cause an incident again."

I accepted his promise under these extenuating circumstances, and reprimanded him only verbally. The older man was very grateful and thanked me in a heartfelt way. I was pleased with my first on-duty decision, and determined that, in the future, I would follow my common sense rather than the strict rule of law, of course without ignoring the law. In practice, this proved effective, and from then on, it became my life's motto.

When I returned to the office, I told my colleagues about what had happened at the construction site, and they, the director in particular, decided that they needed to celebrate my Solomon's decision by taking me out for a cup of coffee at the nearest café. The four of us, including a female friend from the other office, went to the café. She, at a certain point, had a falling out with her co-worker and moved to another table.

There, two strange men joined her. Suddenly, one of them approached me, and demanded that I give him the coat-check ticket. I only had the ticket for my coat. My friend had the girl's ticket. I replied that I wasn't about to give anyone my ticket. He took it as a joke and produced Secret Police identification from his pocket. I tore it out of his hand and put it in my pocket. Knowing the official police regulations very well, I told him that showing his official identification in a public place was a serious violation, as it announced his identity. Now everyone knew who he was. I scared him even more when I told him that I would make sure the next day his boss would be in possession of the document. My friend offered to be a witness, which made him even more anxious.

He turned from an insolent agent into a meek lamb. He apologized and promised that he would not behave that way again. I returned the identification to him as I left the café. He followed me outside and begged me not tell his supervisor of the incident because he would lose his job. I promised him that I wouldn't do that. Of course, I wouldn't even think of stepping into the lion's lair. I was content that I had humiliated an enemy of mine, an agent of the Secret Police, and that was enough for me. Pleased with my achievement, I returned home to 26 Kasztanowa Street.

Soon I began studies at the Evening Higher Engineering College. I had only two hours to spare between my classes and work. I had to hurry to make it on time to the lectures. In the beginning, I wasn't sure if I was up to the new challenge. But in a few months, I became accustomed to my new environment, and my life became a merry-go-round of work, home, college, and home again.

When my first year of college ended, I had more time for recreation, and I returned to my former hobbies. Going to the movies was always a priority. Once in a while, I met with a friend from the Engineering College to celebrate a name day (equivalent to a birthday in the United States) or a passed exam. He had the same positive outlook on life as I did, and we shared the same points of view on many issues. We both felt alike in our element when we went out together to the restaurant or café. Because he was born in Bialystok, he knew the city inside and out. He told me a story, the truth of which I highly doubted, but only because I was not yet familiar with the customs of the city. He told me that each neighborhood followed its own rules and had its own boss who ruled over it. No guy outside a neighborhood could go out with a girl from inside the neighborhood. My friend was very excited to tell me this story, and I was eager to hear it as he began.

"I once walked a girl I had met to her house and then started heading back toward the bus stop. It was already dark, and only the streetlamps lit the street. Just then, five big guys came from around the corner and blocked my way. They asked me the reason for my visit to this neighborhood. I knew what they were up to, and I lied saying that my aunt lived there, and I came to visit her. One of them joked, 'You've got a good-looking aunt,' and he mentioned the girl's name."

"The head of the gang came up to me and said, 'You're going to be punished for lying because you know very well that the girl lives in this neighborhood, and only we have the right to her. Now get on that rock and sing us a love song.' I thought that's not much of a punishment, and I hopped up on the rock and started to hum," Love will forgive anything..."

It looked ridiculous because they looked very serious as they were listening to the song. It turned out that this was only a trick, and when I finished singing, they gave me a harsh beating. I tried to fight back, but I didn't stand a chance, so I ran away. When I came back home, my brothers asked me where I had gotten so many bruises. I told them about my adventure, and they immediately started planning their revenge. I had six brothers, one better than the next, and they were just waiting to beat someone up.

"A week later, I was supposed to go out with the same girl and walk her home again. My brothers were supposed to hide and only go into action when I was about to sing my song because they assumed the same order of events would occur. Everything went according to plan. Once again, the same gangsters surrounded me, and their boss started his speech, 'Well, I see our little lesson didn't serve you at all. Now you'll have to sing two songs, one about love and the other about betrayal!' I looked around, and chills ran down my spine because I didn't see my brothers anywhere. I hoped that they were waiting somewhere beyond the reach of the light of the street lamp. I was about to get up on the rock, when suddenly, my brothers jumped out of hiding. The bullies froze, not knowing what was going on. A few seconds later, they all lay on the ground. This time, the joke was on them."

"What happened next?" I asked my friend with a hint of impatience.

"Unfortunately, I stopped seeing the girl, even though I liked her a lot. I had to steer clear of the neighborhood. She probably married one of the bullies. I never ran into her again, not even accidentally."

I liked the scenario of the story. I thought it would make a great movie, but as far as the facts, I wasn't convinced that they were all true. Eventually, I had a similar adventure myself in another neighborhood.

The café where we often ate was in a two-story building, with dance parties on the lower level. My friend suggested we go there to eat and then dance. Indeed, the lower level was pleasant and the band played nice tunes, which was very inviting. Soon, I noticed that my friend was already spinning a girl around to the rhythm of the song. I didn't want to be second-rate, so I chose a girl who was sitting at a table with two of her friends. I bowed politely, as I used to do, and asked her to dance. The girl got up from the table, and we were about to begin dancing, when some guy came up to me and announced that this lady doesn't dance. I reminded him that the emancipation of women already took place in the last century, and that women had the right to make their own decisions. He asked to speak to me in private, so not suspecting anything, I went with him to the bathroom. I only remember that we entered the men's room, and after that moment, I blacked out. When I came to, I couldn't remember how long the break in my biography actually was. I sat against the wall, leaning on it. Instinctively, I rubbed my face with my hand. I realized what had happened when I saw my hand and my white shirtsleeve covered in blood. In that state, half-conscious, I went back to the dance hall. When my friend spotted me, he left his partner and ran up to me asking, "Which one was it?"

I looked around the room. Just then, I saw him walking down the stairs. I pointed him out to my friend because I couldn't speak. My whole face was mangled. My friend of Herculean strength literally picked the guy up, held him in mid-air, and then threw him against the mirror on the wall, which shattered to pieces. The frame fell to the ground and demobilized him. Now he was the one leaning against the wall, bordered by a beautiful golden frame.

There was much commotion. The café manager called the police. The officer on duty refused to come, probably because he had more important things to do. I had to leave the café without protection and in a sorry state. I asked my friend to leave with me because I had a feeling that something bad might happen. He was sure of himself and didn't take advantage of my offer. He even joked that this time, he wouldn't be singing because there was no rock to be found for this concert.

The next day I felt much better, so I went to my lectures at the Engineering College. My friend wasn't at the lectures, but I wasn't surprised. Everyone had absences. When he didn't show up the following day, I became worried. After class, I went to his house. What I saw was beyond my wildest expectations. His entire head was bandaged. Only his left eye was visible from under the bandages. I was so shocked; I couldn't utter a word.

It turned out there was a trap set for him, where the girl played the main role. My friend was jumped when leaving the club and immediately knocked down by two of the bullies. The girl hugged him with both arms, begging him not to hurt her boyfriend, when he felt a blow to the back of the head with a heavy object. All he could remember from then on was waking up in the hospital after his wounds were bandaged.

During the entire time he was healing, I visited him at home and shared information with him from the Engineering College. We remained good friends until I left Bialystok.

Meeting My Future Wife

It was the beginning of February 1963. The weather had been terribly cold the last few days. During one of those freezing days, I was on my way home from the Engineering School. A few people were waiting at the bus stop; among them was a young girl with a long braid. She impressed me at first sight. I thought hard about how to approach her, and at the same time, I feared rejection. I thought of several things to say, but I finally decided to use the "watch trick." I walked up to her with an uncertain step and asked, "I am very sorry to bother you, but can you tell me what time it is?"

Very politely, she answered me, so I became more confident, and I continued the conversation. I pretended to be unfamiliar with the city and asked her which way would be best to get to Antoniuk. She gave me a lot of information. Just then, bus number nine arrived going in that direction. We both boarded the bus, and coincidentally, or maybe it was thanks to fate, two seats opposite each other were free. We sat down, and we started the conversation again. Her name was Jadwiga. After speaking for only a few moments, it seemed like we had known each other for a long time. I got the impression that she liked me as well, so I asked her if we could meet again. I was very happy that she accepted without hesitating. We set up a time and place. When I said to her, "see you later," I really hoped that I would be able to do just that. I found out that she lived two bus stops further, but in another neighborhood, Bacieczki.

On the appointed day, I went to the place we both agreed to meet in the center of town. I was impatient because it was almost time for her to arrive, but she wasn't there yet. At the exact time of our date, the girl of my choice stepped off the bus. My heart started beating faster, and I felt a strange rush of joy. I greeted her and called her Jagoda, instead of the more formal Jadwiga, and that's how it stayed.

On our first date, we went to the movie theater. That's how our relationship began, which culminated with a trip to the altar the following June. In the meantime, I had a few interesting adventures that are worth describing.

On our second date, I was invited to her aunt's house, with whom she lived. Her aunt and uncle welcomed me warmly. From then on, we met more often at their home, and from there, we would go into town. One day, after walking Jagoda home, I was on my way to the bus stop, and I saw three suspicious guys watching me. I got on the bus, and they followed me. Two of them went to the front, and one of them stood right behind me. I found myself in a difficult situation. I had no idea what would happen next. I thought that they might make me sing on top of a rock, but there weren't any rocks on my way home. Fortunately, one of the passengers realized what was going on, and she came to my defense. She ordered the driver not to move the bus until they got off. In this way, she saved me from my bad situation. A few days later, as I was returning from the Engineering College, the same guys boarded the bus one stop before mine. This time, one of them sat in the front while two stood behind me. They were certain I would get off the bus because I moved to the front with the other passengers getting off, but at the last moment, just as they were getting off, I hopped back and asked the driver to quickly close the door. I went one stop further and saved myself a beating once again. I knew that one day they'd get me.

The next day, after work, I asked around and found out who the boss was of the neighborhood gang. He was a retired pilot with the rank of major. He always "worked" from the local bar. I went to the bar, and the bartender showed me the table where he was sitting. I ordered four beers and joined him. Without hesitating he asked, "What's your problem?"

I explained that I lived in the Antoniuk neighborhood, and three bullies wanted to beat me up. I added that it was because of a girl from the Bacieczki neighborhood. "From this moment on, you won't find yourself in a risky position. You can leave," he replied.

I went to the bartender, asked for two more beers, and ordered them taken to the Major because that is what they called him. I went to the Engineering College full of hope that I had solved the problem. After the lectures, I got off at my stop, as usual, and happy that no one was following me, I went on my way home. When I was near an intersection, in the light of the streetlamp, I saw and recognized that perhaps all of the bullies from the neighborhood were waiting for me. It was too late to run away. I only wondered if the Major was able to pass on the order. I had one more alternative, to cross the street, but that would have been a cowardly move on my part. I walked straight toward the group because they were taking up the entire sidewalk. I was sure that they would not let me pass, and that I would get a good beating. At the last second, the crowd parted, and I found myself in the middle of a hornet's nest. Chills ran down my spine, as I hung my head down low. I expected that at any moment, something heavy would drop on my head. I passed the last two guys, but no one touched me. I felt my head to make sure it was still in one piece. I thought I was dreaming, and after a while, I turned around wondering why no one even bothered me. They were all standing just as they were, in the same spot. I never told Jagoda about my adventure because that would have required me to confess to a moment of weakness, and that was not in my nature.

The next day I went to the bar again to thank the Major for keeping his promise. When I went to his table, of course bearing a beer, he asked, "No one stopped you yesterday, right?"

"Right," I answered. "I just wanted to add that I'm grateful that you probably saved my life."

"Maybe it wouldn't have been so bad, but it wouldn't have been good either," he added. "I told you yesterday that you'd be safe, but you doubted me. From yesterday on, you're under special protection, and you have nothing to fear. I liked that you came to me directly and didn't go to the police, and that saved you." I said good-bye to the major, and with that, we lost touch. From then on, no one bothered me anymore. I accidentally found out from three of the bullies that two of them were criminals who served prison sentences for robbery.

The following Saturday, I went to visit Jagoda on my brother's borrowed motorcycle. I was sure I could go there without any obstacles. After all, the major guaranteed it. Jagoda and I took a ride out of the city. Just as we reached the outskirts, the police traffic patrol stopped us. At the time, the law required anyone riding outside of the city to wear a helmet. Before we started the ride, I didn't plan to go outside of the city and did not have helmets with me. The policeman turned to me, saying that I would need to pay a 100 zloty fine for breaking the law. I leaned over to the policeman's ear, so Jagoda wouldn't hear, and asked, "Officer, would you even think of wearing a helmet if you were taking a girl to the forest?"

I amused him with the joke, and he laughed aloud. Finally, he stammered, "You tickle my funny bone. You're free to leave." Before I even got going, he got on his radio and told the next policemen not to stop me. When we returned home, Jagoda asked me many times about what I had said to the policeman to make him laugh so hard. I didn't admit to what I said because I was afraid she might strongly reprimand my bad behavior.

On Monday morning, I took the motorcycle to work. Just as I turned from Kasztanowa Street, on which I lived, onto Gajowa Street, a boy who looked around seven years old jumped out from behind a parked car straight at my motorcycle. I stopped rapidly, and then jumped off the motorcycle to pick the child up off of the ground. His father rushed over and took the boy in his arms. I was shocked when I saw his head all bloody. I thought that I had killed the child! The hair stood up on my head. Just then, the boy's grandfather ran out of the house and began to yell at me, "You murderer!"

I followed the child's father into their house. In the meantime, someone called an ambulance. The boy was conscious, and that calmed me down. Then his father turned to me and told me that the accident was not my fault, and I could go to work. I told him that I wasn't leaving because I didn't want to be accused of fleeing the scene of an accident. The driver of the ambulance was a witness to the conversation and told me to leave, too. He added that if there were any questions about the accident in the future, he would be my witness.

It wasn't until the ambulance left with the boy that I went back to work. Nevertheless, my conscience was eating away at me, and a few hours later, I returned to see if there were any complications. I was happy to see the boy playing in the yard. His head was bandaged, but the wound wasn't serious. He only suffered a cut from hitting the air valve handle. He would have sustained more serious injuries if I hadn't swerved to the right. I returned to work comforted by the fact that I wasn't a murderer after all, as the grandfather earlier accused.

My girlfriend, Jagoda, and me.

An Adventure with Jurek

In September 1962, my parents moved into a new brick house. I installed a sink for washing dishes in the kitchen and mounted white ceramic tiles on the wall around it. The kitchen looked modern, even though the old coal and wood-burning stove was still used. There weren't any other options at that time. My parents always dreamed of building such a home, and it wasn't until the children moved away that they were able to carry out their plan.

I visited my parents at Christmas. My father had been very sick and was lying in bed. I saw that he had trouble breathing, so I convinced him to visit the doctor. The next day, we took a train to Grajewo Hospital. Despite the closed door, I heard the doctor literally yelling, "Why did it take you so long to come here? The matter is serious. You have a chronic lung infection."

A penicillin injection and prescribed drugs were supposed to help my father get well. He was also instructed to remain in bed until he felt better. We returned home, and I told my mother about the gravity of his condition. Unfortunately, I had to return to Bialystok. I hoped that everything would be all right.

When I visited my parents again, there were no signs that something bad was happening with my father. Of course, he had a hacking cough, but he seemed to be improving. My older sister, Henryka, married a man from the same village and lived not too far from my parents. Henryka and her husband were my parents' greatest support in the hardest of times. Jurek, her husband, helped my parents and took over my father's most difficult work.

I had one of my most memorable adventures with Jurek, even before he and my sister were married. The adventure took place when

I was in my third year of high school. Jurek courted Henryka for two years and took any opportunity to spend time with her.

Every year, Henryka spent the Holiday of Indulgences at our aunt's house in Wrocen. Jurek wanted to come along, and he tried to convince me to accompany him. It was in the autumn, when the Biebrza River overflowed its banks and flooded the area. We put our bicycles on a boat and rowed across the flooded lakes and meadows to the other side of the Biebrza. We had over two kilometers of water to conquer, but we were used to the conditions, and it wasn't difficult to do. We biked the rest of the way to the village. After the traditional ceremonies in the church, we all met at our aunt's house for the holiday celebration. It was well after ten o'clock in the evening when Jurek and I started heading back. My aunt placed pieces of all kinds of cakes to take home to my parents in my backpack. Right before we reached Goniadz, we heard the first rumblings and saw lightning. It got dark, and we couldn't see even a few steps ahead. Because Jurek knew the area well and was five years my senior, he was my guide.

We arrived at our docked boat, once again boarded with our bikes, then embarked from the shore. The storm was quickly coming our way, and soon it started to rain. The thunder rumbled closer; the wind and rain got stronger each second. The waves rocked our boat so hard, it nearly tipped over. An eerie glow of the lightning seemed to directly encroach upon us. The only time I was able to see Jurek rowing was when lightning struck. Otherwise, it was completely dark. The waves were so strong that water poured into the boat. Even without the waves, the rain would have drenched us. I felt that the boat was gaining water, but I was all wet, so I couldn't feel how high the water was inside of our boat. The lightning strikes only illuminated the area for a moment, and Jurek was only able to tell where we were by the familiar objects sticking out of the water. Suddenly, lightning struck so close to our boat that the boat rocked back and forth. As it struck a second time, I saw that Jurek raised himself high. As first, I didn't know what was happening, but I felt myself submerging into the water. I realized that my side of the boat was sinking, and I with it. I had no other choice but to jump out of it. This time, Jurek disappeared from my sight. When I jumped into the water, his part of the boat sunk to the bottom. After a while, I heard splashing and saw him swimming towards me.

When lightning struck again, I spotted the top of a tree. I thought that the bank of the lake must be there, and the water must be shallow enough for me to stand. I swam in that direction in my new suit, shoes, and tie. As I got near the tree, I tried to stand. Unfortunately, it was too deep, and I sank with my head submerged. I had to swim further. A few meters beyond the tree, I tried again. This time, the water was waist-deep, and there I waited for my Holy Day partner, who was swimming in my direction.

The boat, the bicycles, and my backpack filled with cakes stayed behind in the middle of the water. To me the flooded waters looked like one big lake. The storm calmed down a bit, and the lightning struck far away from us. We faced the dilemma of who should haul the boat from the center of lake. Each commissioned the other to do it. Finally, Jurek swam out to get it. He tied the boat to a tree, which stuck out of the water, and we took the bikes and backpack with us. He waded through the water first, and I followed him, trusting him to lead the way. The water was deep, and at points, we were in over our chests. Jurek warned me that somewhere in that area there was a ditch. Then suddenly he disappeared. A moment later, he swam out again and helped me reach the other side. We finally reached Jurek's house, and there I changed into dry clothes. Despite this, I was shivering uncontrollably from the cold.

In the morning, I changed back into my soaking wet suit and rode my bicycle home. My parents weren't home, so I quickly changed and hung my clothes to dry by the warm furnace. When my mother returned home, I wanted to offer her cake from the Holy Day. I opened my backpack and started to laugh, while humming a tune about flour dumplings. The poppy seed cheesecake and other cakes stuck together because of the water. My mother looked at my suit and asked with surprise, "My child, where were you?"

I answered, "I went to celebrate the Holy Day at Aunt Anastazja's house in Wrocen. I told you where I was going."

I didn't say a word about our adventure, which could have ended in tragedy if our boat had been struck by lightning. Our attempt to make our way back in those treacherous conditions didn't predict anything good. It wasn't until I was falling asleep and the words came to me, "Angel of God, my guardian..." did I realize what kind of danger that watery wilderness was that we had put ourselves in.

Jurek; his wife, Henryka; my mother, Zofia; my uncle and former teacher, Henryk; and me at my brother's rectory in Poland.

My Father's Death in the Grajewo Hospital

On the morning of April 5, 1963, Anastazja called me at work and told me that an ambulance came and my father was taken to Grajewo Hospital. Immediately, I took the first train going in that direction to visit him. I had arrived after visiting hours, and I wasn't allowed inside. I was permitted only to talk to my father through the window. This was possible because his room was on the first floor. I remember my father's crucial words, "Thank you for coming to visit me, Henry."

"Dad, of course" I said. "It's normal for children to visit their sick parents in the hospital. Anyway, I'll come back tomorrow, or the next day, and we'll return home together. The doctor to whom I spoke said so."

My father looked meaningfully into my eyes but didn't reply. I noticed that he wanted to say something but refrained. We stood looking at each other for a long time, and I subconsciously felt that, at that moment, my father was saying good-bye. I will never forget that look. My heart filled with sadness. After a while, a nurse came in and ordered him to lie back down in bed. I couldn't move, even as my father disappeared from my sight through the window.

I went to see my mother to comfort her and be with her at this difficult time for both of us. The most troubling experience for my mom was when my father, getting into the ambulance, looked around and said, "Zofia, this is the last time I will see this scene in my life."

My mother and I were talking well into the night when my brother knocked on the door. It turned out that he hadn't been notified until later that day and was mistakenly told to go to the house instead of the hospital. I took the morning train with my brother to Grajewo. I knew which unit my father was in, so we headed straight there. We entered the hall, but a very embarrassed nurse stopped us, and first, turning to my brother, whom she recognized as a priest because he was wearing a cassock, said "Father," and then looking at me, "Sir, your father has passed away. Please go to the morgue where his body was taken. Please take his belongings." She pointed to a bag.

Without a second thought, I took hold of the bag, and without a word, we went where she had directed us. My brother entered the morgue first. When he saw our deceased father, he threw himself onto the body. He began to show deep despair. I thought my heart would break at the sight, so I left to go outside.

I went to find the nurse to inquire about the final minutes of our father's life. Her response surprised me. She said that right after I bid my father farewell, he asked her to put his feet on the bed. She added right away, "Your father had an easy death."

"How did it happen?" I asked.

"When I laid your father back down and helped him put his legs on the bed, that's when he died."

O God, I thought, *that's why he looked at me that way.* I knew subconsciously that it was our farewell. Then my heart ached more, my nerves slackened and sobbing began to jerk my body.

I returned to the morgue. My brother was praying intently and was so focused that he didn't notice me. I thought that our father's death was in a different category than the unfamiliar people he had buried so many times before. It wasn't until then that I realized that we had lost our greatest treasure. We became half-orphaned, despite our maturity.

The funeral was sad, but dignified. None of us cried because our tears had been depleted earlier. My father was a man liked for his simplicity, honesty, active involvement in the church committee, and most importantly, he was the father of a priest, who, by the way, gave a very touching eulogy at the funeral. As my father was placed in the grave, I remembered the time he gave me a delicious slice of bread, thickly coated with butter. When I was a student, he brought me suitcases of food. He had never wronged me, and now he was gone forever.

Although my mother was now alone, she remained strong and decided to continue running the farm. She probably counted on the help of her daughter, Henryka, and son-in-law, Jurek, who lived in the village a few kilometers down the road. She wasn't disappointed; from then on, they always came to her aid.

Misfortunes happened in pairs for my mother at that time. A month after my father's death, the pigsty buildings and barns burned down due to a single bolt of lightning from a spring storm. At that time, three-year-old Barbara was with Grandma. She saw the burning barn and became frightened, not allowing my mother to leave the house, even for a second, to open the barn door and free the animals. A chance passerby did it and saved the animals from going up in flames.

My mother surprised me. She used the insurance money to purchase land for me to build a house in Bialystok. She considered the lightning strike a sign to carry out my father's last wish to help me buy a home. That was an opportunity for my mother to fulfill his promise.

The farm could no longer be managed without the buildings. My brother was appointed to the Grabnik Parish and suggested that my mother move there with him. Of course, she accepted the offer enthusiastically. She gave the house to a hospital attendant from Osowiec, free of charge, in exchange for his care of it. She wanted to help his young children have better living conditions. From then on, my mother was at the presbytery with her son, the priest. She thanked God that her life was directed in such a way that she was able to attend daily mass celebrated by her son. It was a great honor for her, and she was happy.

Dating Jagoda and Our First Years of Marriage

I met with Jagoda as often as time permitted it. I didn't miss any opportunity to see her. Her closeness, her kisses, first shy, then more passionate, made me feel happier and happier. One day I concluded that I was in love. I wasn't sure of her feelings, but everything pointed to the fact that she liked me very much. I found out that the troubles I had with the bullies were caused by the jealousy of her former boy-friend, who turned them against me.

Thanks to my brother, who never denied me his Junak motorcycle, I took Jagoda on all kinds of trips. We went to the beautiful Bialowi-eska primeval forest and even spent the night there. We often went to her parents' home in Wasilowka, near Janow. I asked her to come with me to visit my mother in Budne many times, but my requests were always met with her refusal. I had to use deception. So I asked her girlfriend, who also owned a motorcycle, to take a trip with us to Osowiec and to keep our plan of stopping by my mother's house a secret. Jagoda didn't know of our plan and agreed to the trip enthusi-astically. It wasn't until we stopped in front of my house that she saw through my ploy. Jagoda's friend had a good sense of humor, so the plan succeeded.

I introduced Jagoda and her friend to my mother and uncle, who had come to visit his sister. My uncle knew many jokes, so he started to entertain us. Jagoda's friend worked as a bartender, so she wasn't going to be outdone. She reeled off jokes as well. We had a great time, and as we were about to leave, my mother asked, "Which one of these girls is your girlfriend, Henry?" I started to joke and told her to choose. Faultlessly, she indicated Jagoda.

"How did you come to that conclusion, Mom?" I asked.

"You two simply fit together well," was Mom's answer.

We returned to Bialystok in high spirits. As we said our good-byes, I uttered the special words for the first time, "Jagoda, I love you!"

Then she hugged me and whispered, "Henry, I love you, too."

We fell into a frenzy of love and could not stop kissing. It was hard to part from my beloved that night, and I returned several times to practice my kissing skills. Then she told me a secret. "Usually boys would try to kiss me on the first date, but you behaved differently. I thought you didn't like me, and you just came around for your own amusement."

Now I had to give her the reason for my behavior and put her doubts to rest, so I asked, "Jagoda, do you think anyone would want to harm someone they love?"

"Of course not," was the answer.

"I conducted myself in this manner because I liked you from the moment we met. You had a different impression of my behavior, but you had the right to it. From now on, I'll try to make up for lost time," I added jokingly.

Now all that was left was the issue of an official engagement, and along with it, Jagoda's parents agreeing to the marriage. I wanted the proposal to be special, so I turned to Anastazja's husband for advice. He began to joke and came up with many ridiculous versions of proposals. Finally, so I would never hold a grudge against him in the future, he jokingly told me that instead of marrying at all, I should plunge myself in the Bialka River. I wasn't going to be outdone, so I replied that it would be impossible to drown in that knee-deep stream and asked him why he didn't take advantage of the chance when he was getting married, since the Biebrza River was so close. We never ran out of jokes, but I still needed advice. I turned to my sister, who laughed while listening to our conversation. I relayed my version of the proposal to her. I told her I would be asking for Jagoda's hand. My sister started laughing even harder, and declared that usually it's another part of a woman's body that men want. I left without any helpful suggestions, so I had to think of something on my own.

One spring day in 1964, I bought a beautiful bouquet of flowers, and along with it, a customary bottle of vodka, and headed with Jagoda to her parent's house. That evening, as we sat down to dinner, I got up from the table, and with a bit of a quivering voice, asked Jagoda for her hand in marriage. The decisive moment for her parents to give us their blessing finally came. My future mother-in-law agreed with a smile while my future father-in-law nodded his head in approval. To seal the deal, we each drank a shot of vodka.

We set our wedding date for June 14. On that day, my sister Anastazja organized lunch for twenty of my guests to celebrate, and afterwards, we took five rented cars to my future wife's parents' home, where Jagoda was awaiting my arrival. Our wedding took place in a church in Janowo. There were six priests headed by the bishop. Of course, it was Father Romuald, my brother, who wed us. In this sermon, he touched on the marital problems that are yet to come. We were surprised at these words because we were so happy to finally be together. Then the reception took place at Jagoda's parents' house. At my request, the bishop also attended the party. It was a joyous and festive time, especially since during dinner, my uncles entertained the guests with jokes.

Two weeks after the wedding, Jagoda's entire family was granted passports to emigrate to the United States. Jagoda was issued her own passport because as an adult, she had the right to emigrate on her own. This posed a dilemma. What should we do? I left the decision up to my wife, but the thought of her leaving terrified me. Of course, I could have gone later as well, but as newlyweds, separation did not bode well with us. At least that was how I felt. I was happy to hear that my wife decided to return the passport back to the provincial police headquarters, where the documents had been issued. The officer who took the passport back was shocked, and commented that some people wait a lifetime for such a document.

Thanks to Anastazja and her husband's hospitality, we moved into the attic loft of their home, which her husband remodeled for our comfort and privacy. The only setback was that, in the winter, it was difficult to maintain a steady temperature because we only had a coal furnace. It was warm in the daytime and cold at night, but it didn't bother us too much. We had been used to the conditions ever since we were children.

Jagoda decorated the room, and we felt happy. After work and after dinner, which my young wife prepared, we would go out somewhere. My sister, who preferred a more domestic life, always commented on our outings, "Where is the devil taking you now?"

No, the devil wasn't taking us anywhere, but we enjoyed going out to the movies, to the cafés, or for a walk through the park on our own.

We liked that lifestyle. We spent nearly every Saturday night with friends dancing or enjoying ourselves at a café or restaurant.

At Christmastime, we went to my sister Henryka's house in the village of Budne. My sister informed her small children of our arrival. "Uncle Henry and Jagoda are coming to visit." Jagoda is not only my wife's name, short for Jadwiga, but is also the word for berry in Polish. That evening at dinner my nephew asked, "Mom, you said that Uncle Henry would come with jagoda. Where is it?" Of course, he was thinking about the berry from the forest. There was a lot of laughter until it was explained that it was Uncle Henry's wife, and her name was Jagoda. My nephew was a bit disappointed, but he finally went over to Jagoda and gave her a hug, even though she was not the berry that could be eaten.

Soon, in March 1965, our first daughter was born. We chose the name Beata for her. My mother came right away to see her son's firstborn, her granddaughter. We planned on christening her on Easter Day, but my mother insisted that we baptize her on Palm Sunday, so that is what we did.

On Thursday of Holy Week, we noticed that Beata was sick. The clinic was located nearby, so Jagoda took her to be checked by the doctor. Not suspecting that anything serious was wrong, I went to work. A few hours later, I had a premonition that I should go home and see what was happening. As I entered the house, I saw a terrified look in Jagoda's eyes. I walked up to the stroller and noticed that Beata wasn't doing well because her eyes were darting back and forth. I ran to the clinic and stormed into the doctor's office, out of breath, and she called to me, "Here's a hospital referral for your child. I have it ready."

I ran back home, but Beata was no longer alive. Jagoda was scratching the wall in grief. I took my wife in my arms to calm her down. Despair tore at our hearts. We embraced while we mourned the death of our first daughter. How short was the road from incredible joy to incredible sorrow! Fate took our child away, the child we came to love so dearly. It was April 21, 1965. During Beata's funeral, I remembered my brother's words about marital problems. It was only then that I understood the meaning of his words. But why did our problems have to be so painful?

I began to think about taking the risk of building a farmhouse on our plot of land and living there. We could not afford to build a proper house. It was a risky undertaking because the inspectors could stop the construction, since we were building without a permit. The success of the construction would also depend on the discretion of my neighbors, who could possibly inform the inspectors of our illegal construction. I had all of this in mind, but the well-being of my family won over my reasoning, and I decided to take on the risky project.

It was August of 1966, and Jagoda was two months pregnant. I called together a construction crew, and after preparing the materials, I built the small house within a week. I was able to do that because no one turned me in to the inspectors, and the construction wasn't halted. Thanks to financial support from Jagoda's parents, I quickly completed it, and we moved into the small, but our own, home.

We had a bedroom and a kitchen, which Jagoda beautifully decorated, and we were truly happy to be on our own. First, we bought a bed, and then we bought an armoire on credit. All that we needed was a table for the kitchen. After payday, I went to the furniture store and purchased it. I preferred not to have it delivered to my house because delivery was too costly. I brought the table home myself, carrying it on my back for three kilometers. Towards the end, I had to stop to rest more often because the table was heavy, but I reached my destination, and we ate dinner on our new table.

One day I was called to appear at the local police station on charges of illegal construction of a building. I appeared at the station on the day of the summons. A young lieutenant police officer received me and asked, "How do you explain the matter of illegal construction?"

"Lieutenant, before I start explaining, can I ask you a question?" I answered.

"Of course," replied the lieutenant.

"Do you have any children, and do you love them?"

"I have a son and a daughter, and I love them very much," he answered somewhat confused.

"Sir, I had a daughter whom I loved very much, but she died because of poor living conditions. I know I broke the law, but please put yourself in my place, and try to understand. My wife is pregnant again, and if I hadn't built the house, I would be condemning my child to a certain death. You can do whatever you want with me, even take me to jail, but I only ask one thing of you, do not evict my pregnant wife from the house. I promise that when conditions allow me to build a proper house, then it will be done completely according to the law."

"Please trust me, that as long as I'm in this position, your case won't see the light of day," answered the lieutenant. I was full of admiration for that man, and I thanked him from the bottom of my heart, wishing him every success throughout his entire life.

A few days later a city commission arrived to check if the condition of the house was suitable for living. They were pleasantly surprised by the décor of the small house. One of the female committee members turned to us and said, "We didn't expect everything to be so orderly. You (she turned to my wife) have a knack for decorating. As for the building, we have no reservations. We approve your living here and the registration of the site."

"Thank you very much!" we almost cried from joy simultaneously. It was an unprecedented success, as the inspectors gave us permission to stay in our little house.

On March 19, 1967, our daughter was born, and we gave her two names, Malgorzata (Maggie) and Violetta (Violet). For the first two weeks, she was calm and sometimes whimpered, but that was normal. As time went on, she became more restless and cried more often. We immediately took her to the doctor. The doctor decided that these were colic pains, and they would pass. Unfortunately, Maggie cried more and didn't stop, even at night.

Next, we went for a private visit to another doctor. She gave a different diagnosis and prescribed medicine. To no avail, Maggie only cried more. I watched over her until midnight, and then Jagoda took over until morning. We feared for her health, and one day I took a taxi to three doctor's offices in one day. The first two doctors gave different diagnoses. The last was a professor from the Bialystok Medical Academy. I asked for his help to save my daughter, explaining to him that we already experienced one tragedy and couldn't imagine enduring another such misfortune. I told him that he was the third doctor that day.

The doctor ordered Jagoda to put Maggie on the table to be examined, while we stood aside. As he undressed her, Maggie cried so loudly that she stopped breathing. Jagoda was startled and said quietly to me, "Oh God, she'll die."

"Don't worry, Jagoda she won't die in the hands of this doctor," I answered, although I was terrified myself. Then we heard Maggie's cry again. We breathed a sigh of relief.

The doctor examined her for over half an hour and finally gave a diagnosis. "Your child is fit as a fiddle. Please don't waste your money and time. You can rest easy about her health. Your case isn't rare; her discomfort will pass soon enough." I asked him how long this would last. "Up to a year," was his answer.

We were happy that our daughter's health wasn't in danger. We only had to be patient and wait until the phase passed. It was astonishing because Maggie never cried in Jagoda's arms. She felt her maternal warmth and calmed down. We had no idea how such a little one could know the difference.

For six months, we relentlessly took turns watching over Maggie. One night, we awoke startled that something had happened because she wasn't crying. Morning was approaching, and rosy-cheeked Maggie slept soundly. She had just turned six months old. From that moment on, there weren't any more problems. From that entire assortment of doctors, only one had diagnosed her correctly. That same week, I paid the doctor a visit and thanked him personally and on behalf of my wife.

Everything was going wonderfully in my job as well. I was promoted to supervisor of the mechanical unit. After a few months in that position, I received another proposition. The director called me into his office and offered me the managerial position at the Office of the Senior Mechanic. My responsibilities would have included supervising the overall operations of all of the construction facilities. I was pleasantly surprised, but I wasn't able to make a decision right away, so I asked him for a moment of delay. I approached the office workers in that department, asking them if they were willing to accept me. They accepted me graciously and congratulated me on my promotion. I returned to the director's office and agreed to the offer. The director was very pleased and announced that, in three days, I would take over the duties of the person who was leaving the position. Nevertheless, the General Party Organization (POP) didn't agree to my taking the position unless I joined the Polish Labor Party Alliance (PZPR). The very acronym, PZPR, was revolting to me, not to mention the idea of actually joining this communist organization that I hated. I categorically refused, even though my monthly income would have doubled.

I was convinced that I would never again have the opportunity for a promotion in Poland, so I decided to accept my in-laws' offer and take on the great world by going to the United States temporarily, where I could earn some money and improve our living situation.

It was a new challenge for me, which I decided to undertake. I believed that it would be beneficial to my entire family's life. I was prepared to do anything for my daughter, whom I loved immensely. I wanted to be the best father in the world because I believed that my children would always love me, even as they grew up.

Vacations in America

In October 1967, from Gdynia, I departed on the Polish ship *Batory* to the United States. The farewell was nothing short of dramatic, as the ship set sail from the port. Everyone on the ship's deck wept and blew kisses to those remaining on land. At one point, my wife disappeared from my sight, and all that was left was the sadness and anguish in my heart. Next to me, stood a woman whose lament was particularly loud.

When we reached Copenhagen the next morning, we were allowed to disembark and tour around the city. Copenhagen delighted not only me, but also all of the others who were beyond the iron curtain for the first time.

After we sailed out onto the Atlantic, the Captain's Ball took place on the ship. I felt especially honored to be among the select guests to receive an invitation. At each table was an officer, who answered various questions. Out of curiosity, I asked if there were any threats or dangerous situations on any of the ship's previous voyages. It turned out that there were two such dangerous situations, and one of them nearly sank the ship. The hull was torn, leaving a large hole. Water poured into the lower deck, which contained the passenger's belongings. Most of the baggage was sucked out into the ocean. Two marine orchestras played day and night to muffle the sound of the pumps and keep the passengers from panicking. The Canadian Coast Guard was put on alert, in case of a passenger evacuation. Rescue divers repaired the breach with large metal sheets, and the ship reached Montreal safely.

The lady who wept so heavily during our farewell stayed in the cabin across the hall. I met her one evening. She was dressed in a beautiful ball gown, and with curiosity, I inquired about how today's celebration went. She cheerfully told me of her wonderful daily experiences on the ship. Because I was curious as to her quick transformation, I reminded her of the day we bid farewell. She began to laugh and without any qualms she stated, "Sir, I think because of the damn water I'm losing my mind. I left my husband and three children back in Poland, and I'm having the time of my life here."

I didn't have the chance to chat with the stranger again, but I knew that she was having a great time on the dance floor.

I was interested by all that was happening on the ship, so I stuck my head into every event and peered into every nook, so as not to miss anything. I would often spend time in the ship's swimming pool, where I could show off my swimming skills.

I stayed in a four-person cabin. We slept on two bunk beds. One of the passengers was an elderly gentleman, who prayed the rosary every day. One day I took advantage of our moment alone and started a conversation. I already knew that he was an engineer by profession and held a director's position.

I was curious to find out, knowing the realities of Poland at the time and judging by my own experiences, how such a religious man could be a director in Communist Poland. His answer surprised and fascinated me: "Despite the fact that my mother was a practicing Catholic, I was an atheist by conviction. This did not stop me from mocking believers. Thanks to this, I was promoted to higher positions, until I finally became the director of a rather significant company in Krakow. One day my 10-year-old son became ill. After intensive treatment, the doctors stated that his days were numbered, and I could do nothing more to save him. They recommended that we take him home, where he could die in peace. After this conversation, I was shocked, and in an instant, I realized how powerless I really am as a human being. I was returning home in a daze. When I passed a church, I noticed that its door was open. I went inside, fell to my knees, and feverishly began to beg God for help. I remembered the prayers my mother taught me, and I began to pray. I swore an oath that if my son would be healed, I would return to the faith. What you see here is the result of what happened next. My son got well and has already graduated from college."

I thanked him deeply for the conversation and for the incredible life lesson. For $5, which was the maximum permissible amount to take out of Poland at the time, I bought a few souvenirs and permitted myself a beer at a bar. I had only a dollar left by the time we reached

Montreal. From there, I was to take an overnight train to Chicago. In the morning, right before dawn, I felt hungry and went to the bar to buy something with my last dollar. There were many dishes, but none of them had prices. I chose the plainest and most modest sandwich and pointed to it as I gave away my remaining dollar. I was nervous because I didn't know if it was going to be enough. To my surprise, I received twenty-five cents in change.

When I returned to my cabin, it became dawn. Through the window, I tried to see if I could spot the America I imagined from the movies I had seen, but I didn't see anything special, just some junk yards filled with used cars.

Once in Chicago, I went with the other passengers to the train station. On the way, we passed empty cartons, papers, and trash. I was stunned at the sight, but I didn't have time to ponder because we entered a building where hundreds of people were awaiting the arrival of passengers from Poland. Screams, and sometimes even tears, accompanied the welcomes.

I walked the entire length of the waiting crowd, but I didn't recognize anyone from my family. I turned against the stream of the moving crowd, hoping that someone would finally notice me. Unfortunately, the station soon emptied, and I was left alone. Walking along the empty platform, I thought of what I should do to get out of this "fatal" situation. I even considered returning to Poland. A passerby who approached me saved me from my calamity, asking me, "No one came to get you?"

"I'm not sure why, but unfortunately, no," I commented.

"Perhaps, do you have someone's number who was supposed to come and pick you up?"

I quickly handed him my last twenty-five cents and a piece of paper with a telephone number. He placed the call and spoke in English with, as I later found out, my youngest sister-in-law. After he finished the conversation he said, "They'll be here to pick you up soon. They heard an erroneous announcement on the radio that the *Batory* would be a day late."

I was most grateful to the stranger who was able to solve my problem within minutes, and I thanked him genuinely from within. Soon, I greeted my wife's family joyfully, and I immediately forgot about the unpleasant beginning. We reached my in-law's rented apartment in a Chicago neighborhood called Brighton Park. I finally felt at home thanks to my mother-in law, who took heart-felt care of me from the start.

Soon I found a job at a paper processing plant called Cromwell Paper Company. I received a starting pay at $1.80 an hour and I, one of thirteen Poles, was assigned along with another Pole, as the assistant to an African-American man, who cut the paper on the guillotine according to specific criteria. Our job was to pack the ready-made product and deliver it by a forklift to the warehouse. The boss, our direct supervisor, spoke in broken Polish and started by saying, "Don't forget, in America, we work fast."

We took his words literally and worked like machines. We noticed that the African-American supervisor looked at us with disapproval, so we decided to work even faster. A few days later, our boss praised us, but the supervisor was even more disgruntled.

The boss gave us a ten-cent raise for good work. But after a few days, a woman from another department came and explained in Polish, "Don't work so fast. The guy on the paper cutter has to work even faster to keep you occupied. That's why he's not happy with you."

Now that we understood, we slowed down the pace of our work. The boss, however, didn't like this, and as I was delivering the materials to the warehouse at a normal pace, asked me, "Whatcha got in your pants that you're crawling so slowly?"

No more comments were made after this, and everything returned to normal. We worked like this for three months, until one day, immigration officials came to the company for an audit. It was revealed that thirteen Poles were working illegally. The next day we had to report to the agency to testify. I went there with my mother-in-law's brother, who served as the translator, but I was afraid that I might be deported back to Poland. It turned out that it was only a routine hearing. After it, I asked the official who questioned me if I could return to work. He smiled and cautiously replied, "Only God knows if you can."

Only one of the thirteen didn't return to work. He returned to Poland. Nevertheless, I had to find a lawyer who could defend me in case of another audit. Legal services were expensive; they consumed nearly half of my salary. I had to get a second job. I operated two automatic drills at the same time on the second job. When the first drill finished its run, I removed the finished product and placed the next one on it. During this time, the process on the first drill was nearly finished, and I had to service it just like the first. It looked like a dance, as I stepped from one leg to the other.

At the end of the workday, I barely made it home. Morning was approaching, but it was still dark outside. I entered the hallway and tried to climb the stairs. I couldn't lift my leg, so I crawled up to the top on all fours. Suddenly, I noticed two legs in front of me. I lifted my head and saw my mother-in-law standing there awaiting me. She probably thought that I was drunk because surprised with my behavior, she inquired, "Henry, what in the world are you doing?"

"Nothing, I'm just coming home from work," I answered. "I had a tough day, and my legs are not obeying me."

I overestimated my endurance. I started getting sick. I couldn't breathe through my nose; I felt like I was suffocating. It was worse during the night when my throat dried up, and I had to drink water every hour. I was at the brink of exhaustion and already, after a week, I had to quit my second job. I was extremely grateful to my mother-in-law, who took care of me like her own son. She consoled me and gave me encouragement. She prepared my sandwiches for work and waited for me with dinner ready when I returned each day. Before bed, she brought me a glass of water and talk with me until I fell asleep.

My sisters-in-law, Wanda and Chris, were gracious toward me, and that encouraged me. One Sunday, Chris asked me, "Henry, do you like pizza?"

"Oh boy, do I like it," I answered.

She jokingly meant pica, the Polish colloquialism for an anatomic part of a woman and said, "Maybe you're thinking about something different?"

Of course, this type of meal (pizza) wasn't in existence in Poland yet, but I knew what Chris meant, and we had lots of laughs regarding the convergence of the words which sounded similar in Polish and English. I missed my daughter and wife very much, and in spite of the small amount of money that I was saving, I wanted to be with them as soon as possible. That is why I decided that I would return to Poland sooner.

In the meantime, I paid a visit to my aunt, my father's brother's widowed wife. She was the owner of a prosperous grocery store. She had a beautiful home on the north side of the city and welcomed me warmly, which pleasantly surprised me. She treated me to a lavish dinner, and thinking that I was socially uncultured, she sat next to me and whispered hints into my ear, "Take your knife in your right hand, and your fork in the left."

I nearly burst into laughter, but I held it back. I quietly explained to her that I knew how to behave at a table, and I had frequented restaurants since I was young. I didn't have any ill feelings toward my aunt because she didn't want me to be embarrassed in front of her dinner guests at the party. After the party, she joined me and my brother-in-law in the car as we drove a few blocks to be taken home. When we stopped at a red light, she didn't hesitate to inform me that we had to wait for the green light to go again. I was surprised at how little Americans knew about Poland. I concluded that they had the right to think Poles were ignorant because Poland was located behind the iron curtain, thereby practically cutting it off from the rest of the world.

At my request, my father-in-law sent an invitation to my brother for a temporary stay in the United States Earlier I had arranged accommodations for my brother at the presbytery with Bishop Abramowicz, the head of the local parish. It just so happened that I was only able to see my brother for one day because I returned to Poland on the same passage of the *Batory* on which he had arrived. In Montreal, while on the ship, I noticed that I easily breathed through my nose again. *Could I already be in Poland?* I thought.

I was happy returning to the people I loved the most—my daughter and wife. In Copenhagen, I bought a beautiful car, which arrived with me on the *Batory* in Gdynia. I intended to sell it in Poland for double the profit. Unfortunately, I arrived in Poland on July 4, and on July 1, new customs laws were enacted that I wasn't aware of. In light of the new regulations, I couldn't sell the car for another three years. My plans were ruined, and I was forced to use the car myself for some time.

When I was still in the United States, I decided that I would never come back. I repeated my father's words in my mind (which I heard after his return from Germany after the war), but in the context of a different country, "I shall never set foot on American soil again."

When I caught a glimpse of Gdynia, seeing my beloved homeland, my heart jumped with joy. I missed my country and the people who I loved most, my wife and daughter.

First, however, I was in for an unpleasant surprise at the customs station. Everything was taxed, and the inspector's lack of lenience was disconcerting. After nine months in the United States, I now felt the harsh realities of communism more profoundly than ever. My car was not returned to me. I had to report for it a week later. This dampened the joy of returning, but when I saw my beloved wife, I forgot about the unpleasant experiences. Happy, we boarded an overcrowded train from Gdynia to Bialystok and sat on my suitcases for the entire overnight ride. Nevertheless, this didn't bother us much because we were happy to be together. Finally, we arrived in Bialystok. We went to the train station, caught a taxi, and arrived home. It was early in the morning, and Maggie was still asleep, but I couldn't stop looking at her and thinking about how beautiful she was. She was already a year and four months old. The noise and commotion awoke her, and when she saw me, she smiled and said, "Feniek," and this name stuck with me for a long time. I took her in my arms, and we hugged for a long time until Mom invited us for breakfast. We were happy to be together in our home in Poland.

When I was still in America, I received a letter from my brother-in-law, who lived in Budne, that our parent's brick home had burned down. The hospital attendant, to whom we rented the house, testified to the police that I was the one who burned down the home in order to get an insurance settlement out of it. After the police checked my records and determined that I was abroad at the time, they had no basis to suspect me of wrongdoing. The suspicion fell on the tenant himself because the fire broke out at night after everything had already been removed from the house, so he didn't sustain any material damages. The beds, linens, wardrobes, clothing, shoes, pots and pans, and other belongings were standing far away from the house. The case was dismissed because he wasn't caught red-handed.

One day I decided to go to Bialaszewo, eighty kilometers away, to the local police station that was investigating the case. I wanted to testify and clear my name after the investigation. In addition, I wanted to reopen the investigation against the hospital attendant who falsely accused me of the crime. As I exited my car and headed toward the police station, someone pulled me from behind by my suit jacket. I wondered who it could be, so I turned around, but no one was there. *I must be imagining things,* I thought and continued walking. I took a few steps and this time, unmistakably, I felt someone pulling my jacket. This time I turned around to catch the culprit, but no one was behind me. I turned around again, but I could not spot anyone, not even in the distance. I decided that it was my Guardian Angel warning me not to go through with it. I turned back from the front of the police station, got in my car and returned to Bialystok.

Soon, the hospital attendant was stripped of his right to practice his profession because he issued a work release to someone for over a three-week period. A hospital attendant was not allowed to issue work releases lasting more than two weeks. Moreover, he was sentenced to a two-year suspension for another offense. His wife and children left him. He was alone and living on the riverside in a grass hut that he built himself. After a while, he went mad and died home-less in complete seclusion. A passing tourist discovered his remains.

When the news reached me, I realized that the tugging sensation in front of the police station wasn't just an illusion but a clear warning. I was relieved that I didn't add to the attendant's misfortunes, since his life on this Earth ended so miserably.

"Angel of God, my guardian..." thank you for warning me in proper time.

Company Director

Before I left the United States, I wrote a letter to the company that employed me in Poland and asked if I could return to work three months before the end of my one-year unpaid leave. I received an immediate reply: My job was waiting for me, and I could return to it at any time.

After retrieving my car, for which I had to borrow money to pay customs fees, I reported to the director. After squaring matters with the Personnel Department Supervisor, it was decided that I would begin work the next day. I was never late to work, and this time, I was already sitting at my desk earlier than usual, looking over the documents I had taken from the drawer. At exactly seven in the morning, and at the start of our workday, the telephone rang and the secretary announced, "Mr. Henry, the director would like to see you."

With mixed feelings, I stepped into the director's office. I noticed the anxious look on his face. Then I heard him say, "It isn't my fault or my decision, but I cannot hire you back. Please don't take this the wrong way, but I can't. I just can't."

"Sir, I was never fired. I have employment continuity in this position. I was only utilizing my unpaid leave."

"I repeat, it isn't my fault or my decision," the director repeated. This time he looked down at the floor.

I left the director's office very dejected. I began to regret that I didn't accept the head boss' offer at the Cromwell Paper Company. He personally came from the headquarters of the downtown Chicago office to the factory with an offer to sponsor me for permanent residency in the United States The company was going to cover the expenses. They also guaranteed that within nine months, my wife and child could join me. Longing for my homeland, however, prevailed. To the boss' disappointment, I rejected his extraordinary proposition, which he proposed only to me, even though there were eleven others working illegally in the factory. When I bid farewell to the African-American who was my direct supervisor at the paper-cutting machine, he whole-heartedly invited me to come back to the United States. He added that if in the future I needed any help, I could count on him. His words touched me deeply. During the nine months we had worked together, we got along well, excluding the unfortunate beginnings when I wasn't yet familiar with American customs.

After I left the office building, I remembered that before my departure to the United States, the director in Poland offered me a promotion. Despite my consent to take over the new position, three days later, he hired another person with lower qualifications, but who was a member of the Communist Party. At that time, I didn't complain because the "Communist Party was the guiding force of the nation," and the director was given no choice but to hire a Party member over me. But now, I was certain that the Security Office had surrounded me with their special "care."

I didn't have to wait long because after my dismissal, a certain man came to my house and told me he was from the Main Police Headquarters and that he would like to speak with me. Since I just started the construction of the proper home, and just poured the foundations, I didn't want the cement to harden, so I asked that we change the meeting date. He replied angrily, "I will come again, soon." I was surprised that he did not even set the date of the next appointment and walked away.

From the money I had earned selling the American clothes, I was able to buy building materials for a new home. I managed the construction and built everything myself. Once in a while, I would hire someone to help. Soon the money ran out, and my wife decided to head to the United States to earn some more. Grandma Zofia cared for Maggie.

In October 1968, I said good-bye to Jagoda at the port in Gdynia because just like I had a year earlier, she was traveling on the ocean liner *Batory*'s last voyage. As I took the train back to Bialystok, I felt sad. I kept hoping that the water wouldn't cause her to "lose her mind," like it did to the lady who sailed with me.

A few days later the same man from the police station came around again, but this time, I immediately stopped the construction work, and we went inside. He explained that he was fulfilling the duties of the

Deputy Commander of the Civic Police in Bialystok. He was interested in everything I was doing abroad. I had nothing to hide, so I related the entire course of events to him. He kept insisting that I was offered something there. When I denied it, he wasn't completely satisfied with my explanation.

Soon, I was summoned to appear at the Main Headquarters of the Civic Police. This time a different man questioned me, dressed in plainclothes just like his predecessor. I knew that it was the Security Officer. The agent held me at the station for several hours and took notes at my interrogation. At the end he asked me to sign them. When I started to read them he became distressed, but I politely explained to him that I had signed many documents in my life, but I never did so without first reading them. Finally, I refused to sign the notes altogether because there were many "distortions" in them. At this, I thought that he would go into a rage, but instead, he left the room, leaving me alone. He returned two hours later and handed the notes to me to sign once more. I couldn't do it. Unfortunately, if I had signed them, I would have sentenced myself, and I categorically refused. Then he only stammered, "That's fine, we'll meet again under other circumstances. You're free to go, citizen."

I returned home depressed. I cheered up at the sight of Maggie, who as usual sat at the window awaiting "her Feniek." It wasn't until I took her in my arms that I was able to regain mental balance after the grueling interrogation. I didn't expect it, but that was just the beginning.

One time, as I was buying groceries at the store, the cashier placed my purchases on the counter and started serving another customer. I asked her to bag the items because I didn't bring a bag with me. In my mind, I was still subconsciously living in America where an employee was hired just to bag purchases. The cashier replied that they didn't have any packing paper. I asked to speak with the manager.

"What do you need a manager for?" she asked.

"So he can carry my groceries home," I replied without hesitating.

Everyone in the line burst into laughter, but surprisingly, the packing paper was found under the counter, and the cashier herself packed everything up. The arrogance and disrespect were apparent. Despite the short time I spent abroad, I was already used to the quality of service I had received there.

I returned to my car and was about to open the door, when a policeman standing on the sidewalk asked if I that was my car. "Yes," I replied.

"Sir, you should check if anything is missing because just a moment ago, someone was rummaging through it."

"I saw it too," added a passerby, who was listening in to our conversation.

I was upset, having concluded that someone was out to steal my prized possession. After all, I was the only one in Bialystok who owned this particular model.

However, a few weeks later I learned the truth. In a restaurant, I met with a friend who was a well-known figure; he had contacts everywhere, including the police. He took me aside and said, "Henry, if you buy me a round, I'll tell you something."

"I'll buy you not one, but several rounds, and you don't even have to tell me anything."

"I'll tell you anyway. It's about what happened in the situation with your car in front of the grocery store," the friend said.

"I know all about it," I answered. "They wanted to steal my car."

"Falsehood. They were changing the batteries to a listening device. Your house is also bugged. Watch out for yourself and be careful."

After saying this, he quickly left the locale.

I came to understand why the policeman (the one who told me about the break-in to my car), when I met him by chance the next day, didn't want to give me any information. When I asked him about it, he only answered, "Sir, I don't remember what happened in front of the grocery store." I assumed that he was warned by the Security Office not to meddle in their affairs.

From the moment I received the warning about the listening device, my wife and I were careful with our conversations, both at home and in the car. We never said a disparaging word about the People's Rule or the Security Office.

Summons to appear at the provincial police headquarters were now an everyday affair. Frequent interrogations also took place at restaurants, where unfortunately, payment of the bill was left up to me.

My search for work didn't bring about the desirable effect. My applications were accepted, but after checking my records, I was always met with refusals. I was now blacklisted. My former boss, who worked as the Mechanic General at the Provincial Association of Cooperatives (WZGS) found out about this. He knew me well as a man with a sense of humor. It was at the Bureau of Public Projects that I wrote "Breviarum Romanum" (a daily prayer book used by priests), on the cover of his Polish Labor Party Alliance (PZPR) party handbook. He asked three times who had written it, but no one ever turned me in, and that's how it ended. It wasn't until he left the position for WZGS that I admitted to the deed.

This time, just as I was losing all hope of finding anything, he personally came to my house in his official Volga car and offered me the position of inspector in his department. Because he ranked high in the Communist Party, his recommendation enabled my hire. Only a day later, we were on our way to perform an inspection at the Polish Association of Regional Cooperatives (PZGS). Because it was my first inspection, he wanted to show me what the job entailed. The PZGS President received us in his office, asking the secretary to brew fresh coffee while he took out a bottle of fine cognac and a chaser from his bureau. I was a mere student this time, so I observed my teacher to see what he would do next as I followed along. Every time my boss reached for his glass, I did the same. By the end of the first workday, the bottle of cognac was emptied. We went to sleep in a hotel.

The second day was similar to the first. I began to worry about the consequences of this. I gently shared my apprehensions with the boss. "Please don't worry. Tomorrow we'll start the inspection. I'm here to show you what the whole process looks like in practice."

Indeed, on the third day we did not go to the president's office, but to the PZGS site. We meticulously checked all that was in the realm of our inspection. Three days later, we finished the job and returned to the Bialystok office. There we wrote up a report, which we submitted to our director for approval and signature. The director called us into his office. He wanted to verify that the site was as dire as the report alleged it to be. Unfortunately, it was the bitter truth, and my boss did not agree to tone down the language in our document. On leaving the director's office, I reminded my supervisor of the two bottles of cognac and the lavish reception the PZGS President prepared for us. His answer satisfied me entirely. "Mr. Henry, he hosted us out of his own will, and we cannot take that into consideration. Our job is to write the truth, and that's just what we did. In the future, please don't give into any pressures because from now on, you'll be doing the inspections on your own."

I had to admit that he was right, and that's how it remained.

When the PZGS President took notice of my car, he suggested that I make the inspection rounds in my own vehicle, and the cooperative would pay me per kilometer. The only caveat was that inspectors from other departments could ride with me, if the need arose. I welcomed the offer, since it meant additional income in my pocket. The president himself accompanied me on my first inspection at a PZGS cooperative. I couldn't believe my eyes when I saw the reception that was prepared for us. After a few such inspections, I came to the conclusion that such lavish receptions were the norm. As an inspector and driver, I couldn't accept any alcohol, even though in some cases an inspection would take days to complete. I was content with this because I wasn't forced to drink, as was the Polish custom. I went for inspections usually once a month, and the rest of the time was consumed with office work.

One day my friend Marek called to tell me that he was summoned to speak with someone from the General Police Station (similar to the FBI) regarding a matter concerning me. I asked Marek where he was supposed to meet this person, and I went to the place also. On the way to the spot, a man with a worn briefcase walked in front of me, and it turned out that it was he who arranged to meet with Marek in the park. They met and went further into the park, while I sat on a bench at the park's edge. Suddenly, a gypsy approached me to tell my fortune. I gave her 100 zloty, rather than the usual 20, to tell the fortunes of the two men sitting nearby. I only warned her not to say anything about me.

I laughed to tears as I saw them gesturing for her to go away, but she wouldn't budge because she didn't want to lose the money I gave her. When they finally got rid of her, and the meeting ended, I met with Marek in our former workplace. Knowing that my work phone was bugged, and I didn't want to answer any of Marek's questions about the situation, I let him know why our personal meeting was so important. Marek gave me the following account:

"He asked me if you drink, if you had changed after returning from the United States, if you have any acquaintances, friends, strange phone calls, letters, and so on…"

"What did you tell him?"

"What should I have told him? The truth, that you don't drink at all, that you're an all-around good guy, full of energy and a sense of humor. I noticed though that he wasn't happy with the way the conversation was going."

Soon I headed to Warsaw to attend a Central Cooperative Committee (CRS) Conference with our managing unit. There one of my superiors asked to speak with me in private. I think he knew listening devices were in the office, and this is why he probably asked me to step outside into the corridor. He said to me, "Sir, did you know that your position is meant to be terminated?"

"I know nothing about it," I declared truthfully.

"I'm telling you this so you can defend yourself because in reality, it's about you, not the position. After all, you're a very good employee."

I thanked him for his honest advice and explained to him that this was a game of politics and any attempt to fight for the position wouldn't amount to anything. I wouldn't stand a chance of winning. It was sad, but true. I had a good reputation at work, but in our country, anything was possible. I was thankful to that man for revealing part of the secret, and we parted ways like old friends.

Not even a month had passed when I received a summons from the director, who spoke bluntly, "I am forced to let you go due to the elimination of your position."

I was already prepared for this conversation, so I replied with a smile, "You cannot fire the only breadwinner of a household because that would be against Polish law, and the law is strictly observed in our country," I mocked him, looking him straight in the eyes.

At first he was stumped because he couldn't find the answer. Finally he blurted out, "Your dismissal has been decided."

I replied, "I have nothing more here," as Henryk Sienkiewicz's famous literary character Michal Wolodyjowski liked to say. Genuflecting exaggeratedly to the director, I left his office. I noticed the rage in his expression, but that just amused me even more.

I found myself unemployed once again, as the summons to report to the Security Office and the interrogations multiplied.

In the beginning of September, just before my wife's arrival from the United States, the same man from the Security Office came by and asked who it was that I knew at the customs office in Gdynia. When he received a negative reply, he became very upset. He questioned me again about everything and probably had his sights set on catching me saying something incriminating. I was surprised when he returned to the topic of Gdynia. I knew that this was connected with my wife's arrival, but he didn't mention any of that.

I turned for help to my friend from the police department, who had warned me in the past about the police's plans and saved me many times from imprisonment. I asked him to come with me to Gdynia and help me to enter the customs station when my wife would arrive from the United States. Without a moment's hesitation he agreed, and two days before my wife's return, we went to Gdynia. He packed his police uniform as a precaution, but in order not to raise any suspicions, he went in plainclothes. When the *Batory* docked at the port, we went upstairs to the customs station. My friend flashed his police badge, and the guard let him in without reservations. Walking behind him, I was stopped. Then my friend whispered to the guard, "This citizen is with me."

With an air of unwavering confidence, I entered the customs officials' booth. I saw that I was observed by two men who were taking turns watching me. They followed me everywhere. I steered clear of my friend, so I wouldn't cause him any problems. We pretended we didn't know each other.

Finally the ramp was lowered, and the passengers of the *"Stefan Batory,"* the new Polish ocean liner, began to disembark to the customs station. Suddenly, I noticed my wife, and my heart started racing. We fell into each other's arms. Eleven months of separation was eleven months too long. We missed one another very much. Jagoda was happy that I was able to welcome her at the top of the dock and didn't even ask how I got there.

"I'm glad I asked you in that letter to take care of customs issues because I brought a lot of things."

"What letter are you referring to? I didn't get anything from you lately." Then I told my wife about the interrogation, and I just assumed she would need my help. I asked her to lower her voice if there was anything else she wanted to tell me.

"You know, I have gold coins inside my heel," she whispered in my ear.

"Give me the shoe, but in a bag," I quietly said.

We were still standing and embracing the entire time, so it looked like for a half hour we couldn't get enough of each other, although we didn't really have to pretend.

I took the bag with the shoe from my wife and slipped it to my friend as we passed him. I returned the other way to let him know what was in it. I noticed that he went to the bathroom, and when he exited, he went outside. I knew that one big issue had been solved. The other still remained, to hand the inspector a bribe, so that he would cut us some slack on the customs fees.

I approached one of them and made an offer. He asked me my wife's name, and when I told him he stated, "I can't" and lowered his head.

I immediately walked away and approached another customs inspector. This time I raised the amount of the bribe significantly because I was under the impression that my previous offer was too low. Despite this, after hearing my wife's name, the answer was the same. Only the fourth inspector said, "Your wife has been directed to personal inspection. I could do you a favor and ask my supervisor to relieve your wife of this burden, but then I would have to levy customs fees on literally everything."

I agreed to it without hesitating because I didn't want my wife to be degraded and disrespected in such a way. The inspector went to the director and returned with good news; his supervisor revoked the decision of a personal inspection.

Unfortunately, he had to do as he said. I paid 80,000 zloty of duty for the items, which would have been $800 in black market prices, and my wife brought $1,700 with her.

"It would have been better to leave it all to these crooks," I remarked about the customs inspectors.

We arrived home happy that it was all behind us. We were extremely grateful to our friend, the policeman. Without his help, the gold coins would have been confiscated, and the customs fee would have been even higher. The penalty could have also included being arrested and sent to jail. What was more important was that Jagoda escaped a personal inspection.

The whole truth emerged two weeks later when a letter came from the United States, whose sender was Jagoda. The letter was held by the Security Office for thirty days. In it, my wife requested that I find someone at the customs office to help with the many items she intended to bring back. That explained everything. In this way, the Security Office wanted to show me that I was under their constant watch. Otherwise, the letter would have simply been destroyed.

The Horror of Relentless Persecution Continues

Thanks to the new flow of income after Jagoda's return, I put all my energy towards the construction of the house, especially since I was fired from my job without cause once again. Only my family and my building our home gave meaning to my life.

One morning, at around five o'clock, someone knocked on the door. Drowsily, I lifted the curtains and spotted three men in civilian attire. When I opened the door, one of them shoved his badge in my face and declared, "This is a search!"

"Why, do you have a warrant?" I asked.

"I'll claim responsibility for this search. We'll come back with the warrant later," they answered, but of course that never happened. The search was entirely unlawful.

After my home was turned completely upside-down, I asked the man with the badge, "What exactly are you looking for? Perhaps I can help."

"Heaters," they sarcastically replied.

"Not a problem. They are in the attic," I replied in a serious tone. Getting to the attic required scaling a ladder. One of the men held it steady as another struggled to get up. When the "badge guy" finally realized that I was playing around at their expense, they called off the search and went on their way. I am still not sure what they were looking for, but luckily they didn't "drop off" anything incriminating, and I avoided arrest.

The situation brought back memories of the wartime horrors of my childhood. Although this was no longer wartime, I couldn't find peace either. There was blackmailing and provocation. I was tightly surrounded by the Secret Police and under surveillance at all times. On several occasions, I was forced to enter a random stairwell to get them off my back. Sometimes the tricked work, sometimes it didn't. I had nothing to hide, but the constant surveillance was unnerving. After a while, I got used to it and stopped noticing their presence.

Nevertheless, I found myself in several uncomfortable situations. One time, as I was calmly waiting at a bus stop, a stranger began to insult me. I knew that he was just trying to provoke me, so without reacting, I calmly boarded the bus. Although only a few people were on the bus, I noticed a false overcrowding around me as passengers pushed me from all sides. I had to leave the bus immediately.

Another trick they used was to turn people against me, those whom I regarded as my friends. One of them asked me to buy $100 from him. Not suspecting deceit on his part, I agreed. As he handed me a one-hundred dollar bill, I noticed that it was counterfeit. I requested that we go to a secluded place where I could pay him the black market price. He agreed, and we made our way to the agreed-upon spot, which was close to a provincial police headquarters. When he saw where I was heading, he began to apologize and explain that he was forced to make this deal with me. He revealed that after the transaction, I was to be arrested based on the fake one-hundred dollar bill. I didn't blame him, but rather felt pity for him. I asked my friend to stop cooperating with that bunch of crooks. I told him to tear up the fake currency, which he did on the spot. Proof of the alleged crime ceased to exist.

It was inside the Police Headquarters building that I was interrogated by different officers, but outside of the headquarters it was inevitably the same man, the one who after my return from the United States, came to my house and introduced himself as the Deputy Head Commandant of the Provincial Civic Police. Soon, I found out his name but couldn't confirm whether it was his real name. Surely, he held the rank of colonel. He often asked me to take him somewhere, and I never refused, treating his requests like an order. One time he asked, "What is that hanging from your rearview mirror?"

"It's a rosary," I replied

"Why do you have it in the car?"

"I have been a driver for three years now, and I believe that this protects me from accidents because until now, there hasn't been a scratch on my car," I declared.

The following Sunday he demanded I meet him at a bus terminal to drive him to Sokolka. That Saturday I went with my wife and Maggie to visit my mother and brother in Grabnik, where my brother served as a pastor. On Sunday, we left two hours before the appointment, so that we could drive the 120 kilometers without hurry. I brought my wife and Maggie home, and I went to meet him alone. He was already waiting for me. He walked up to the car, opened the door, and saw that the rosary was still hanging there. His face became red with anger and he said, "I'm not going anywhere with you!" He slammed the door and walked away hurriedly.

This time I lost my temper. I put the car in reverse and slammed on the gas pedal. For a few seconds, the wheels turned in place, and a black cloud of smoke escaped from underneath the car. The tires were screeching. After a while, I came to my senses and calmly made my way home.

A few days later, I was scheduled to report to the finance department to settle accounts for the expenses related to the construction of my house. It turned out that only the financial director was available to take care of my case. I had to wait for the "lord and master" to assist me. Finally the secretary announced that the director was ready to see me. When I entered his office, he didn't bother to ask me to sit but asked, "Did you bring the receipts for the house?"

"No!"

"Why not?"

"You simply had no right to call me in for an audit. It's too early for that. I'm surprised that you're not familiar with the regulations."

Consternation followed. The director was silent for a moment. I wasn't concerned with his opinion. I never fawned over any bureaucrat, knowing full well that he was just a puppet set up by the Security Office and patronizing him was beneath me. I was familiar with the law, and it surprised me that these ignorant bureaucrats, who only held their positions thanks to Communist Party promotions, didn't have the same knowledge as I had.

"I don't know what you're talking about," the director finally stammered out.

"It's simple. I'll explain it to you, if you don't know. The settlement of accounts should be carried out only when the house has a roof. My house, according to the blueprint, is a two-story home, and it doesn't even have a ceiling above the first floor yet. I know very well who ordered you to do this, but it's a shame that you were willing to break the law. If I wasn't familiar with the regulations, you would have succeeded," I told him without hesitation.

"We will call you in at the right time; we'll wait," he replied arrogantly and rudely.

The bureaucrats saw themselves as omnipotent at the time. I had to be as tough as steel if I wanted to achieve anything in that world of lawlessness and hatred toward non-party members.

There were shortages of building materials everywhere. Unfortunately, sometimes I had to resort to buying black market materials. The most profound were chronic shortages of cement. Drivers of the cement trucks would offer to sell the scarce product. One time, I took advantage of the opportunity and bought two tons of cement on the black market.

Not more than an hour after the transaction, a taxi pulled up to my house. My friend, the policeman, stormed into my house and yelled, "Henry, put the stolen cement away. They're coming to search your property. One of the guys who unloaded the cement was part of the Volunteer Reserve Civic Police. I just happened to be in the office when I overheard him reporting you to the lieutenant."

Then my friend jumped into the taxi and left. When I heard his warning, I began to sweat so profusely that even my hair was dripping wet. I ran to my neighbor's, who had two young sons, and asked him for immediate help. I gave them 500 zloty to carry the cement to their storage area. They did it in fifteen minutes.

They had barely finished the job when a whole bunch of cops appeared in my yard. Their search for cement yielded no evidence, and the supervisor of the police raid only commented, "Where in the hell did you put it?"

With a surprised expression I asked, "Who are you looking for? Maybe I know him; maybe I can tell you where he is." I held a good face to a bad game.

The policeman made no reply; he only smiled and drove away with his team. I could relax somewhat, but I swore to myself right away that I would never again buy any materials on the side. If they had found the cement, I would have received two years in prison since surely I would refuse to work with the secret police. That evening my friend, the policeman, paid me a visit. This time it was a personal visit in order to explain what the police raid was all about. Once again, it was a setup. That's why the cement was brought directly to my house with the offer to sell it at a reasonable price. I was still naïve enough to take the bait, even though I was well aware that I was under tight observation. Unfortunately, we learn from our mistakes, but sometimes these mistakes cost us dearly. From then on, I walked on eggshells.

All of my job applications were accepted with the assurance that my qualifications were high. All that was needed was the director's approval. I hoped that the news of my blacklisted status didn't reach everywhere. Unfortunately, each time I applied, after a few days, I was rejected again. When I asked about the reason for the decision, all I got was an evasive answer. I lost all hope and stopped searching for a job altogether and focused all my energy on building our house.

When it was near completion, in my absence, two men approached the building site introducing themselves as my friends. The plumber, despite my warnings not to let anyone in, showed them around the whole house. Afterwards, the plumber told me about how my friends showed interest in everything. The consequences of the visit were apparent a few days later when I was called in for a construction material audit.

I reported for the hearing as scheduled. When I saw three officers, ranking from lieutenant colonel to captain, sitting behind the table, I knew that this was going to be an interrogation, and chills ran down my spine. The documents I presented to them were inspected thoroughly. Then a harsh cross-examination began. Many charges were brought up against me. In their opinion, several things didn't match up, and I was sure that I would go straight to jail. So I began to explain the discrepancies, one by one. Finally they decided, "You used more cement than the receipts indicate. Where did you get the rest?"

"The additional material came from national public construction lots. I took it with the director's permission. I was permitted to remove the excess hardened cement and rocks intended for my construction, so that's just what I did. Go ahead, check the petition. You can find it in the documents I presented to you." They found the document, and each of them inspected it carefully.

Once again I succeeded, but I walked out of the provincial police headquarters with trembling legs. I was happy that I could return home. I gained respect for the director. I valued him for signing my petition for the cement because before signing it, he thought about it and said to me, "Sir, I will sign this for you, but this can turn against me one day. My only hope is that if we wind up behind bars, we'll go together."

My happiness did not last long. A few weeks later, no sooner was the last sheet nailed to the roof than I received another order to report for a financial audit again. I expected it, so I had my documents in order, so that there wouldn't be any reservations. I was received by the same official, and without any introductions he declared, "I don't need any of your documents today. I will give you only two weeks to sell your car. I suggest you mind the deadline, otherwise, you know what will happen."

"I know," I replied and left very frustrated. I was reminded of what happened after the audit. One of my interrogating officers arrived at my home in a Syrena car and offered to exchange cars. He probably counted on the fact that I would fall for the foolish transaction before the deadline. Of course, I made it clear to him that ten of his Syrenas would not have been enough for me to agree to the offer.

Now I understood how much the Copenhagen-bought car bothered the Communist Party and Security Office. They couldn't permit a man who neither belonged to the Party nor collaborated with them to own a luxury car and have his own house.

To the governing entities at the time, Catholics, believers in God who practiced their religion, especially family members of priests, were automatically labeled enemies of the "people's" nation. Those were times when the rule of law disappeared amid the inhumanity, disdain for fellow man, and mutual hatred. I wasn't able to accept the falsehood and duplicity of the leaders and representatives in power. What troubled me most was that many of my countrymen lost their human dignity in exchange for certain positions or for a passport. To fulfill their forlorn desires, they destroyed others, conscious of the fact that those people would suffer in prison or die a martyr's death.

As I returned home, I thought of what I would do next. The ground under my feet was becoming unstable, and I started to think about leaving Bialystok, but I wasn't sure where I would go. America wasn't a permanent solution because I had decided to never return there. It hurt me to see that this was not the same Poland I longed for in America. I knew that I could not hold my country accountable for this, but the association was inevitable. I was terrified to see people losing hope for a better tomorrow and become more complacent in the face of this abhorrent Communist system.

Despite this, on Saturday, I went with my wife to our favorite restaurant, the Astoria, to enjoy ourselves a bit and forget about the week's difficulties. After all, we spent every Saturday away from home, and that was our weekly ritual. We were young, and life still had much to offer. At the restaurant, I gave a generous tip to the orchestra and requested the song "Red Poppies at Monte Cassino." It was a forbidden tune, but despite this, the orchestra began to play. All of the patrons put down their silverware and delighted in the patriotic melody. Just then someone, most likely an agent, stood up and started dancing on the floor. I reacted right away. I approached him and reminded him that this melody was not meant for dancing. A couple of men jumped out of their seats and ran up to him as well. He was swept away from the dance floor before he could even turn around. I didn't see him in the room anymore. We left the locale because on Sunday morning, I had to head to the Warsaw auction to sell my car. After all, the man from the finance department gave me only two weeks.

Unfortunately, I wasn't able to sell my car the first time because prices fell drastically that day. I had one more Sunday to spare, so I returned to the auction, and, despite the low price, I made the sale. I had no other choice.

On Monday, I reported to the finance department with the car sales contract. The director looked over the document and clearly satisfied, whispered in my ear, "Now, you can buy yourself another car."

What insolence, what lawlessness, I thought and left the office.

Since I still didn't have a job, I was able to finish our house in no time. My wife was in her element because she was once again able to decorate the house according to her own taste. We enjoyed the comfort of our new space. Two beautiful crystal chandeliers illuminated the salon, while the grand piano added to its splendor. Although Maggie was still small, she was already learning to play it. Life couldn't have been better, from that respect. However, the Security Office, which still had many more tricks up its sleeve, would try to enslave me and force me into collaboration.

One day I received notice that I was to report to a restaurant called Luksus (Luxury) to speak with, of course, the lieutenant. At the time, I was taking a break from drinking alcohol. I asked a friend from high school to come at the agreed-upon time and pretend to accidentally bump into me there. He did just that. When the lieutenant and I were eating dinner, my friend approached us, and of course, acting surprised to see me there, he asked if he could join us. I agreed, but the Security Office man was not excited about it.

I immediately ordered a bottle of vodka, and after a few glasses, we struck up a conversation. My friend was a history professor, so he knew how to lead a conversation to everyone's contentment. After the first bottle, another was finished. They were both drunk. I paid the bill and motioned to my friend that it was time for him to go. The agent grabbed me by the arm, and we walked outside. He started to speak informally with me and announced, "Henry, we refused to issue you a passport so you could go abroad, but starting today, you can count on the door being open for you. You can even keep your passport at home, and you can go as you please." Normally, after each trip abroad, a person was required to return their passport to the police station.

I was shocked, and at first, I didn't know how to respond. My only thought was, *Why the sudden change? Could they have gotten tired of bringing me down and humiliating me?* I propped him up so he wouldn't fall because he was very drunk. Finally I said, "Thank you very much, sir. I am very grateful."

"A favor for a favor," he said, "You will have to take a few letters there. They will already be stamped. Your job will be to put them in a mailbox in the United States. That's all." By agreeing to the proposition, I would, in effect, agree to be a spy.

Oh God, that's the catch, I thought again, but I knew the law. I replied, "No problem, just as you wish. I'll take the letters, but according to the customs regulations, they must be open."

"In that case, you won't even go to Czechoslovakia!" he furiously declared and walked away straight as a pole. He sobered up right away.

I stood on the sidewalk hypnotized. I couldn't move. My suspicions were confirmed. They wanted to make me a minion for the Communist regime, which was strong at the time. That is why they deprived me of employment, put wiretaps in my house and car, and denied me exit from the country. That was the reason I was audited, interrogated, summoned, spied on, and tormented, so that I would finally succumb to their pressures. As a last ditch effort, they even tried to ensnare me with the tactic most difficult to refuse, the ability to keep my passport so that I could travel freely. That is how the secret police were most effective in recruiting agents. I couldn't live in Poland anymore; the only choice left was to go to America. I still could not believe it. I was an optimist by nature, so I counted on a better destiny, even in the most tragic moments.

One day, a taxi driver I knew brought us a repatriate from Russia. The driver knew that my small house was empty, and the woman was looking for a place to live. She came to Poland only with her twelve-year-old daughter because her Russian husband was afraid. We agreed to take her in, provided that I could obtain a permit from the town hall. All of our neighbors had tenants in their houses, but I could not afford to do anything illegal because I knew I was under constant observation. I went with her to the presidium, but they referred us to the Communist Party Unit within that agency.

An elegant gentleman received us in a modern office. He asked us what had brought us there, so my responsibility was to explain the matter. "This lady came from a country friendly to us, the USSR, and I hope you can help her. We will let her stay in our house for six months free of charge. After that we will charge her nominal rent. The decision is yours to make."

"Fine, I agree to it. Go ahead and rent the house to her."

"I'm sorry, but I will have to have that in writing," I bore deeper into the matter.

"I give you my word that not a hair will fall from your head," answered the Party representative.

"I would trust your word if you were the only person behind that desk until this lady buys an apartment. But I know quite well what life is like; I experienced it myself. Let's suppose that tomorrow you are fired from your position, like I was at one point, and you no longer work here. Then what? The problem will fall on me, and I have enough of them. I'm not looking for any new ones."

Meanwhile, the "great" leader of the Party Unit became very pale and answered me with unhidden anger, "Please wait in the secretariat."

While waiting in the secretariat, I heard the sound of an employee's running footsteps as the Communist Party official called for him. I recognized him as my friend. He was so frightened that he didn't even look at me, even though we knew each other well. I felt pity for him because he was an engineer, the supervisor of a construction department. People were degraded while being fed the belief that the Polish Allied Labor Party was the strength of the nation. In my opinion, they were all scoundrels and traitors, who robbed Poland of its crowning glory. Unfortunately, these were difficult and hopeless times. I trusted in the prophecy of Our Mother of Fatima, which says that communism will rule the entire world, but only briefly. I only feared that in historical terms, "briefly" might mean two hundred years.

They debated for over half an hour. Finally, I was called into the office again and notified, "Sir, we will issue you the permit in writing, although it is against the law." My friend pretended not to know me, and I didn't want to cause him trouble, so I thanked them and left.

When I told my tenant that everything had been taken care of, she literally jumped for joy. I told her that my wife and I decided that she need not pay rent for six months. On that same day, she bought silverware and plates. It turned out that in Riga, where she had lived, they had only one plate, from which they took turns eating. They could only eat soup at the same time. She worked as a chemist, and her husband was a teacher. I couldn't imagine life in such primitive conditions. After a while, her husband came from Russia and became enchanted with life in Poland. Poland was their America. I was celebrating my name day at the time and invited them. Many guests showed up for the lavish party. He couldn't imagine such a celebration, and afterwards, he commented, "Where we live you wouldn't even get to the end of the party before you'd be taken straight to prison." He enjoyed living in Poland very much, but feared staying because he would always be called a "kacap" (an offensive name for a Russian), and such treatment was a blow to his honor.

At that time, Jagoda's parents came to visit from the United States. They did not have the chance to get to know Poland before they left. I wanted to show them the most interesting places it had to offer. My brother lent us his car, and we went to "see the world," as we grandly called it. We visited first Warsaw, then Krakow, and Zakopane where we ascended to Kasprowy Peak. There we had dinner and drank tea with rum. My in-laws were impressed by everything they saw. For the first time in their lives, they were able to travel around Poland. On the way back, we nearly ended the trip in tragedy. Cruising at 120 kilometers an hour, the rear tire suddenly exploded. The car swerved back and forth across the whole width of the road. Fortunately, no one was coming from the opposite direction, and we avoided a head-on collision. A moment later, I regained control of the car and safely pulled over to the side of the road.

When I got out of the car, it seemed like my legs had turned to rubber. I couldn't move, and it took me a few minutes to regain my composure. I thought, *What a trip it would have been for my in-laws if our car had crashed into incoming traffic or fell over a precipice.* The view over the side of the road gave me goose bumps. Fortunately, the Guardian Angel was with us and watched over our safety. The rest of the way home was without incident.

Hope and Fiascoes of Finding Work

My attempts at finding a job always ended in a fiasco. I lost all hope after my last conversation with the Security Office Lieutenant. I knew that I was tightly surrounded, and the noose around my neck was growing tighter. My wife began fearing for my life because a friend, whom I played bridge with, the president of a cooperative, was murdered. His wife was the director of the Polish National Savings Bank and was determined to find the killer, but she was not able to in time, since a month later, she died of unknown causes at the hospital. The couple left two young children to the grace and disfavor of life. Those who failed to recognize the People's Rule, and especially those who opposed it, ended up that way.

I searched for a way out of that difficult situation, and more often, I found the only feasible solution was to emigrate to the United States with my family. Various individuals came to my house offering ways out, but I never trusted any of them and told them "to go to hell." Despite my strong refusal, one of these men came again. When I categorically refused his help, he resentfully replied, "How wicked people are. You try to lend a helping hand, and they push it away, only to lose the chance that fate unexpectedly brought."

After a time, I was called into court to testify against this man. It turned out that he had exploited over one hundred people and scammed them out of large sums of money. When I entered the courtroom, all of the seats were filled with people that fell for his scheme. I greeted them loudly, "My dear would-be Americans, I welcome you wholeheartedly."

No one replied to my greeting because everyone was wondering if they would get their money back. Unfortunately, no one recovered their funds. "Mr. Arranger" got five years in prison, and that is how the matter ended.

I believed in the next man, however, since he was recommended by a friend. We drove to Warsaw's Neighborhood Civic Police Station where a woman in plainclothes, with whom we had an appointment, came out to meet us. My friend referred to her as "Captain," but in my view, she was too young to hold such a rank. The next moment he got out of the car and approached the kiosk to buy cigarettes, I took the opportunity to ask her about her rank. It turned out she was only a corporal. I asked her about her contacts at the Ministry of Interior, and if she was able to help me.

"My connections, unfortunately, are few," she replied honestly, "but I'll try to make a contact."

By this time, the original man returned. When he settled into the car, he began the conversation with the words, "Captain, please arrange for this man to leave for the United States as soon as possible."

She didn't reply. I turned the car around and took her back to the police station. Because the man didn't know what had happened in the meantime, he demanded 10,000 zloty upfront. I stopped the car and told him to get out of the car, without any explanation. He was angry that he had lost so much time, and that I treated him in that way. I made my way back to Bialystok. I immediately started inquiring about my friend's contacts and who recommended this "arranger" to him. It turned out my friend was an informer. I severed all ties with him, even though he had been in my home many times before for my wife's or my name days. My circle of friends was shrinking; the cause was most likely envy. For those times we were well off and that was a splinter in the foot of the Security Office.

Third time's the charm, as the famous saying goes, and that's what happened in my case. One day in a restaurant in Warsaw, I accidentally met a man who turned out to be a high official in the Ministry of the Interior. I became acquainted with him, and he even invited me to his home. I didn't mention my plans of going to the United States because I thought we hadn't gotten to know each other well enough to stir up the topic. I even visited him at a special resort for ministry officials. He had to personally come up to the gate so that I could enter. A special pass was required, and everyday mortals were forbidden to enter. The place was quite luxurious. My only thought was, *There are people and then there are folks,* the latter being in higher spheres of power. There he introduced me to his supervisor, the Minister of the Interior himself. I enjoyed myself thoroughly, although it was the first time I found myself in such company. The phrase, "don't judge a book by its cover," came to mind.

Once he invited my wife and me to a performance at the Warsaw opera. The crème-de-le-crème of modern society was there. During intermission, I spoke with the minister again and introduced my wife to him, and he introduced his to me. The evening was enjoyable, and I came to the conclusion that in Warsaw, I was able to resolve many matters. As time would tell, I wasn't mistaken.

Meanwhile, I still lived in Bialystok, and I had to grapple with many difficulties. Well, "many situations happen to people," and that saying applied to me as well.

One September afternoon in 1970, I met a friend and former co-worker of mine. We both were glad to have run into one another. Then he asked me in a friendly manner, "What have you been doing lately?"

"Nothing; I'm looking for a job." I answered.

"Man, you fell from heaven! You're just the man I'm looking for; I need a worker like you right away."

"What type of job is it?"

"It's for a dispatcher in the transportation unit where I am the chief. Now I work at Bialystok Sanitary Installations Company. My base is outside of town on Ciolkowski Street. Please be there at seven in the morning, and we can discuss the conditions of your hire."

"Unfortunately, I can't take the job because I've never worked in the transportation sector, and I may not be able to handle the responsibilities. I wouldn't want to betray your trust in me," I replied honestly.

"Don't worry. We've known each other for a while. I know what you're capable of. It'll be a piece of cake for you."

"I'm very grateful for your confidence in me. I'll be at work on time tomorrow," I answered, mentioning nothing of my blacklisted status.

The next day I arrived as we agreed at the transportation hub with my employment application in hand. My future boss took the application, and in his official car, went to the directorate located in the city center. He was supposed to return in less than an hour, since it was just a formality. I waited for eight hours, and before the end of the shift, at three o'clock in the afternoon, the manager returned and said, "Sir, I apologize for your long wait, but I did as I promised and arranged for your hire. Unfortunately, I wasn't able to negotiate a higher salary. If you accept the lowest, I will make it up to you with bonuses, which are mine to give."

"I must admit that I can't believe I was actually hired. I keep thinking that it's a dream. Thank you very much, and I promise you will not be disappointed in my work."

After some time, I found out about what went on behind the scenes of my hire. Mr. Richard went through a lot of trouble. They categorically denied him permission to hire me, following the recommendation of the Security Office. Then he gave them an ultimatum, either I would be hired or he would resign from his position. He put his career on the line to keep his word and help a friend. I will be grateful to him for the rest of my life for all that he did for me because there aren't enough people like him.

During the course of my job, I often picked up my supervisor's telephone calls. I assumed that they were from the Security Office because the director immediately left the office, announcing that he would not return that day. This would take place several times a month, but he never mentioned anything about it. Everyone stuck to their duties.

I was employed as the Senior Inspector in the transportation hub, and I liked both the job and the staff I supervised. Whenever there were problems, I solved them face-to-face, rather than go through higher management.

I gave the drivers their dispatch passes from my office window, which was made for that purpose. One day one of the drivers placed a beer on my desk for me to drink and announced happily, "Sir, I found out that we had the same girlfriend. Now she's your wife."

I was surprised not only by his statement, but more so by the beer during work hours, which was beyond disciplinary norms and considered rude behavior.

"Please take the beer off my desk and report to me at the end of the line," I told him. When I dispatched all of the drivers, I went out to the hallway myself. "Do you know what you did? It's not about the common girlfriend; that's not relevant. I'm referring to the beer during work hours. Drinking on the job is grounds for dismissal from your position, or I could suspend you on a disciplinary basis from your job."

The young man began sobbing like a child. I consoled him, ensuring him that I would not fire him but give him only a verbal warning, so that he would remember for the rest of his life that alcohol wouldn't be tolerated during work hours, no matter what kind. I gave him the dispatch slip, and he happily returned to work.

After I returned home, I told my wife of the incident. She was surprised that he regarded her as his girlfriend because she only met him once in her life, when he was the driver of a private taxi which her uncle leased. Of course, I didn't delve deeper into the matter, and that's how it ended. The driver tried to avoid me and never mentioned it again. I didn't have any resentment toward him. All he wanted to do was gain my trust, but he accomplished just the opposite.

Another time, I got a call from the police that one of our delivery trucks had burned, but the driver was unscathed. It happened in the field, and the driver was away on duty, so I took the company car to the site. It turned out that the driver went to his parent's house without permission from the construction supervisor, and during the night, the truck caught on fire for unknown reasons. The police and forensic photographer were already on the scene. It was a criminal matter, and the driver could face not only a fine but prosecution and a prison sentence.

When I arrived at the house, the driver of the damaged truck ran up to me and looking at me pleadingly, began begging, "Sir, please save me."

"I can't promise you anything because the matter is in the hands of the police, but I will do whatever is in my power."

That was all I could say without knowing the whole case. The policeman and photographer approached me, so I introduced myself. A thorough inspection of the vehicle didn't yield any evidence, and we still couldn't determine the cause of the fire. The policeman suggested that we go to the house and write up a report. The driver whispered in my ear that he had some vodka and chasers at home to bribe them with somehow. I gave him a stern look, and he understood it. We entered the house. What I saw next was beyond my expectations. The policeman and photographer must have had the same impression because they both looked at me. It was a miserable sight. The floor consisted of dried mud. We sat down at the makeshift table.

"What do you make of all this?" I inquired.

"I'll write the report in such a way to give you room for a decision, and you can do what you will," replied the officer.

With the completed report, I went to the hub and ordered the delivery of the burned car to our repair shop. There I called a company committee, which deemed the electrical wiring to be the cause of the fire. In the report I indicated that it was I who permitted the driver to park at his father's home. I found out that the driver was the only breadwinner of the family, and he had three younger siblings. Based on our report, the courts dismissed the case. In effect, the driver was not held responsible. He came to me and said, "Sir, I will not forget this for the rest of my life."

Right after that, I experienced a tragedy which I cannot forget about to this day. Although I wasn't involved in it personally, I feel partially guilty about what had happened.

In our fleet, there were two Lublin cargo trucks. Because of their small dimensions, I had to order two large PKS vehicles (state operated bus system) to deliver oversized sanitary equipment. A Zubr truck with a trailer was delivered. The driver reported to me, and I referred him to the construction supervisor who needed the vehicle. According to procedure, each of the construction supervisors ordered a particular delivery vehicle, and I was responsible for processing the order according to his needs. The construction supervisor would use the car from then on. That is what happened in this case. Later it turned out that this particular vehicle was needed to deliver sanitary installations from our hub where the production facility was to make these products for a construction site in the field.

A while later one of our employees ran up to me and yelled, "Come quickly! There was an accident. The loader fell off of the truck."

I ran after him only to see an ambulance that I had called taking away the loader of the truck. He was still conscious because he tried to pick himself up from the stretcher, but the doctor gently held him up and laid him back down. The next day, when I arrived at work, I got the news that the man had passed away. It was a deep blow to me.

A few days later a five-member commission arrived accusing me of causing the accident because I had not trained the employee at his worksite. Each member of the commission questioned me individually, and one of them was particularly relentless and questioned me the longest.

While I was responsible for training our own transport employees under Labor Safety and Health Hygiene (BHP) regulations, and I did so according to the rules, the training was a general one held in my office, rather than at the sites where I sent my drivers. I had over twenty vehicles myself and leased additional ones each day from other companies. Training each employee individually at the worksite would be impossible, which is exactly what I testified before the commission.

After my testimony, I contacted one of my colleagues in the supervisory unit to find out the identities of the members of the commission. It turned out that one of them was a gentleman from the Security Office, the one who had the most questions. A week later, they came to interrogate me once again. This time, I told my wife that I was involved in a lawsuit and that I would most probably be charged with neglect at the workplace, which resulted in the fatal accident. I was devastated. Even though this person's death did not rest on my conscience, something bothered me. I wasn't at fault for not training him at my worksite because I didn't know where the construction supervisor would send him. In addition, even my own employees weren't trained onsite because that would not be feasible. If it were necessary, the responsibility fell on the site supervisor. I told the commission all of this, truthfully and without laying any burden on anyone.

A month into the investigation it was found that the duties of my position did not require training under BHP (occupational safety standards) for leased vehicles. This was outside of my area of responsibility, and the case was dismissed with the assumption that the ordeal was just an unfortunate accident.

One time, I went to the director's office because I had a personal matter to tend to. I was refused help. Then I turned to the Labor Union, which every worker was obligated to be a member of. The leader arrogantly remarked, "We don't help dissenters like you."

"Dissenters? What have I dissented against?" I asked surprised. "If you want to know the truth, you're the one cooperating with the dissenters, not me. Please take me off the Union membership list effective immediately, and mark in the report that 99.9 percent of employees are members, not 100 percent."

However, the Union's quarterly report indicated that 100 percent of employees were members of the Union because everyone was required to be a member. I went to the headquarters and filed a correction. I was certain that I was one of the first Poles to resign from the Communist Labor Unions during that time.

They tried to convince me to join again, but I never faltered in my decision. The news spread like wildfire, and many people warned me that it could end badly. Soon the company organized a reception for their employees at a restaurant for our good performance at work. The director of the vehicle workshop, whom I worked with on a daily basis, was present as well. At one point, when he was fairly drunk, in front of all of the celebrating guests, he turned to me at the table and said, "You blood sucker!"

"Whose blood am I drinking or did I drink?" I asked. "Maybe yours?"

There was an awkward silence. No one wanted to interfere, so as not to cause a scene.

"Now I'd like to add something more," I went on, "You are a well-known and a much- disliked secret agent and informer in our company. It's reasonable that this word fits only you. Do you want to clear your own conscience by accusing others of what you are doing?"

His face became as red as a beet. I thought that he would lose his temper, but he said nothing because I denounced him. I didn't stop at that, but added, "Sir, if you were younger, I would punch you in the mug. But I respect your gray hair, and I won't do that. I have to add that you don't possess a face but that which I just described a mug." Then I stood up and went home. Later I found out that everyone at the table waited for a reaction from him, but he left the restaurant livid.

It didn't take long to see the effects of the incident. A few days later, a Volga (at that time, a luxury car made in Russia) arrived at our house to take my wife to the Provincial Civic Police Station for a hearing. Jagoda was in her last month of pregnancy at that time. The men at the Security Office were not concerned with her state or the effect of stress on a pregnant woman or her fetus. What mattered to them was degrading people to the point where they were willing to give themselves up and cooperate. They promised to bring her back home after the interrogation, but this did not happen. I didn't know about the incident because I was at work at the time. As it later turned out, after the interrogation, I was picked up from work for an interrogation as well, in what was most likely the same Volga. I was questioned by the same man who questioned my wife. It was intended that we not meet in the meantime. He interrogated me for over two hours and finally declared, "You are lying!"

"I'd like to know how you can be so sure that I'm lying," I replied to his accusation.

He was convinced that, this time, I would not escape their clutches, and he gave me my wife's testimony to read. That was his mistake. I knew what line of defense I should use, although I wasn't sure that I would return home. I was interrogated so many times that I was immune to their attacks. Despite this, I always got chills down my spine because they didn't need a strong reason to put an innocent person in jail. Judging from the type of questions he asked, I was certain that, for the most part, he used conversations from the wiretaps installed in the car and house, which at first I didn't know of. That was my greatest burden because they knew all of my secrets. They picked a cunning way of catching us lying, and our testimonies really did differ greatly. To weaken and minimize the effects of my wife's testimony, which in his view looked contrary to mine, I asked, "Sir, do you know what your wife is doing right now?"

"Of course I don't know," was his answer.

"I don't think any man knows what his wife is doing away from home. I'm no exception. I'm sure you know the saying, 'women tend to change' and sometimes her head is in the clouds."

Point-by-point, I addressed all of the inconsistencies in her testimony. I probably didn't convince him entirely, but he lowered his tone. I did not sign the protocol from the hearing. I never did this because it didn't reflect the truth of my testimony. Then I added that my wife had done it for me already. I thought that he would burst into a rage, and he exited the room while threatening me that it was a shame that I didn't say good-bye to my family. Minutes passed, which seemed like hours, and he didn't return. This time I was actually scared. I even started to talk to myself, "Guardian Angel, my guardian..." but I didn't finish because my interrogating officer returned and announced, "You are free to go."

I left the building anxious that another trap would be set for me behind its walls. I returned home safely, but late. My wife was afraid that something had happened to me, especially since she was at the hearing herself. She explained how they harassed her there and didn't bother to take her home, and it was difficult for her to take the over-crowded bus. I decided not to worry her further because she was about to give birth soon, so I told her that I was late coming home because I was held up at work. I didn't tell my wife everything so that she wouldn't get upset because she had a child, was pregnant, and had household responsibilities. In addition to that, she was finishing her last year of high school in the evenings and planned to begin evening college courses.

After a while, my wife asked me if I wanted to take a walk and get some fresh air. I knew something was amiss. When we went outside, I found out the truth. The matter involved the nanny who watched Maggie. She asked that I fire her because she didn't even want to take Maggie for a walk.

"Do you know what she said to me when I told her to take Maggie outside?"

"You'd better tell me because I'm sure I won't guess," I replied.

"She told me she wouldn't go because she would get her heels dirty."

Despite the difficult experience earlier, I burst into laughter. I couldn't stop, and my laughter infected my wife. In spite of the harsh experience of going through an interrogation for the first time, she started to laugh as well. We decided that I would dismiss the nanny from her job the next day, but I would pay her for an extra month. The next day when I told her about losing her job, she asked that I let her stay another night. It was good that she did because it was a night of revelations.

"I lied to you when I said that I loved children," she confessed. "I hate those brats. Imagine that when I served as a nanny for one of the doctor's children, they even made me sleep with their brat in one room, while they made love in the other."

We were relieved that we fired her because she could have harmed our children. We hired our cousin, and she proved to be a wonderful, loving nanny for our children.

Soon the sun rose over my horizon too. It was March 29, 1972. On this day, my beloved wife gave birth to our son, Robert John. It was a grand event for both of us, but especially for me because I became the father of a much-desired son. Now we constituted a complete family. We had two loving children, Maggie, who was five years old already and extraordinarily smart, and a newborn son. I knew that our family line would not disappear.

A few days before my son was born, my brother brought Maggie to his home because she wanted to stay with her grandma. Two days later, she missed being home. My brother had no other choice. He had to bring Maggie back. It was good timing because when he arrived, my wife went into labor. I borrowed his car and drove Jagoda to the hospital. Also, I took his timely visit as an opportunity to ask him if he would be the baby's godfather. My brother joked that if the baby were to be a son, he would agree. The next day I went to the hospital, and it turned out to be a boy. Families, even husbands, were not allowed in the maternity ward during those times. I only got to see my wife through a window. When I returned home, faking a disappointed frown, I asked my brother, "Guess what the baby is?"

"Of course, it's a daughter," my brother replied.

"You almost guessed it, but you're going to be a godfather after all," I teased.

"But I told you that I'd be a godfather if it's a son."

"Well, that's the problem. I have a son, and now you can't take your word back."

We couldn't stop joking, but my brother still wasn't sure if it was really a boy or a girl. Finally, he asked, "Now tell me seriously because I can see by the way you're acting and the way you're answering that it's a girl."

"Alright now I'm serious. You will be a godfather. We have a son. I mean it, a son."

My brother kept his word, and on April 9, 1972, he held his god-child, Robert, as he was christened at St. Roch's Church in Bialystok. Soon after the baptism, my neighbor, Jozef, came over with a wonderful proposition. I concluded that he must have been able to read my mind. He suggested that both of our families move to the coast to the tri-city area (Gdansk, Sopot, and Gdynia). This left me with one problem because land and houses were much more expensive on the coast than they were in Bialystok, and I wasn't able to figure out a financial plan before I sold my house. My neighbor had already thought of that as well. He offered me a loan without interest. He was a wealthy man, making his fortune selling delightful ice cream, the recipe of which he invented himself. The following weekend we went in his car to Gdynia. We looked around and made a final decision to move. I had been in love with the tri-city area ever since I was a student; the idea gave me wings again. I hoped that living on this wealthy coast would keep the Security Office away, and I wouldn't be compelled to go to the United States, which I didn't miss one bit. My wife confirmed the necessity of leaving Bialystok for Gdynia. She feared that one day I would die in a fake car accident or in some other unfortunate way.

Besides, I didn't want to endanger a great man, my boss, Mr. Richard, who put his job on the line for me. I thanked him dearly for everything that he had done for me. He then confessed, for the first time, that the mysterious telephone calls that I picked up because I had a direct line to the city were for him from the Security Office. I already assumed this because I unmistakably recognized his tone of voice after the calls each time. He was called into the police station or restaurant, and every time they posed the same question: "Why did he hire me?"

In addition, they were interested in whom I knew, why I stopped drinking alcohol after my return from the United States, and what my position was towards the people's party and the Soviet Union. He was forced to drink alcohol, even though he was abstinent. They called for him at least once a week during the entire duration of my work at

BPIS. In that way, they tried to force him to fire me. He was a great man, not only because he did not fire me, but he also didn't even mention all of this to me until my last day while we bid each other farewell. This proved detrimental to his health because after my departure, he had a stroke. Unfortunately, after a few years, he died.

"Richard, you were a righteous man throughout your entire life. You helped me in the hardest of times. May God reward you for your wonderful deeds."

I said good-bye to my staff as well. One of the drivers, who served a five-year prison sentence for "the people's rule," followed me into the office. When I closed the door, he kneeled before me and pressed my hand to his face. He was an elderly man nearing retirement, and he truly shocked me with the gesture. I felt so touched that I fell to my knees also, and we embraced. What a marvelous gesture. It was like parting from my own father. As he left my office with tears in his eyes, he said, "Director, I have lived many years, but I never had a boss like you. I know that you have to leave, and I wish you all the best," he added at the end.

"You are a great man and employee. Your actions and words touched me deeply, and I will never forget it," I told him from the bottom of my heart.

I bid a hearty farewell to the rest of the staff. The farewell was a great joy for me and made up for the humiliation that the party members and secret agents put me through. It lifted my spirits and gave me the strength to make efforts and face further life struggles. I left Bialystok without regrets to begin a new life in a city close to my heart. I had gotten to know the tri-city area of Gdansk, Sopot, and Gdynia during my studies at the Institute of Technology in Gdansk, so it felt like I was returning home.

My neighbor bought a home near the city center on a beautifully situated place near the ocean, where he intended to develop a part of it to open a café. Thanks to his loan, I was able to purchase a land lot to build a house in Gdynia-Orlowo, an equally beautiful spot. It lay only one hundred meters from the Baltic Sea and had a pier just like the one in Sopot. I believed that, in affluent Gdynia, my life would turn for the better. I still had many unresolved matters, so I would go back and forth between Bialystok and Gdynia with my neighbor in his car.

My brother-in-law, Anastazja's husband, obtained two wooden kiosks from the company where he was director that I intended to bring to Gdynia and set up on the lot, so that I would have a place to live while I finished the construction of a proper home.

I contacted PKS (Truck Company) and ordered a large truck with a trailer because I had to haul tools and other construction equipment, in addition to my kiosks.

Thanks to the fact that I worked in the transportation sector, I had extensive contacts, and the truck came right on time. With the help of my neighbors and friends, the loading did not take long, and in the evening, we were on our way. The driver warmed up the truck, and I went to say good-bye to my wife and kids because we would be separated for a few days.

As we got on our way, a police car pulled up and blocked the driver. Without any explanation, I was told to get in the police car, where two officers were sitting. The car drove off immediately, and without a word, I was being taken into the unknown. Without losing any time, I asked, "Where are you gentlemen taking me?"

"You are under arrest," replied one of them.

"Arrested? For what and why? Please tell me because I am not guilty, and this must be a grave misunderstanding," I tried to save myself. "Officers, I left a rented vehicle back there headed to Gdynia," I explained on the way to jail. "It's costing me a lot. Who's going to pay for the waiting time? I'm not going to let this go."

I was determined. I knew that this was an illegal arrest, but they had their way of doing things, and I couldn't predict anything. I saw that one glanced at the other, and at that moment, I had an inkling of hope that everything could be solved amicably. Knowing how corrupt the regime was I asked, "Gentlemen, how much will it take to let me go?"

They glanced at each other again. I sat in the back seat, so I could easily see their reactions. I was sure that they would be tempted if I offered them a significant sum. So without hesitating, I offered, "Would a thousand be enough?"

They pulled over to the side of the road, and after taking the money, they told me to get out. They didn't take me back home, so I returned by bus. My terrified wife and anxious driver, who had no idea what to do next, were overjoyed to see me.

What a nice good-bye. I thought of my life experiences in Bialystok, and I told the driver to get going right away. We drove through the night, and right before Elblag, the truck broke down. I was out of luck, but we had to act and not brood over it.

There were local transportation repair shops nearby, so that is where I headed. I reported to a manager and laid out my problem. "Unfortunately, I'm unable to help you because bus number two has to begin its route in a moment, and it is now in the pit for repair," replied the shop manager.

"Where is the liquor store?" I asked the manager.

"Don't bother, that won't help. The director will kill me if number two doesn't make its schedule," he replied to my question.

Despite this, I went and bought a bottle of vodka and a snack. Upon my return to the repair shop I asked the manager where I could sit down, so I wouldn't be disturbed. In the meantime, I called the repairman over to where the manager and I were waiting. They each had a few shots, and the manager turned to the repairman saying, "Pull out the number two and haul in this man's truck."

It turned out that it was a serious repair job because the transmission was broken. In a few hours, it was replaced with a new one, and we headed out again toward Gdynia. We arrived at night and slept in the cabin of the truck until morning. The driver was grateful that I arranged to have the truck repaired so quickly. He intended to pull into the lot as far as he could, so we could unload all of the heavy parts of the kiosks in the right spot. Unfortunately, as it was spring, the ground was wet. When the driver backed the truck up onto the lot, the wheels sank axle-deep into the ground. There was no way the truck could move.

The driver began to panic. I reassured him that I would get help, and everything would be all right. My experiences in transportation taught me about life; these and other problems were my everyday responsibility.

First, I put together a crew to unload the truck. Then I arranged for a tractor, which pulled us out onto hard ground. On the way back, we took the spare parts I had ordered through the truck company from Gdansk. Thanks to that, I only had to pay half of the bill for renting the truck because that was what the rental contract specified. When we stopped for the night, the driver asked me, "Sir, how do you know all of this? I'm in awe of you. You're such a savvy man."

"Oh life has taught me well, and how," I replied and left it at that.

In the meantime, my neighbor finalized the closing on his house in Gdynia and suggested that I come live in his house if I needed to. Of course, I took him up on the offer. I was happy that there were good people in this world after all. Not only did he lend me money, he ensured me a place to live.

When, in Bialystok, the news spread that we were selling our house, buyers were a dime a dozen. Of course, I chose the one that seemed trustworthy and offered the highest price. In those times in

Poland, the government had the primary right of purchase. My transaction was risky because the contract reflected a lower price than the actual selling one. If it turned out that the administration of the local council took advantage of its right to purchase it first, I would only receive the price indicated in the contract, and the sale would be a loss. Everything turned out well and was arranged without problems. We sold our house for an even one million zloty. At that time, it was the highest lottery win one could have. It was the dream of every Pole. We turned that dream into reality, and in reality, we were millionaires. We arranged with the new owner, that for a price, Jagoda could remain there for another six months.

I could calmly go to Gdynia and put all my effort into the new construction site. Once again, I went with my neighbor to Gdynia in his delivery truck. Jozef brought with him various valuables, and we were on our way. We took turns driving. Unfortunately, when I was driving, the traffic police stopped us. They checked out what we were hauling and demanded documents for the items. My neighbor announced that they were his valuables, but that he could not document that he was their owner because he didn't even know it was necessary. Then the policeman remarked, "We have no qualms with you, just with the driver, and we have to detain him until the case is resolved."

My neighbor again started explaining that I was just driving the truck at his request and that I had nothing to do with it. What is more, the truck was registered under his name, and he was the owner of the vehicle, which the registration card stated. My neighbor didn't know that I was in their records and that their motive was to degrade me. It wasn't until we had spent several hours negotiating that we were released.

I saw Bialysok as the "road to suffering," so I abandoned it without regret. I knew that it wasn't the city's fault, but the fault of the Communist regime itself, which enslaved and degraded many people that lived in it. Nevertheless, when I walked across the threshold of my home for the last time, despite my efforts to clench my teeth, tears involuntary fell from my eyes. I had become attached to it because I put my whole heart into building it.

Gdynia, My Favorite City

Finally, Gdynia, my city. I took advantage of Mr. Jozef's hospitality and stayed with him. Our wives and children remained behind in Bialystok, and we hit the ground running and worked hard. We met up in the evenings or late at night. We were both very busy, and there was no time to talk. On Sunday, we went to a restaurant where we could chat a bit. Two weeks later, I thanked Jozef for taking me in, and then moved into my little hut rigged together from the two kiosks. Since I lived on the construction site, I didn't lose any time commuting.

I had a kitchen and a bedroom. In the kitchen, I placed a coal-heating furnace and a gas stove with a tank for the use of the construction crew. I hired two masons and three assistants. I befriended the neighbor across the street, and he lent me his cement mixer and hoist-crane. This made the construction work much more efficient and cut down on the time.

I focused on delivering the building materials, which sometimes proved nearly impossible to get. I had to resort to "prohibited tricks" and be clever. A curse came about me at the time, an omen if you will, "May you build."

On the day that the building materials were being distributed, I went to the Local National Council and was taken aback by the crowd waiting for the doors to open. Standing in the back of the line, I had no chance to get a share of the materials. I decided to use the side entrance. I hoped that it would be opened at the same time as the main door. I stood there alone because others, most likely, didn't know of its existence. When the doors to the building finally opened, I burst in like a madman. I ran up three steps at a time and reached the third-

183

floor office first. The rest ran behind me screaming, trampling over one another, and took their places next in line. I felt guilty for having tricked those people, but in those times, the creed was: may the best man win! And the methods used? That was another matter altogether.

The economic situation in Poland was tragic. The communist regime formed destructive economic policies with premeditation. Concerned for providing an adequate life, families obscured higher goals for people, such as the struggle to restore freedom and democracy to Poland.

People were forced to search for just the main necessities. There was a shortage of everything in the stores from furniture to meat, eggs, and toilet paper. There was even a running joke in the country, "Why isn't there enough toilet paper? Because newspaper readership would fall in Poland." Unfortunately, people bought newspapers and used them instead of toilet paper. It was sad but true.

There were lines everywhere. Lines would form in front of the butcher shop at four in the morning with people waiting to buy something. The people's enslavement was at its height.

Thanks only to ingenuity was I able to get the allowance of all the necessary building materials, which were administered and appropriated by the Local National Council, those materials being metal products (reinforcements and beams for the foundations). Other materials would have to be obtained elsewhere using another method.

As a sign of gratitude to three ladies working in the office, I bought them each a bouquet of flowers. The manager was pleasantly surprised, and she said, "I've been a manager here for twenty years, and you are the first one to come and thank us for our efforts. You brought beautiful flowers. If you are in need of anything in the future, don't hesitate to ask. We'll handle the matter firsthand." I thanked them, but the allowance proved sufficient, and I didn't have to take advantage of their graciousness again.

The cement on the other hand, came from my brother in Orzysz, which was located in a different territory over five hundred kilometers away. If any work on the house was going to get done, the illicit procedures used by the Communist system, in which contacts, connections, bribery, and cleverness was the name of the game, had to be taken advantage of. The cement, which arrived commissioned from PZGS in train cars according to the needs of the province, wasn't even unloaded there. The receiving station was changed to Gdynia, where my address was written in, and in that way, a few loads of the state-regulated product ended up in my hands. I had to pay for the delivery through a few provinces and for the unloading in Gdynia. This tripled my expenses, but there wasn't any other option. I was happy that I had any cement at all. After the unfortunate attempt to buy cement on the black market in Bialystok, I didn't even think of trying that again. I found out that my neighbor, a few houses down, was caught attempting that type of transaction, and he went to jail for it. He was probably given an option: cooperation or jail. In that way, many people chose to cooperate with the regime because jail time was not the most pleasant experience. I personally knew of a few such cases, so I preferred not to take any more risks.

I ended up overpaying for the hollow blocks and bricks as well. It looked pretty suspicious because the manager of the company would inform me the previous day when the delivery would take place. He told me not to stand in line, which was always very long, but to come in the afternoon, when they announced that everything had been sold out. Then I sprung to action. When my head appeared in the window, the manager personally opened the door to his office and invited me in. He simply asked, "How much do you need today?"

I always made jokes, so I showed him the sign, which announced The Sale of Materials Has Ended.

"If so, then you can close your office, and we can go have dinner at a restaurant. But perhaps you still have some bricks and hollow blocks left?" and I added the amount I required.

The price was prearranged. For each brick, I paid an additional 10 groszy and for the hollow block, 1 zloty more. The sum that ended up in his pocket was significant, but despite this, we were both pleased.

Because I had the money, the construction of my twin home (two connected houses) moved at a rapid pace. My building crew performed very well. I didn't have to supervise it because the crew's boss, a man I handpicked, held everything on a tight leash and didn't permit laziness. I was responsible for arranging for the materials and delivering them to the site. The task consumed so much of my time that "night ran into day," that is, I left in the morning and didn't return home until nighttime, if one could call the shack a home.

One day my wife came to visit me. The children stayed with the nanny for a few days because she proved to be an excellent caretaker. We trusted her, especially since she was the sister of my brother-in-law, Anastazja's husband. It was the first time Jagoda had come to visit me to see how the construction was going and to look at the area. Up until then she had only heard my opinions of it, that it was one of the most beautiful neighborhoods in Gdynia. She took the night train, so I took her on a quick trip around the city at night. We arrived at our little house late at night and went straight to sleep on a mattress on the floor. When Jagoda woke up the next morning, she complained that something was piercing her back during the night. It wasn't until later that she realized she was lying too close to fiberglass, and that's what made her uncomfortable. In the morning, I had to run errands as usual, and when I returned, I didn't recognize my house. Everything looked different. The clean floor was covered with a rug, curtains hung in the windows, and beautiful pictures hung on the walls. I peered into the bedroom and saw a big transformation. The insulation had disappeared without a trace. My wife moved it to a different spot and covered the mattress with new, colorful bed sheets. I was pleasantly surprised and only remarked, "Jagoda, you should be an interior designer."

At least in Gdynia I experienced some peace because the Security Office didn't know my whereabouts. I registered in Rumia, which bordered Gdynia, but I lived on the Gdynia site. I paid 400 zloty per month for the room, but the owners never met me, since someone else delivered the payment to them. The police inquired about their tenant's whereabouts, but they couldn't tell them because they didn't know themselves.

A new dilemma arose. I got an allergy, which caused a blockage in my nose. I had difficulty breathing, the exact same symptoms as in Chicago. The doctor, whom I saw, told me, "Sir, I think you will have to go back to where you came from. The best climate is where you were born."

What now? I thought. *I already sold the house in Bialystok. I'm almost finished building and now to go back?*

I pleaded with the doctor to think of another way to treat my symptoms and save me from my predicament, since I found myself in a situation without a viable solution.

"Dear sir, I will order some French medicine for you, and if that doesn't help, I won't be able to do anything more." After taking the medicine, I felt better, and soon the symptoms subsided entirely. I was happy.

During this six-month separation, I visited my wife and children a few times. Finally, it was time for two-year-old Robert and seven-year-old Maggie to come with Jagoda to Gdynia permanently. We still lived in the small house, but the proper one was almost finished. I sold half of that proper house (which was a twin house) in its crude state for 750,000 zloty. We couldn't complain about our financial situation. On the contrary, we were very rich again. Soon we moved into our beautifully finished house.

The new owner of the second half of the house managed according to his own preferences. He picked up sand from the yard, hauled it across the street, and dumped it onto an empty lot. In no time, I was summoned by the Administrative Council about the matter. I notified the new owner of this, and he immediately agreed to be my witness and plead guilty, as well as reimburse me for the 5,000 zloty fine I incurred from the case.

On the day of the trial, we both reported to the Administrative Council. I was called before the committee. Since it was the first time that I stood in front of an administrative body, I was surprised at how many people were involved in a committee. The head sat in the middle. To his sides were the members, then a policewoman and a transcriber were to the side of the room, six in all. Each of them looked at me as if I was a hardened criminal, but that didn't make a big impression on me. My experiences in Bialystok toughened me. I looked at each of the committee members as if I looking at the talking head from the Gdansk circus.

The committee head turned to me with the question, "Does the defendant know why he was summoned before the Administrative Council?"

"I know," I answered, "but I cannot comprehend why I am called the defendant when it's not I who should be the accused, but my witness, who came with me to testify on my behalf."

"May the defendant explain what he has in his defense," continued the council head.

I declared that I wasn't the one who hauled the sand, but the new owner had done it, and he came with me to affirm the truth of my testimony. They showed me out of the room and called my witness (and neighbor), who confirmed my testimony. I stood before the Administration of Justice. The committee head, despite my evident innocence, began with the words, "What does the defendant have to say in his defense?" He repeated the formula.

This is nothing but ridicule, I thought to myself and answered, "The defendant asks in his final statement that the Administrative Council acquit the witness," I replied without hesitating.

First, there was commotion. A moment later, everyone burst into ringing laughter. I stood in place with a stone face, which made them laugh even harder. The committee head, finally able to speak in between laughs, said, "Get out, sir! Get out immediately!"

In a slow, rhythmic step, I left the courtroom, and the sound of their laughter accompanied me until the moment I closed the door. My "witness," hearing their laughter, asked what the reason was for it.

"I asked them to acquit you," I answered.

"What have you done?" my neighbor commented.

We waited a long time for the verdict, and I started to have doubts about my sense of humor having the effect I was going for. An hour later, I was placed before the judiciary committee again. I saw their eyes red from tears. As the head looked at me, he lowered his eyes, and holding back his laughter, gave us the verdict. "After looking into the case," he began, "we acquit the defendant from the charges brought against him, but the defendant must report to the Provincial Administrative Council to obtain a reimbursement for the fines incurred."

With all seriousness I said, "Thank you from the bottom of my heart. The High Administrative Council saw to my innocence and pardoned my witness. Because it will be Easter Day in a week, I wish the High Council a Happy Easter (in Communist times religious affairs were not permitted), and wish each of you bon appétit with your eggs, and especially to the ladies here who saw my innocence." (Eggs in Polish slang meant the same as testicles or "balls" in English.)

That time everyone simultaneously burst into laughter. None of the committee members were able to spit out the words that it was the end of the hearing and release me, so I waited patiently, greatly satisfied that everyone was content, including the plaintiff and the defendant. This lasted for a long while until someone laughingly burst out with the words, "Get out, sir, finally. Get out immediately!"

My response was immediate, and I loudly announced, "With great pleasure."

Following these words, everyone fell against the table holding their sides with laughter. While I strode rhythmically toward the door, I left the courtroom again. When I opened the door, my neighbor and witness, hearing the laughter, again asked, "What is it now?"

When I told him the whole story, he only repeated what he had said earlier, "What have you done?"

That ended the case in the first stage. Unfortunately, I still had to report to the Administrative Council in Gdansk. It was just a formality, and my money was refunded. My witness was never held accountable, but each time we met, he reminded me about what I had done. This time we were the ones who had something to laugh at.

The Bialystok Security Office most likely communicated and transferred my case to the Gdansk unit because I was soon summoned to appear before the Military Commission. It seemed strange that none of the commission doctors examined me. One of them told me, however, to report to the last uniformed officer. There I was forced to sit nude in a chair. I was placed in category C (fit for duty with restrictions), and I was certain that it would be written into the military booklet again. I followed the officer's direction to give blood and get clothes from the locker room. There one of the recruits opened his booklet and cursed.

"They changed it," he said, "from category D (never fit for duty) to A (fit for duty without restrictions)."

Then I checked mine as well. The same words I just heard incidentally came out of my mouth. I was also classified as category A, with an allocation to a unit to which I was to report in six weeks. Then the other men noticed the same thing in their booklets. It turned out that we were all the enemies of the People's Republic, and we had to be rehabilitated somehow.

The next day I reported to the private office of the director of the Regional Clinic and instead of the 50 zloty the doctor usually charged per visit, I put 500 zloty on the table and presented him with my dilemma.

"We'll take care of the matter," he reassured me. "Please come to the clinic tomorrow for some testing. The nurse will be aware of your arrival. Please appeal to the Provincial Military Commission right away." I appealed and did as the doctor told me, but never received a reply. I was held in limbo.

Soon afterward, my youngest sister-in-law from the United States visited us again. This time she came with a friend. We all traveled in a car, which I had borrowed from my brother, and visited Krakow, Czestochowa, and Zakopane. Her friend, a United States native, liked Poland quite a bit. My sister-in-law insisted that my wife come to visit them. It was after this that Jagoda took the familiar *Batory* ship to see her relatives again in the United States.

In her absence, the children and home were taken care of by a wonderful elderly lady, a nanny, mistress of the house, and housekeeper all in one, Maria Paluszko, a woman with a big heart and great wisdom. I respected her and treated her like a member of the family. I owe much to her because I know that she treated our children like a true grandmother. So she would feel like she had freedom to lead the household, I gave her allowances regularly to do her shopping and never checked her expenses. In the stores, I pre-arranged to pay an additional charge, a bribe, in reality. In the morning, Maggie would take a list with our daily needs to the cashier, and in the afternoon, Ms. Paluszko would go and pick up the items that were prepared for pick-up. That way, I had no problem supplying the home with necessary food items and other things as well. Those were the realities of the time. Whoever had the money was able to subsist but overpaid for everything.

Ms. Maria took the children on various trips. What Maggie and Robert enjoyed most was taking the hydrofoil to the Hel Peninsula. She loved the children so much that she set aside her eventual lottery winnings for them. I joked that she would have to win first, but that didn't change her desire.

Her life probably changed positively and one day, when I returned from the university, she said, "I am so grateful that you took me into your home and treated me like a human being. I have served with many people before, but there is something unique here."

Then she added, "Master of mine, God of mine."

I became upset at her comparison and asked her not to insult God because I was a worthless creature and that what I was doing was simply my responsibility.

"I'm very pleased that you have such a good opinion of me, but I don't want to be indebted and I would like to state: you are a very good soul, one of the best I have ever met."

Then she asked if I would like to hear the story of her life. I agreed readily because each of us could describe the story of his life, and each story would be extremely interesting. She began her story.

"I remember everything since I was three years old. At that time, my mother had already passed away. My father would wake me in the morning, so I could take the cows out to graze. I was so tired, I would fall asleep under the cow's belly. My father had two children with my second mother. When I was six years old, World War I erupted. We had to run away. I was hungry, but there wasn't anything to eat. Everyone cried. On the way, my father left me in a village to work as a servant. There I was told to tend to the cows, weave, sweep, and wash the dishes. The woman of the house had three sons out to war, and her daughter-in-law had four children. The elder woman was often drunk. She would throw me out into the snow at night if I didn't take the cows out on time, or if I didn't wash the dishes well enough.

A reason was always found. When I was outdoors, it was very cold. The temperatures fell below freezing. I slept beneath a bale of hay. I was dirty, ragged, and nearly blind. I could see no further than three meters in front of me. So I wouldn't lose a grazing cow, I held onto a rope, which I tied around the cow's neck. I lived like that for four years.

"Every day I cried and lamented that everyone from my family had died in the war, but one day, my older sister came and took me back. Our house had burned down. My father built a new one. I went to work for priests and for the more well to do farmers. In the winter, I would clear stumps and chop wood. I threshed wheat, and I did all that I was told to do. It was very grueling work. Eventually, my older sisters left, and I was left with all of the chores. I couldn't manage. I almost never slept. At age seventeen, I ran away from home to my aunt's house. I was ragged. My aunt didn't have means either. She took me to a teacher's home, where I worked only for the clothes on my back. There they had a farm and horses. I would also clean the schoolhouse. Two years later my father passed away, so I returned home.

"My stepmother was pregnant with her sixth child, so the responsibilities of supporting the younger siblings fell on me. We had no field to work on, so I had to go from house to house to make money so my sick mother and siblings could eat. My baby brother died after birth. Another teacher hired me to work her farm. I had to tend to the cows, pigs, chickens, and anything that had legs. In addition, I cleaned the school. I worked there for six years, until the death of the teacher's husband. I was twenty-five years old at that time. For six years, I worked only for my clothes. I didn't have any money. I returned home but not for long. I walked all the way to Jaroslawie, intending to find a job there. During the twenty-one kilometer walk, I stopped at each holy figure placed on the side of the road and fervently prayed, wishing to be taken in somewhere as a servant. I couldn't see the road through my tears. I could not read or write. I was hired at a job I had prayed for, working for a butcher. The place had a store and a restaurant. There wasn't any time to sleep; sometimes I would only get two hours a day. One time, I fell asleep while walking and fell to the ground. Four of us slept in a bed. A year later, I left because I found work with a barber. It was on the fifth floor. I had to carry water in a bucket, do laundry, clean, and cook. Cooking was the worst because the food was to be prepared from a cookbook, but I couldn't read. Whatever I ruined was deducted from my pay. Not much was left.

"I finally found a job with a rich Jewish man. I was treated well there, but soon World War II broke out. The Germans took me away to a factory in Bavaria. I worked there for five years as a slave without pay. After the end of the war, I returned to Poland on foot. I slept in sheds. One night I was robbed of my documents. A Russian patrol took me for a spy and arrested me. A few days later, I was released. As I continued on my way, I came upon a Polish family, who hired me in exchange for food. The lady helped me find my sister in Gdynia, and I came here, stopping on the way to make money for food. You saw my little room in the attic. Here I have everything. I live as if in a castle. I feel free, and most importantly, you treat me like your own mother. Now, you should not be surprised that I refer to you in this way."

My heart was filled with sadness, and I had great empathy for her. Even after my wife's return from the United States, Ms. Maria kept the house running like clockwork, and everyone loved her. She was a truly magnificent woman. One day she confessed that she would reveal her life's secret to me, but unfortunately, she took it to her grave.

Working at the Gdansk University

During this timeframe, I received a job at the Gdansk University Transportation Department. The working environment was clearly different from the Bialystok Company. The work schedule and regulations were almost a dream. The office in which I worked was located in the Gdansk Dean's Office in the Przymorze. The vehicle shop, of which I was director, was located in Sopot.

My job at the Gdansk University brought me many surprises but much satisfaction as well. Most of the time I had an official car at my disposal not only for university matters but also for my own private use. The transportation was under my direction and subject to the socialist rule, "what is yours is mine." I would even take my official Volga car out for a beer in the Grand Hotel restaurant in Sopot, the most exclusive hotel and restaurant in the tri-city area. Those at the top stole millions; those at the bottom took whatever they could. The drivers usually rotated the meters forward to make money on gas. It was a well-known fact, but one very difficult to prove, unless someone was caught red-handed. It was my responsibility to perform such audits, and from time to time, I conducted these.

One day, I arrived at work earlier than usual and caught one of the drivers rotating his meter. I closed his car door and turned to walk toward the office. The driver followed me, cut me off in the office building hallway, took hold of my hand and wanted to kiss it. Of course, I couldn't let him do that, and I asked, "Sir, do you know the rules I live by?"

Silence followed. He probably thought I would give him a disciplinary suspension. Then I explained to him, "My educational method is to give people a chance for improvement, to make amends for what they have done."

I noticed that he didn't understand what I said, so I explained directly, "I will not discipline anyone for the first incident, so you can sleep easy, but the second time there are two choices: either you resign with my good recommendation, or I fire you, and I would have to justify it. I don't think we have to discuss the consequences. Do we understand each other?"

He returned to work content, and I never caught him committing any other transgression. Everyone knew about this, and I was convinced that preventive education was more effective than disciplining each transgression.

As I mentioned, rotating the meters was a recurring activity. Department directors or professors who used the transportation service would sign anything that the drivers handed to them. The drivers added excess kilometers, by rotating the meters. The result was an excess of gasoline not used, which they then sold on the side, and the transaction gave them raw cash in their pockets. It was a vicious cycle. The drivers were afraid to rotate the meters on the university parking lot because I would do sporadic checks there. They never knew when the audits would take place, and that is why they took risks outside of the workplace.

One day, when I was substituting for the dispatcher, I received a call from the Gdynia police that our driver was caught rotating a meter. He was arrested and would await a prison sentence. The policeman on duty accused me of not having enough control over our drivers and that they did whatever they wanted to do. I asked him if the seal had been removed from the meter. Then he proceeded to lecture me that we couldn't even properly seal the meters.

It was my responsibility to seal the meters, but only when a vehicle was leaving after being repaired at our workshop. Then I would send the particular vehicle to the Standard Weights and Measures Center, where the specialists would seal it again, even though my seal was installed properly. I had to be careful and avoid any accusations of cooperating with the drivers. I would rather be overly cautious and perform my duties according to the regulations.

Because this was a criminal matter, and the driver was under arrest, I reported the incident to the director. The director asked me to do everything I could to get the driver released from jail. Unfortunately, the situation looked hopeless. I went to the Gdynia Local Civic Police Station, where the driver was being held, and I reported to the officer on duty. He was a major and seemed overly confident. As soon as I stepped into his office, he spoke to me in an arrogant way and began to reproach me saying that we didn't even know how to seal our meters. I acted as if I was humiliated and admitted that it must have been my fault because I bore the responsibility of sealing the meters, and I probably missed something. I turned to him and politely asked, "Major, would you be able to help me solve this issue? As the leading specialist, you're very familiar with these matters, and it will only take you a few minutes to instruct me on the proper way to seal a meter."

I counted on him taking the bait, and I wasn't disappointed. I noticed that he put his hand under his desk, and he probably pressed the call button because the corporal appeared immediately, stood at attention and announced, "Yes, Major, sir."

"Bring the Gdansk University Star vehicle meter from the safe."

"Yes, Major, sir," the corporal answered and disappeared behind the door.

A minute later, the meter was on the major's desk. Without hesitating, he began to instruct me on how a meter should be properly sealed. I followed his instruction. Because I knew the procedure well, each time I took the wire out from the meter, the seal remained intact. When his last guaranteed test of my ineptitude failed, without comment, the major nervously said, "Take the meter! I'll give orders to let your driver out of jail, and you can go back to the base. However you do it, make it right."

Of course, I promised that I would do as he wished, and I went out into the hall where I was to wait for the driver. The wait was prolonged, and I finally saw the driver approaching, assisted by a policeman. The policeman turned over the driver to me and allowed us to leave the station.

When we were out on the street, the driver asked, "Sir, can I touch you?"

"Why do you want to touch me?" I asked, taken aback by his request.

"I simply can't believe I'm free. What did you do that they released me? How can I repay you?"

He couldn't stop talking. He was so nervous; he didn't know what was happening to him. I wanted to calm him down, so before I let him get behind the wheel, we went to a restaurant for coffee. It was then that he began to believe that he wasn't dreaming, and that he was really free.

When he completely calmed down, I gave him some advice for the future. I cautioned him that it was only by a miracle I was able to pull him out of that trap, and that it was the first and last time.

"I think freedom is agreeable to you, but if that's not the case, then next time you can save yourself," I added. He swore to me that it would never happen again.

By that time, it was after work hours already. When the director asked me the next day if I was able to get "that fool" out of jail, I simply replied, "I managed," and left without comment.

Not long after this incident occurred, the phone rang. This time it was from the Sopot Civic Police Headquarters. The officer asked me if I had instructed my driver to deliver a spool of wire from one construction site to the next. The driver didn't have the documents needed to deliver the material and insisted that he only had my verbal orders to make the delivery.

I knew that the driver was caught illegally transporting the material and was looking for my help. I confirmed that I had directed the vehicle to the construction manager, and that the manager probably forgot to give the approval document to the driver. I told him that I would check on it right away. I asked what type of wire it was and what size. The policeman gave me the information, and only then was I able to arrange something. The construction managers' offices were on the opposite side of the hall, so I went there to present the matter to them. One of the construction managers gave me the needed documents, and with the manager's approval, I went to the Sopot Police Station. I had to sign for the pick-up of the driver from the police station; only then was he released.

It came to be accepted in the People's Republic of Poland that if it lay on the ground, take it, since one day it could become useful. Even if it wasn't useful, then it wouldn't hurt to have it. Everything was for the taking. This time I ordered that the wire should be taken to our vehicle shop because it happened to be needed to repair the holes in the fencing. I also gave the driver a lesson, and it went in one ear and came out the other because soon after, he stole a ton of coal from the university warehouse. This time, he stood trial and was sentenced to two years probation. I was on vacation at the time. Despite this, the dispatcher came to my house and said, "We need your help. Otherwise, the driver could go to jail for theft."

"Why don't you take care of this situation?" I asked, "It's in your hands now. Please leave me in peace when I'm on vacation." My principle was to help once, and the limit had been exhausted.

The courts sentenced the driver to two years probation and appointed me as his guardian. After this incident, he didn't steal anything again. He was lucky that I took care of his problem with the first theft, and that a report wasn't written on the issue. Otherwise, there would have been no avoiding the jail sentence.

Another time, I found out that gasoline was being stolen from the vehicles parked overnight in the university parking lot. I reported it to the police, and the officer who arrived suggested staging an ambush, in which I would be a participant. It didn't suit me to be out of the house at night, so I proposed another way to solve the problem. If that failed, then we would devise a trap. The policeman didn't even ask about my idea before agreeing to a month's trial period.

I conjured up my plan. I told one of the drivers, in secret, that we were planning to trap the thief. I asked him not to tell anyone. I knew that, within an hour, everyone would know my intentions. The gasoline theft was never repeated again, and I could sleep well at night.

There were many incidents of theft. There were some that occurred without my knowledge because some of the drivers were able to handle it and keep it under wraps in their own way.

In another case, I defended a driver in court. That time he was threatened with a hefty fine or even a jail sentence. Thanks to my testimony, he was freed. As we exited the courtroom, the driver said, "Sir, I will do anything you wish."

"Certainly. I wish one thing," I quickly answered, "but it involves you. In the future, please behave in a manner in which no person can make a claim against you. I did whatever I could, but according to my principles, it was the first, and unfortunately, the last time. It's late already," I added more gently. "My wife and children are getting impatient wondering why I'm not back yet, so please take me home. I am satisfied with your gratitude, and I'll consider the matter closed."

I didn't have a particular problem with any of the workers from my car repair shop, but exceptions did occur. One day one of the mechanic's wives came to my office. She came with what must have been her two-month-old child in a stroller. She told me in confidence that her husband was having an affair with a much older, but rich woman, who owned a foreign luxury car. I promised to speak with her husband, but I couldn't guarantee anything because it was their own private matter. Then she asked if I could watch the child for a moment, since she wanted to speak with the director on the matter. I knew that this might be a futile hardship on my part, and yet I couldn't refuse her. I agreed to be the caretaker of her child, especially since it was only going to be for a moment.

After an hour, she still hadn't returned. The baby began to whimper, so I gave it a bottle of milk, and I had a moment of quiet. Two hours passed, and she still didn't return. This time, the milk didn't help, so I turned to my secretary, who worked in the other room, for her assistance. The secretary changed the baby, took it in her arms, rocked it for a bit, and laid it back in the stroller. She started to joke and finally said, "And what if she had left you with the baby thinking that, as a supervisor, you were responsible for everything, even for the family?"

"I took that into account and already weighed that possibility," I answered seriously, "It's going to be worse if I arrive home with a baby in my arms. I'm worried that before I can explain myself to my wife, she'll throw my bags out the door. Then I'll come to your house with the baby, drop it at your doorstep, and ring the doorbell. Then I'll run away, and we'll see what your husband has to say about it."

We started joking, but time passed, and the lady didn't return for her child. The situation stopped being funny. Fortunately, right before the end of the workday, the young mother came to pick up her child. She looked very upset, so I didn't ask about the outcome of her conversation with the director. The next day I went directly to our vehicle repair shop in Sopot and called the culprit mechanic in to talk.

We went to the student cafeteria next door, and I laid it all out for him: "Sir, you have a beautiful wife (she really was quite pretty). Meanwhile, you're looking for adventures behind her back. What's most important is that your wife forgave your 'mishap.' You should be grateful to your wife and apologize to her. You have a beautiful baby boy, for whom I was honored to personally baby-sit, and for the good of the child, your marriage should last forever. Please think it over a hundred times before you repeat this mistake because it will be an irreversible mistake. You will lose your family, and your family will be vengeful towards you for the rest of your life."

I don't know if I talked some sense into him, or if my authority worked on him, but he promised me that he would go back to his wife and begin their married life anew. That's just what happened, and I was happy that I was able to somehow resolve their marital crisis.

Soon the dispatcher resigned. He was related to a certain minister from Warsaw (in my opinion, this was the only reason he was able to keep his post). A retired aviation major was hired to replace him. The major was forced to retire because during a control check of airspace over the Baltic Sea, he noticed two West German planes that entered Polish airspace. He reported to his superior commander that he would launch an attack on the enemy aircraft, but the commander categorically refused to allow it. The major turned off the radio and took the initiative of preparing the attack, but he failed because the West German planes had already abandoned the Polish airspace. The pilot was threatened with jail time, but since he had the right to retire, he was discharged into civilian life.

The drivers were terrified that the major would instill military discipline in the shop. Unfortunately, the opposite proved to be true. The new dispatcher was unable to coordinate their work. More complaints emerged regarding the transport under this new dispatcher than under his predecessor. The major was a good man and lived through a lot in his life.

I remember when he told me about a disastrous landing, during which his rudders jammed. "I saw my life flash before my eyes as if it were a film. I tried many ways to correct the landing, but all my attempts were futile. I was close to crashing to the ground, when miraculously, the rudder unblocked itself, and the plane stopped far beyond the runway in a field. I couldn't move, so a rescue crew opened the cockpit from the outside and pulled me out. That was the last flight in my life," he explained.

I liked him and helped him many times, since he was honest with me, but the job of a dispatcher was too stressful for him, and he wasn't able to handle the responsibilities.

The director asked me if I could take over the dispatcher's responsibilities until a new one was hired. Of course, I agreed without hesitation. After all, in Bialystok I brought their transportation department to perfection. I hoped that, until they hired a new dispatcher, I would be up to the task.

I gave the director one requirement: that he would not meddle in my work and that he would give me a month before he judged the effects of my work. He agreed to the condition. He was probably surprised that he received more complaints than ever regarding the transport department. He called me and asked, "What is happening over there? I have received many complaints about you from the professors. You're sending two, even three people in a delivery truck to pick up the books, papers and office supplies when there's only one seat in the cabin."

I explained to the director that, of course, only one could go, but the two other men could give the driver permission to deliver the supplies with their signature. If they insisted on going to the destination, then the train passed by every fifteen minutes, and they could use that mode of transportation.

"Our delivery trucks aren't meant to transport people," I concluded.

A moment later the director asked, "What should I tell them? They're waiting on the other line for my decision."

"Sir, just as I promised you, in a month, you'll have no more complaints. What you want to tell them now is not my business."

I don't know what he had told them, but he never called me in again to report complaints, although I knew that more existed. A month later, two vehicles stood in the lot for university use, and all other issues were resolved as they occurred.

The director called me into his office for coffee. After a loose conversation he said, "You were born to be a dispatcher. I'll give you a raise, and you'll keep the position."

"Is it an offer or a condition?" I asked.

"Of course it's an offer because you're a great manager of the vehicle repair shop, and I'd like you to work there. Unfortunately, the two positions can't be reconciled."

"I'll be honest with you, director. I prefer my old job because there I'm able to make official trips, and I like to travel. As a dispatcher, I'm stuck in my seat."

"That's a pity," answered the director, "because the problems will begin all over again, and I was so relieved when the complaints stopped."

One day, the administrative director called me into his office and took out a real estate blueprint for plots of land near the lake saying, "You're the first university employee that I will give the right to choose a lot, and that's because when I requested a car, I didn't even have to wait five minutes, whereas before, I had to wait a whole week. These lots will legally be assigned to the university, but as you can see, only the lucky ones can take advantage of this. The director agreed to give you the first choice of plots as you wish." I chose one with direct access to the lake. The director praised my choice and told me that it was one of the best ones.

Soon a new, young dispatcher was hired, who was full of energy and confidence. I filled him in on the secrets of effective transport management, and he handled it excellently from the beginning. We quickly became friends, and there were no secrets between us. As a gesture of gratitude, he invited me out for a beer several times. During those times, we discussed many political matters. I never concealed my views, and I always spoke my mind. I knew that this was a poor practice, especially in times of totalitarian rule, but I couldn't change my personality, and I haven't changed it to this day. Because of this, I made many enemies because the truth hurts.

It wasn't until a few months later that a coincidence opened my eyes. When the friendly dispatcher reached for the telephone, I saw a gun hanging under his arm. This struck me like a bolt of lightning. I realized that I had not escaped the persecutors; that only in the tri-city area, other, less obvious methods were used, and not as obtrusive as the ones in Bialystok.

I still wasn't sure what to do, but I was increasingly pursued by the thought of leaving Poland for the United States I finally had wonderful living conditions, an equally great job, and transportation at my disposal. All in all, a life worth living. What's more, I had additional income from the rental of my house. My family and I occupied the basement, the garage, and the first floor ourselves. I rented out the two remaining floors as a hotel to my workers from Slask Miners, with whom I had a contract during the three-month summer season. The rental income was greater than my entire year's salary at the university. In addition, I received an offer to rent out my basement, which was to serve as a cafeteria for vacationers. For a three-month usage, I received an offer of 55,000 zloty, plus full board for us. I struggled with what to do in this case. I was already familiar with America, and I knew what was awaiting me there. Living there didn't enthuse me.

Nevertheless, I wanted to find out if the Gdansk Security Office took over the role of the Bialystok Office, and as a test, I applied for a passport for a temporary trip to the United States. Of course, I was refused. I personally went to the director of the passport department in the Provincial Civic Police Station (KWMO) in Gdansk for an explanation of this decision. His answer upset me greatly: "You will not go anywhere; forget about obtaining a passport at any time to depart abroad."

The boom fell, I thought, and felt like a prisoner in my own country.

Soon a commission arrived. Its goal was to appraise our assets and levy a one-time tax on our earnings, better known as the Gierek tax. They taxed us 120,000 zloty, but thanks to the corruption of the officials, we were able to decrease the amount of the fine. It turned out that it didn't apply to everyone, only to the "enemies" of the People's Nation.

I was curious about the role my "friend," the dispatcher, played in my life. I didn't let it show that I saw the gun under his arm. On the outside, if appeared that nothing had changed between us.

One day I invited him and the director simply for coffee, as it was commonly called, to the best private coffee shop in Sopot. The invitation was accepted. In an elegant and extravagant atmosphere, with a beautiful décor and lit candles, I seemingly enjoyed the get-together. At one point, I leaned across the table to be face-to-face with the dispatcher and posed the question, "For what purpose were you sent from the Security Office to work at the Gdansk University in the very office I work in?"

There was a deathly silence. Even in the candlelight, I noticed that the dispatcher paled significantly. The director probably was aware of whom he hired or knew that he could not reveal the secret. In a knee-jerk reaction he wanted to say something, but he hesitated and remained silent. There was complete confusion. I paid the bill and left. The next day at work the dispatcher asked me, "When do you intend to depart for the United States?"

"I don't know yet," I answered, "but when I decide it is right, please believe me, nothing will hold me back."

This time it was he who invited me for dinner at a restaurant. I didn't refuse because I was curious about what he wanted to tell me. I had nothing to lose but much to gain in the conversation. I was surprised when he began to tell me about the training he received before he started working for the Security Office. He suggested that he would repeat everything that the people sitting even four desks away from ours, would say. He began to relay entire sentences of what they talked about. He was able to read lips.

Two weeks later the dispatcher was officially transferred to the position of director of the university dormitory. He already did what he was instructed to do in our office, maybe not entirely, but his identity was revealed, and leaving him in that position didn't make sense. His superiors from the Security Office transferred him, so that he could investigate the student community, where he wasn't yet known.

My neighbor didn't have close contact with other neighbors besides us. He invited us to his name's day party as well as the Commandant of the General Civic Police in Gdansk, the head of the Provincial National Commission (WRN), also from Gdansk, and other city officials. The neighbor managed a private firm in Gdansk, so his contacts were crucial to managing his interests.

When, after a few glasses, everyone "broke the ice," many different topics were brought up, starting with politics and ending with the church. The leader of the WRN began to strongly criticize the church and priests. This infuriated me. I immediately began a discussion with him, and at one point, I asked him outright, "Sir, this conversation is leading us to a dead end. Perhaps I should start from a different angle altogether. Please answer my question honestly. I am tolerant toward both believers and nonbelievers. What counts to me is the person and his good deeds. Besides that nothing matters, especially the words uttered for public use. I am curious about one thing. Why is it that those who battle the Church, when death looks them in the eye, always call for a priest and want to unite with God, against whom they fought throughout their lives, usually for the sake of their careers?"

Everyone was silent; no one wanted to be the first one to answer my question. I continued my argument, "I am surprised at all those who hold their high posts who in the cover of the night, baptize their children, get married, and in the public eye show disdain for the church and religion. I would respect those who hold their own, from beginning to end, and don't bend in whichever direction the wind blows."

I looked over to my paled neighbor. I felt sorry for him, but it was too late to fix anything. The next day he commented, "Mr. Henry, what have you done?"

I answered, "I am positive that you will never invite me to your name's day celebration again, but at least now you know that I say what I think, and I don't beat around the bush."

I was wrong because we were soon invited to his wife's name's day celebration. This time, there wasn't any criticism, and the guests had a good time.

A few years later I found out that the leader of the WRN began to officially attend church, but he was punished for it severely. His son, a Polish army officer who held the rank of lieutenant was murdered, and his body was never recovered. That is how the Communist regime took its revenge on insubordinate citizens. I don't know why, but to this day, I feel guilty in part for the death of this man. Could it be that my arguments determined that his father turned back to the faith, and his son suffered the highest punishment? God's judgments remain a mystery, but we have to accept them.

One day I received a surprising offer. On one hand, I was very happy, on the other, I felt an incredible weight of responsibility. I had the chance to obtain passports for the entire family, but only if I were to decide to leave the country within two weeks. I was sad to leave everything so suddenly. We were wealthy, had a beautiful house, happy children, and a nanny. To add to this dilemma, my sister, Anastazja, moved with her husband to Gdynia to be closer to us. How was I to abandon all of this and leave?

My wife pressured me, but the decision was mine, so I took my time as the hours passed to our disadvantage. I knew what was awaiting us in America, and I knew what I was leaving behind in Poland. I was aware that in Poland, I faced annihilation, if the regime decided to do so. In America, I would at least be free and alive.

I decided to leave the country, and for 120,000 zloty, I received the passports. But before I left, I had to re-register myself in Bialystok and leave the country from Bialystok, as opposed to Gdynia. I needed to show that I was not a property owner from where I left. Otherwise, I would be forced to sell my home in two weeks, and I did not have enough time to do so. I already had visas for the whole family to stay permanently in the United States, thanks to my in-laws.

At work, I requested my rightful leave, during which I intended to go abroad, knowing that I didn't have the means to return. I informed my mother and brother a few days before my departure and told the rest of my family at the last minute. Their surprise was enormous, but the decision had been made final. My wife's entire family awaited us in America, so we weren't going into the unknown or to strangers.

On March 18, 1976, from the Warsaw airport, I sent via post office my resignation from work, and we all made our way to the document and customs checkpoint. Each of us was separated, except for three-year-old Robert, and went through a personal search. We were stripped naked. Not even my eight-year-old daughter was spared. They forced me to hand in my wallet, take everything out of my pockets, and place the contents on the table. I noticed that some of the Polish gold coins lay on the surface, but they were hidden because along with them, I had American cents, which resembled gold coins. Despite this, I knew that if the customs official was to discover fraud, I could say good-bye to America. I stood naked in place and didn't make any moves. At this time, the customs official left the room with my wallet. I didn't move, knowing that I was being observed by cameras. After twenty minutes, the customs official returned to the room and holding my list with names, addresses, and telephone numbers of my closest family and friends, he only asked about one person. He wanted to know how I knew the man from the Ministry of Interior, whom I had become acquainted with in the restaurant in Warsaw. After all, he was their supervisor.

"He is my friend," I replied truthfully.

"I'm terribly sorry. Please put your clothes on and leave the room!" the official answered. They stopped searching my wife and daughter and left us alone. I met the customs official again in the hallway, and I thanked him for the "wonderful" farewell and added that this event would always remind me of Poland for the rest of my life. He looked at me but didn't answer.

We took our seats on the plane, not telling our son that we were going to America, since he absolutely did not want to go to the place that had taken his mother away from him several months earlier. After Jagoda's return from America, he did not leave her side. He even followed her to the bathroom; no persuasions helped. There wasn't another solution, and we told him that we were going to the Canary Islands, to which he agreed enthusiastically. We also requested that our youngest sister-in law, who visited us in Poland, not greet us at the airport in Chicago because of Robert's aversion to seeing her.

I left with mixed feelings. Did I do the right thing by leaving my country? At the same time, I was convinced that the damned Communist system and its faithful minions would not let me live in peace in Poland.

Pictured is my home that I built in Gdynia, Poland, with balcony views of the Baltic Sea. We had to leave this beautiful house and escape to America.

Escape to America

We arrived in New York. At that time, green cards rendering permanent residency in the United States were issued at the airport. The official who issued the cards called me several times, pronouncing my last name "Sadzieski" (as read in English). It wasn't until later I realized that it was me he was referring to, and I picked up the document. Because of this small oversight, we barely boarded our plane to Chicago.

We finally arrived at O'Hare Airport, where my sister-in-law, Wanda, greeted us. Chris, my other sister-in-law, came too, but she couldn't show herself to Robert because we were certain that despite being almost four years old, he would recognize her and trouble would begin. Unfortunately, on our way to the in-law's house, our cars ended up driving side-by-side. Recognizing his aunt, he probably felt painfully deceived. He began to scream, "We didn't come to the Canary Islands; this is America. I want to go to my home! To Gdynia! To Orlowo!"

Nothing could persuade him otherwise. For the next three days and nights he screamed and repeated the same thing, "I want to go to Gdynia, to Orlowo." We were afraid something would happen to him. After three days, he realized that everyone, especially his mommy, was with him, and he calmed down.

After two weeks, we rented an apartment on the second floor of a two-family house. It was nothing compared to our house in Gdynia. Here, we felt misery and despair, but at least we were independent, and that counted. The furnace for heating the apartment was connected with a pipe to the chimney exactly like the one in Gdynia in the kiosk where I temporarily lived during my construction. The light came on by pulling a string.

Joachim, my wife's cousin's husband, arranged a job for me at the same factory I had worked for before, the Cromwell Paper Company. This was convenient, since the factory was located close to our home. I walked to work, and we didn't have to buy a car. Shopping was the most difficult because my wife carried the groceries a long distance from the store. Two weeks after our arrival, I became very ill. Once again, my allergies started up. I had difficulty breathing, and my nose was congested. The pain from my sinuses radiated to my back and was unbearable. I couldn't work, and the doctor's visit and medication consumed a lot of money. A month later, I returned to work, since we needed money to live on. It was a real ordeal. I could not sleep.

The truth is that bad things are quickly forgotten. I forgot about the persecutions in Poland, and the good memories returned to my mind like a boomerang. I would have bouts of depression. I played tapes with patriotic Polish recordings and tears streamed from my eyes. To cheer myself up, I repeated, "Whatever you do, you'll regret it," and these words of a Greek sage somehow gave respite to my restless soul.

I could return to Poland, but I would be sent directly to prison. The thought of this did not fill me with optimism. I had to stay. I hoped that the day would come when I would finally see a light at the end of the tunnel. One day, when I turned on the tape, I heard my daughter Maggie's voice, "Robert, come quickly; Daddy is going to cry."

Because he was slow to get up, she pulled him over, and they stood facing me. They looked me straight in the eyes and waited for me to begin to cry. This time it amused me so much that I took them in my arms, and instead of crying, I began to laugh. My little ones helped me to understand what was most important in life. It was for them that I had to face my problems, so that they would have the opportunity for a better life in a free country.

After a month, the owner of the house informed us that, in the near future, she would sell the property. Once again, terror filled us because with two children, no landlord was eager to rent their apartment to us. In this case, my in-laws lent a helping hand and offered to give us a loan for a down payment on the house. The remainder was willingly lent by Jagoda's sister, Wanda, and her husband, Henry. We were back on our feet again, and we were convinced that our family would never leave us in trouble. We had come to America in March, and already in May, we were the owners of a two-family, wooden house. Now we had tenants. We lived there for free, since the rent of the tenants covered our mortgage payments.

Within a year, we were able to pay back the loans to my in-laws and brother-in-law, and we were on the straight and narrow once again. My rash began to subside, and the visits to the doctor took place only once a month. Finally, after a year, there were only occasional outbreaks.

The factory in which I worked was called a paper mill. The paper was processed and manufactured according to the orders. I was the assistant at a machine that processed paper in such a way that anything wrapped in it would be protected from rusting. The main recipient of the product was the military. The machine was rather complex, and its operation wasn't easy. The operator of the machine didn't want to reveal the secret of its operation. He even hid the report, which he filled out before finishing work. I signed it without knowing what was in it. He even shielded the paperwork with his hands at times while writing. He was Polish, and the Polish community never lived in harmony. This was most painful, especially for the newly arrived immigrants.

After a while, that operator was planning to take a vacation, and the manager told me to follow him around in order to learn how to operate the vats in the basement. There were three types of liquids in them, and the correct one had to be used according to the order. When the operator realized that I was following him, he turned around and sneered,

"Why are you coming with me? Get out," and he added a couple of curses.

I stopped following and didn't even report the incident to my supervisors because I dislike snitching. By the end of the workday, as usual, he gave me the report to sign. Then he rudely informed me, "You know what, Henry, I'm sure I won't be on vacation for long because no one but me knows how to operate the machine."

I didn't comment on this, but only thought, *Blockhead, you're going to sit at home for six weeks waiting for a call from the factory, but no one will call you in that time.*

The next day I went to work a half hour earlier, and the first-shift operator showed me what I needed to know. He was Polish as well, but the two operators were vastly different. He was a truly kind man.

For the first few days, I had a lot of trouble because I had to learn the functions of all of the buttons on the dashboard and how they changed the operation of the machine. Later the machine worked for me as it should, and the original operator never did receive a phone call to return from his vacation and operate the machine. He spent his leave at home left alone. When he returned, he no longer covered the report with his hand, and I had the chance to read what he wrote. I thought I would burst into laughter, but I held it back and only said, "You're using some kind of unknown language because it's neither Polish nor English."

He became upset with me and said, "I've been writing like this for thirty years, and no one has ever said anything to me."

Then I gave him a "cheat-sheet" listing all of the variables of the machine's functions. It didn't surprise me that my operator didn't know English because over half of the employees were Polish speaking, including the manager, who spoke to us solely in Polish. We always spoke Polish at home, and in the neighborhood stores, nearly everyone spoke our language.

Despite this comfortable life among Poles, I decided to learn English, and I enrolled in a course. I knew that speaking English would help me in my job and with life in this country.

One day, when I became an operator, a smiling African-American approached my assistant. Patting him on the shoulder, he began to curse profusely. He used very strong language, and since my assistant didn't understand, he smiled back at him. I stood behind the machine out of sight. When the African-American walked away, I asked my assistant what they were talking about.

"Actually, we didn't talk about anything," he answered. "He praised me and patted my shoulder, which meant I'm a good guy."

Then I explained to him what the matter was really about, and I offered to be his witness, but the assistant didn't want to "seek justice" as he put it. In a way, I wasn't surprised that we Poles were treated in such a way. It seemed we didn't stand up for ourselves. I was upset by jokes about us, and even the Polish Alliance's objections were to no avail, not to mention the efforts of a single individual. Not only did Poles not help one another, they put obstacles in each other's way. In this environment, one couldn't demand respect. What is more, I had never seen an African-American come drunk to work, but I did often see Poles in that condition. The manger, a Pole himself, tolerated this order of things, and it was a vicious cycle.

After a while, Jagoda decided to work as well because it was difficult to live on my paycheck alone. An opportunity arose, and she was hired in my factory for the first shift. We didn't need anyone to care for our children because we relieved each other since I worked the second shift. After a few days, when the other employees found out that my wife was hired there, they protested. Most of the Poles went to the office in a group, and in a vulgar and rude way, insulted the human resources lady, cursing at her relentlessly.

She commented on the event later saying, "Never in my life have I heard anyone use that type of language toward me." They were known as the old generation of Poles, who, unfortunately, hated the young, intelligent, educated Poles arriving in the United States.

My wife was let go because the company didn't want any problems. I must emphasize that among the group of protesters, one not could find a single American or African-American, only Poles. I came to the sad conclusion that at that time, Poles were united only by a whip made from thick leather hanging above them. Jagoda soon found a job in another factory, but the ordeal left her resentful.

The children, on the other hand, quickly accepted the American way of life, and even Robert began to play with the neighborhood children in the yard. In the beginning, it all looked amusing because he spoke Polish and the rest spoke English, but they had a lot of fun. Three months later, Robert no longer had trouble communicating, and he began to speak English in complete sentences.

When we left Poland in March, Maggie was in the middle of second grade in the Gdynia Primary School. In order for her to be with her own age group, we sent her to the third grade, knowing that she would manage because she was very clever. The decision proved to be the right one because Maggie finished the third grade with honors.

My health began to fail once again. This time I was troubled with hemorrhoids. The family doctor sent me for testing, and it turned out I would need surgery. In the meantime, I found a doctor on the north side of Chicago—I lived on the south side—who did the procedure without a need to go to the hospital. He completed the procedure at intervals, until the hemorrhoids were completely healed. From my point of view, this was the way to go since I was able to avoid missing work. Each day counted because we couldn't afford to cut our household budget. I made an appointment and drove to my first visit. It turned out not to be as easy as it seemed.

After the procedure, I hardly made it back to the car. When I started to drive, I felt a mounting pain, and this was only the beginning of my ride home, not to mention making it to the south side of town. I entered the highway in the middle of rush hour. I was stuck in traffic, and instead of driving home in an hour, the drive took three. I felt intense pain because I had to sit behind the wheel the entire time.

Once I was home, I immediately lay down to bed. I knew that something was not right, and I called my father-in-law. He contacted the doctor and relayed the situation to him. The doctor directed me to hold the swollen spot with my hand and not permit it to surface, as it could burst and be fatal. If in a few hours, it didn't stabilize, I was supposed to call an ambulance.

Fortunately, I only missed work that one day. The next day I felt better, so I went to work to "bring home the bacon." In America there isn't time to be sick, and according to a Polish-American saying, "You work, nap, and work again." One has to work to the brink of exhaustion, sleep a bit, and go to work again.

The next three procedures were equally as painful, but I was already used to it and suffered less. Although it was very difficult, I went to work after each of those procedures. After all, I had to support my family and pay the bills.

We lived in Brighton Park for only three years. Next, we bought our second house, this time, a one-family unit, in a better neighborhood on 61st and Keeler. After Maggie finished Catholic elementary school, she began her studies at one of the most renowned public schools, M. Curie Sklodowska High School.

Because she wasn't offered a typing class, I asked my neighbor to go with me to the school and help me enroll my daughter in that course. The neighbor explained the matter, but the secretary answered that there weren't any more open spots in the class. I went into action and asked her who was enrolled in the class. The secretary's answer upset and worried me. It turned out that the children whose parents were politicians or worked for the police or fire departments had first priority to enroll.

Without looking to my neighbor for help, I began to explain the situation and said, "I came to the United States from a communist country with the hope that I would find justice and freedom here, but I was wrong. The same discrimination is evident here. I don't think that my child is worse than the other students, whom I see being treated as privileged."

Silence followed. After thinking it over, the secretary announced that she would give me an answer the next day. When we left the school, the neighbor began to lecture me in a quivering voice that I was not allowed to say that. She was pale and frightened because she thought we would be arrested. I comforted her that I didn't say anything offensive, and I was only demanding my rights. Indeed, at nine o'clock the next morning, we received a telephone call from the school informing us that our daughter was accepted into the typing class.

Certainly the secretary had no regrets about her decision because after her first year of studies, Maggie was the best student in the school. Her homeroom teacher even came to our house, congratulating us, which was a great honor.

We had very good neighbors. The husband of the helpful neighbor was Polish and spoke Polish quite well. He helped us run errands, speaking English for us many times. One day, as I returned from the bus stop, I noticed him as he left his house and entered his car. He didn't move but waited for me. When I drew closer, he motioned me to come and began to talk with me. He looked at me strangely, and I felt that he was saying good-bye to me. At first, I couldn't recall when I had been in a similar situation. When I told my wife of the incident, I remembered my father had looked at me a similar way right before his death. Three days later the neighbor's wife came to us bearing the news that her husband was in the hospital. In order not to dishearten her, I didn't tell her about my premonition, which unfortunately, proved to be correct. Two days later, the neighbor died in the hospital.

I went to the funeral home, and it just so happened that his family members or friends were not present at the time. I felt a deep sadness, and I began to weep loudly. The owner of the funeral home approached me and asked, "Was he your brother?"

I shook my head no, so he continued to inquire, mentioning close relatives. I replied negatively to each of his questions.

"Well then, who is he to you?" he asked anxiously.

"He was my neighbor," I stammered, when I recovered a bit.

I didn't know what he was thinking, but he nodded his head and left me. It was probably the first time he saw someone weep after the loss of a neighbor.

Three years passed when we bought a new house from a developer, paying cash. This time the house was located on the outskirts of Chicago, in Burbank. Maggie finished her last year of high school there, and Robert finished Catholic elementary school and Catholic high school.

At this time, my wife and I both lost our jobs for eighteen months. It was hard, but we were in good spirits. We even went to Las Vegas. Government aid helped us to survive.

We finally found jobs and soon bought a four-unit apartment building in Orland Park. Life returned to normal, and it seemed that everything would turn out better from then on.

I began a job in a small printing shop, where there were only a few employees. Occasionally, I had to take a paper sample from the conveyer belt and check the quality of the print. I don't know how it happened, but at one point, my hand got stuck between the rollers that pulled the paper. I was lucky that the power button was within my other arm's reach, and I stopped the machine. Because I reacted quickly, I saved my hand from becoming completely crushed or severed. Unfortunately, the hand was already pulled in halfway. Part of my hand was crushed. I called for help. A few workers immediately ran over, but they didn't know what to do to free the hand from the rollers. Meanwhile, I was in incredible pain. The only way to free my hand was to dismantle and take out the top roller. They immediately took to dismantling it. Unfortunately, this took over an hour. The ambulance was already waiting for me, and I quickly found myself in the hospital. The nurses gave me tranquilizers and painkillers. I experienced a great ordeal by the time my hand healed enough to leave the hospital.

After a long period of recuperation, I returned to work. I saw the job as only a temporary position because the factory was located in a very bad neighborhood. In the meantime, I applied for a job in another factory, and the human resources manager, assessing my qualifications, assured me that I would be hired during the next hiring phase. A year later, he called to tell me that I could start immediately, if I was still interested. Of course, I was thrilled, and the next day I reported to the office.

I was sent for a medical checkup, and the results had to be delivered within two days. I was very surprised when it turned out that I had high blood pressure. The doctor told me to report to him a week later for more tests. My employment was on the line. From the hallway, I heard someone speaking Polish in the office next door. I took a risk. I knocked on the door and went inside. I told the Polish doctor of my dire circumstance. He helped me and went to the doctor who saw me just a moment earlier. He came out happily and said, "Today please take this blood pressure medicine and come back tomorrow. I approved your check up for your job application."

I was happy that he was able help me with such an important matter and thanked him. At the same time, my high blood pressure worried me, and I concluded that this was a temporary state of things due to stress.

Most importantly, I was hired. I worked twelve hours a day, seven days a week. I made a good income because of the amount of overtime I worked.

A year later, the factory decided to implement a Japanese-style work environment. Eight workers were chosen for special training. I was honored that I found myself among them. From then on, instead of going to the factory, we went to the local library, which granted us use of their facilities for that purpose. Coffee, sandwiches, and cookies were included in the training. After the three-month-long training, our responsibility was to execute the new methods.

Soon all of the machines were modernized, and a computer system was installed. It seemed that the factory's future was not threatened, but as it always is in business, sometimes it's up and sometimes it's down.

The same was true of my health. Soon I had prostate surgery, which led to some complications, and I had to remain in the hospital longer than my medical insurance allowed. I called the insurance company and informed them of this, so that I wouldn't be responsible for paying the high medical bills later. The lady who received my call was surprised that I was still in the hospital, when I should have been home by then. As usual, I joked that it wasn't a problem; I could find a pair of scissors to cut my tubes and cords and go home.

The lady on the other end of the line took my words seriously and yelled, "Don't do it! I forbid you to do that!"

"Then, what am I supposed to do?" I cordially asked.

"Please call me tomorrow."

"Tomorrow is Saturday," I reminded the lady.

"Then please call back on Monday, and I will extend your stay in the hospital until then."

I didn't call again because on Monday, I was released from the hospital. The high bill was paid without a hitch. Medical regulations are very complicated in the United States, and it's necessary to first verify them to understand them. Many people unnecessarily pay out-of-pocket, which could be avoided were they familiar with the regulations.

Less than a year after this surgery, it was decided that I had to go through another surgery on my hernia. I again found myself in the hospital and had to suffer through everything fate had gifted. Despite this, I never complained because I was convinced that what was meant to be cannot be avoided.

My daughter, Maggie.

My son, Robert.

Deteriorating Health

Family life began to bloom with joy and success. Maggie graduated from Loyola School of Dental Surgery as a dentist in 1993. She and her eldest child, Sarah, celebrated the beginning of a new life. Robert began his studies at Ripon College. Five years later, Maggie's family became bigger. Anthony and Erica were born. Life seemed very good. But as we made long-term plans for the future, I felt that something was not right with me. Medical tests indicated that I was healthy, but despite this, I didn't feel well. My wife made a decision and took me to the hospital. Initial tests showed good results, but I was not released and stayed in the hospital overnight. The next day they performed a coronary catheterization, and surprisingly, it turned out that two arteries were completely obstructed, and two other ones were 75 percent blocked. They performed a procedure but couldn't unblock them. I had a heart attack, but fortunately, it occurred in the hospital, and they were able to bring me back to life.

During the heart attack, one of the nurses accidentally ripped the needle from my vein and blood spurted onto the ground. It wasn't until one of them slipped that they noticed the error. There was a moment of panic because they weren't sure of the amount of blood loss, and they wanted to give me a transfusion. Fortunately, it turned out that I had a sufficient amount of blood, and the transfusion proved to be unnecessary. In my groin area, where they entered the vein to get to the heart, there was an enormous bruise, and a bag of sand was placed on it to prevent a rupture, which could possibly lead to death.

I spent nine days in the intensive care unit, and I could not move at all. Two weeks later, I was released from the hospital under the condition that I would return for another coronary catheterization in order to open the remaining two arteries. This time my Guardian Angel was watching over me, and I left the hospital alive.

Maggie took the matter into her own hands and signed me up for another coronary catheterization at Loyola University Hospital and set up an appointment with a professor at the university. She trusted the university; after all, she had graduated from there.

After I left Christ Hospital, I had chest pains, which I didn't have before the procedure. I reported it to the professor at Loyola who would perform a second opening procedure of the remaining two arteries. His answer calmed me down, "The chest pain is not from your heart. If it was, you wouldn't be alive."

Nevertheless, the pain did not subside until April 30, 1997, when I was taken to the room where coronary catheterizations were performed. The procedure usually takes a maximum of forty-five minutes. Mine took two hours and forty-five minutes. Finally, the very irritated professor said to me, "We have an unusual situation here; we have to do a bypass. Despite my efforts, I do not have a method to repair anything."

At that moment, he literally yelled to the nurse, "Take him to the operating room immediately."

There was great commotion. They transferred me onto a gurney, and running alongside of it, they transported me to the operating room. Just then, I saw a tearful Maggie, who tried to comfort me by telling me that everything would be all right. She was so nervous that she spoke to me in English.

I only had time to say, "Maggie, honey, please forgive all of the wrongdoings on my part, forgive me and...good-bye!"

She only had time to yell out, "Daddy!"

In the hallway, a doctor ran up to me as they were pushing me toward the operating room and introduced himself as the anesthesiologist. He said that he would put me to sleep soon. A moment later, I disappeared behind the doors of the operating room. At that moment, I regretted only one thing—that I didn't go to confession before the procedure. I wished to receive Holy Communion. I asked God to forgive the sins I had committed against my loved ones. I only remember being transferred onto the operating table, and then I fell asleep.

The operation lasted six and a half hours, and three arteries were replaced. I awoke in pain. There were three patients in the room, and my wife only recognized me by my feet. That is how swollen I was. I suffered the most during the daily change of sheets. It took four nurses to do it, but despite their professionalism, I felt like everything would burst inside my chest. After four days, I was released from the hospital because that was the deal the hospital had with my insurance company. To my wife's questions they answered, "You can bring your husband back even in an hour, but you have to take him today, otherwise you will have to pay the hospital bills out-of-pocket."

Terrified, we both returned to the new home we had bought before my illness. We liked it best because we had it built according to our needs. Seven days later, my wife drove me to a post-surgical consultation. The appointment was set for seven in the morning, and Jagoda, as if feeling something was awry, took me there an hour earlier, especially since the day before I had to take nitroglycerin due to chest pain. As soon as we got into the waiting room, I felt worse again. Just then, the nurse called me into the office. She sat me on the bed and left. I had just enough time to tell my wife that I was feeling weak, and I lost consciousness. The doctor at the clinic called an ambulance and stayed with me until I regained consciousness.

The attending doctor at the clinic went with me to the hospital in the ambulance, holding my hand the entire time saying, "No one has ever scared me that way, but you are extraordinarily lucky because you chose the right time and the right place."

She only let go of my hand after she transferred me to the doctor at the hospital.

This was my second heart attack. Life did not spare me troubles, stress, and tension until my heart wasn't able to handle the pressure and had to, for a moment, stop beating. This time, I survived again. The question is, thanks to whom?

"Angel of God, my guardian dear, to whom God's love commits me here, ever this day (night), be at my side..."

In May of 1997, Robert graduated from Ripon College, but unfortunately, I couldn't attend his graduation, although I wanted to very much. I only watched the video from the celebration. My heart beat faster when Robert received his diploma from the school president. I was proud to read a letter in which one of the professors wrote, "It was an honor to have Robert in my class. He was an honest, intelligent, disciplined, clear-minded, and enthusiastic student. It was the first time in my long career that I had such an extraordinary student in my class." This gave me the strength to battle against my illness.

The real horror began with the influx of hospital and doctor's bills. It was about $200,000 in total. The insurance paid half and began to bill me for the rest. It wasn't legal, but nevertheless, the hospital tried to charge me the rest of the total. I went to the main office and demanded to speak with the manager. I presented him with the whole stack of bills, and I began to explain to him that he was unfairly burdening me with them and that I didn't owe them a cent.

"Please read exactly what is written," I demanded.

He read one of them and said, "I am right, and you have to pay the sum out-of-pocket."

"Listen," I said, "if you can't read English, get someone who knows the language because maybe they can help you and explain what is written here. I'd like to add that I had two heart attacks, and you will lead me to a third one with your ignorance. After all, it's not about $100 but about $100,000. I fought for a correction for a few months now, but interventions via telephone are not effective. That is why I came to see you personally."

At this moment, I showed him a bag full of medication and stated, "Nothing remains to be said but this: I have to put your name on my list."

Nervously, he said, "What kind of list?"

"That is not your concern," I said.

At that moment, I thought he would call the police but he only said, "Please show it to me again."

After a second look, he turned to me and said, "You're right; you shouldn't have to pay this."

Then I began to mock him and said that such a sudden change could have an effect on his health! I added that he should fix the error not just for me, but for everyone else as well! I also told him that by leading people into bankruptcy in this way, he is harming his own soul and could end up in hell! I demanded that with each bill he should write that it is in error, and that I owe nothing to the hospital or to the doctors. He angrily said that he would sign one of them, and the rest would be taken into consideration as well.

"Listen," I said without any qualms, "you have to sign all of these, or I will not leave this office! Or pay me the difference that I am supposed to pay, and then I'll leave."

He began to sign, but his hand shook violently, and it took him about an hour to finish. I left his office without saying good-bye. I knew many people who paid because they weren't able to fight for their own interests, not knowing the regulations, and the audacious bureaucrats took advantage of this. I don't know why, but a year later, I received a letter from the hospital, apologizing that they erroneously burdened me with the costs of medical care. Why they apologized in writing, and why it wasn't until twelve months after the fact was surprising to me, but better late than never. Unfortunately, that didn't aid my health; it had quite the opposite effect. The stress would reveal its negative effects in the near future.

I never returned to work. I had worked for eleven years at the last factory. In a strange coincidence, it was closed down, and all of its workers were laid off on April 30, 1997, the day of my heart surgery. Despite not being officially laid off, since I was on medical leave, I couldn't return to work. The factory no longer existed in its original form. Fortunately, I was able to keep my medical insurance, although at a greater cost to me.

Soon I began to receive disability payments. Unfortunately, fate did not spare my suffering, and I had to undergo prostate surgery once again. This time it took place in a clinic, and after the procedure, my wife brought me home. I wasn't able to urinate. I called the doctor's office, and the nurse, most likely due to her inexperience, advised me to drink a lot of water. This was supposed to help.

After a while, I felt sharp pains. Fortunately, Maggie was there visiting me. She called the hospital and explained the situation, telling them she was a doctor. She was told to take me to the emergency room immediately. They ensured her that emergency personnel would wait for me at the door. Indeed, they admitted me, despite the long line of people waiting. They took me to a room where I underwent a procedure. The doctor who came in to give me the results asked in a nervous tone, "Who released you from the clinic after the procedure?" He didn't wait for the answer, but said, "An hour later and your bladder would have burst. I don't think I have to mention the consequences."

Well, Guardian Angel, my guardian, this time too, you held my hand.

My wife's family, The Rogalski's, with her parents sitting at center.

Europe—Normandy

In June 2004, Maggie went with her husband and children to Europe in order to be in Normandy for the sixtieth anniversary of the attack of allied forces on the fortified coast, which was defended by German occupants. This was especially meaningful to Ron, my son-in-law, because his father took part in the attack, during which he was taken into German captivity and detained until the end of the war. The event was honored by the President of the United States, George W. Bush. Ron spoke as well and read his father's memoir from that time. This was an important experience for the whole family.

From there, they went to Hamburg for a few days and then took a train to Poland. The most important goal of Maggie's trip to Poland was visiting Grandma, who seemed to be delaying her death. She desired to see Maggie, as well as her great-grandchildren, from abroad. A few years earlier, Grandma Zofia met Sarah, since Maggie had sent her with me to Poland. This time everyone visited Grandma, including Maggie, Sarah, Anthony, Erica, and Ron, whom she wished to meet as well.

That summer I flew to Poland to serve as their guide and advisor on Polish land. We got together in Poznan, where we transferred to a train for Gdynia. There my role as a guide began. The grandchildren were delighted to see me, and I was even happier that they could see Poland and get to know the places where their Grandma and Grandpa were born and raised.

I was very moved by Maggie and her family's visit with her Grandma Zophie. The ninety-five-year-old woman, as I describe my mother, was overjoyed as she took each one into her arms and hugged them close to her heart. She had only one leg, and she sat in a wheelchair. Despite this, she tried to lift herself up a bit in order to highlight the importance of the moment. Out of her humble disability pension, she even bought Anthony and Erica a chalice used for Holy Mass, so that they could offer it to a missionary church when they made their First Holy Communion. The joy that I experienced during these moments of interaction among several generations of my family was enormous.

Ron and Maggie rented a car and took my brother and me on a "voyage" around Poland. We visited Krakow, Wieliczka, Oswiecim, and Czestochowa. On the way, we stopped at all of the attractions. Ron drove the car the entire time. I admired his patience and orientation through the terrain, as well as his safe driving on Polish roads, which, unfortunately, were congested due to a lack of highways.

Maggie, and especially Ron, liked Poland. I was surprised myself with the changes that occurred after Soviet occupation left. This was not the same Poland I was forced to leave thirty years earlier and that I was very familiar with since in the past, I often went on business trips and felt I knew it quite well. This time Poland was different. Ron even enjoyed McDonald's, which was an upscale one from the ones in the United States. The meals were served in a totally different way, and its interior was decorated more exclusively.

At the end of our trip to Poland, we visited Warsaw. Maggie and her family left late in the evening to return home, stopping in Paris and London on the way to Phoenix. After their departure, I took a train to Gdynia for a few days, and I returned to Chicago on July 3. Unfortunately, for a long time after my return, I felt exhausted because we toured around Poland at a dizzying pace, exceeding my normal physical capabilities.

I wasn't given much time to rest because on August 25, at three in the morning, we received a call from Poland that my mother had passed away. When I bid farewell to my mother just a month before, she asked me for the first time if I would come to her funeral. It seemed odd, but of course, I agreed because earlier I had decided that I would. The day after the phone call, I flew to Poland. This time, I felt the difficulties of the journey more severely. I even had the feeling that this may be the last trip of my life. I didn't feel well; I had chest pains. I was forced to take nitroglycerin more often to keep myself alive. The depression and stress caused by the death of a beloved person and the funeral itself, which took place in Osowiec about five hundred kilometers from Gdynia, had a real effect on me.

I ordered a large tomb and financed it myself with the conviction that, along with my parents, I would be buried on this piece of Polish land where I was born. I gave myself up to God's will. Nevertheless, God's intentions were different, and two weeks later, I came back and landed in Chicago. Unfortunately, day after day I felt worse. At that point, eight years hadn't even gone by since my first heart surgery, and everything should have been fine. A few months passed in that way. Because the pain didn't subside, I finally told my wife about it. Jagoda reacted right away. On Sunday, February 21, 2005, she forcibly took me to the emergency room at Loyola University Hospital. After the decided angioplasty procedure, the doctors were surprised that I was still alive. Two arteries were 95 percent blocked, and the most important one was 100 percent obstructed.

The next morning, on February 22, 2005, I underwent another open-heart surgery, and this time three arteries were replaced, a triple bypass. Because I never lost my sense of humor, right before the surgery I told the surgeons a joke. "There was a man who was terrified to have a surgical procedure. His friend convinced him that he had had the same procedure as well, and everything turned out fine. They went to a mutually acquainted surgeon, who presented the surgical plan to him this way:

"'It's nothing to be afraid of,' he said, "First we will put you under anesthesia, and it will seem like I'm going further away, until you fall asleep. After the procedure, it'll be the opposite. I will come closer, and I will say hello, and it'll be over.'

"It happened just as the doctor said, but when the man awoke from the surgery he was greeted by someone else. It was a balding man with a beard. He was much older and didn't offer any greeting. The man turned to him and asked, "So, the doctor who operated on me couldn't come, and he sent you instead?

"The balding man answered, "I am not the doctor; I'm Saint Peter."

With this joke, I not only made the doctors laugh, but the entire staff as well, and I soon fell asleep.

I woke up in the intensive care unit, and the doctor passing by yelled to me, "Henry, I'm not Saint Peter." The scene repeated itself each time one of the operating doctors passed by my bed.

I was taken aback by what I experienced during the operation. I had a vision that fascinated me. Around me, I saw glowing rectangles with radiant bright circles in the middle, like little suns. At first, the lights were very far away. Suddenly, this mass of light surrounding me began to draw closer to me. In the first phase, moving slowly, then quicker, and in the last moment it reached incredible speed. I felt that I was absorbed in it, and I was turning into light myself. At that moment, I felt a great relief. I experienced an amazing joy. I wanted to stay there forever. The magnitude of joy that I experienced cannot be compared to any natural phenomenon because there aren't words to describe it.

Suddenly my eyes opened, and with horror, I saw that I was in the hospital's intensive care unit. I felt disappointed that I had returned to Earth. I couldn't gather my thoughts; why this had happened, and why the great joy, which I had experienced, had burst like a bubble. The thought haunted me for the next two weeks, and I couldn't come to terms with reality. I didn't tell anyone about it because I didn't know if my family and friends, who were happy that I was alive, would understand my sadness.

I concluded that God must have different plans for me, and I soon came to terms with my fate. I thanked my Guardian Angel for interceding and for extending my life again in the mortal world.

I received wonderful medical care in the hospital. Maggie, despite her urgent activities, flew down from Arizona to ensure the best conditions for me in the hospital and to lift me up psychologically with her presence. Robert visited me regularly. His presence was crucial to me, and by all means, very necessary. Jagoda was the stronghold in my suffering, not only with physical pain. Most of all her trust in that everything would be all right gave me the strength to fight my illness. I was grateful to Monika, Jagoda's cousin, who visited me every day after work because she worked in that very hospital. She lifted my spirits as much as she could, and she did it wonderfully.

I am full of admiration for my doctor, Professor F. Leya, to whom I owe my life. He took over my care following my second heart attack, and since then, he takes care of me treating me as he would his own father. His wonderful care and special concern for my health helped me survive difficult moments with dignity.

I recovered slowly. There were more complications, and instead of staying four days, I was released from the hospital after seven days.

Soon thereafter, the relentless sky-high bills began to arrive again. It was very stressful, even though I now had experience in settling these matters.

The post-surgical rehabilitation caused me pain. I wasn't able to perform all of the exercises that the program required. I struggled, but somehow I managed to reach the end of the program. Life went on and returned to normal. At least that's what it seemed like to me.

One day, I received news by phone from my mother in-law that a woman was looking for me via a Polish radio advertisement. She was very worried and asked me directly, "What does this woman want from you?"

"I don't know; it's the first time I've heard about it. But knowing women, it probably has something to do with child support," I joked.

There was a long silence at the other end of the line. My mother in-law took my answer literally. I quickly then followed with an explanation that it was probably someone from Gdansk from my student years, and child support did not enter into this equation.

The next day I called the radio station, and I was given the telephone number of the person who was searching for me. I found out that that woman was only an intermediary; it was actually someone else who was looking for me.

It turned out that the person searching for me was the landlord from Gdansk when I was still a student. She currently lives in Germany and is a citizen of that country. She wanted to find me for two reasons. The first was that I had given her a bouquet of flowers for saving me from my dilemma when two girls had come to visit me at the same time. It was a significant event for her because never before, nor ever again, did she get flowers from a stranger.

"And the second reason?" I quickly asked out of curiosity before she could tell me the whole story.

"The second is that my daughter remembers you well, although she was a child at the time. You brought her candy, and she waited in the front yard every day no matter the weather, or she came out to meet you at the tram stop. She liked you a lot, and, of course, she expected to receive something at that time. She was the one who initiated the idea to find you and to find out about your life."

Of course, I called Germany. We pleasantly reminisced about our young "foolish" years. Her daughter was married and had four grown children. I sent my best to both ladies and thanked them for remembering me. It was good to know that one time in my life, I was able to please someone through such a small gesture.

Life is made up of such inconspicuous episodes, which give meaning to our existence. The more deeds we do to please others, the more we will be valued. It isn't possible to count either the good or the bad deeds we do because sometimes, even unknowingly, we could make someone happy or miserable. Glory to whoever can make others happy consciously. Good deeds always count, but it isn't until the end of our life's road that they bring enormous satisfaction.

The next piece of news surprised me again. I received a letter from Germany from Olga Doerfling, maiden name Czajewski. She was born in the former Soviet Union, married a German, and currently lives in Germany. When she tried to recreate her ancestral history in order to create a family tree, she found my name on the internet. She contacted me not only via mail, but via telephone as well. It turned out that her great-grandfather was married to a Polish countess named Olimpia. My great-grandfather was from Eastern Europe, and the possibility that they were related was enormous. It was a large family because Olga's great-grandfather was one of twelve children. Before the revolution in 1917, they were quite wealthy, and there were a couple of doctors in the family. Her grandfather, Damian Czajewski, was Lenin's personal doctor (this saddened me, although as a doctor by calling, he had to provide medical care to everyone who needed it). One of the members of the family, Piotr (Peter) Czajewski, immigrated to the United States and was the owner of a film production company named Lancaster. A few others found themselves back in Poland as the borders changed after the revolution. It's possible that this was the family of grandfather Czajewski. I am personally convinced that they were related.

Jagoda's sixtieth birthday was coming up, and my wish was to throw a surprise party. I had thrown one already for her fiftieth birthday, and everything turned out well. This time I had my doubts, due to my deteriorating health. I felt worse each day. I just couldn't put my finger on why. After all, it had only been a few months since my last bypasses, so I was sure that it had nothing to do with my heart.

I asked Jagoda's sister, Chris, and her husband, Stanley, to help me organize it, and in fact, they took the initiative from start to finish. Thanks to their help, the party turned out wonderfully. Maggie surprised us by flying in from Arizona for the celebration. Over thirty guests were invited.

Chris "dragged" Jagoda out shopping. Meanwhile, all of the invited guests came to our house. When Jagoda entered the house after she returned from the shopping trip, she was very surprised. She didn't know what was happening, and only everyone singing "Happy Birthday" made her realize that it was a celebration in her honor.

I wanted to play an active role in her celebration, but despite my good intentions, I felt that something bad was happening to me. I was afraid of only one thing—that something would happen to me during the party. I even had a bit of cognac and felt better. It helped to confirm in my mind that my well-being was related to my heart because cognac has similar effects as nitroglycerine and expands the veins.

Some of the guests were surprised that I was not my usual self, full of energy, and with a sense of humor. Fortunately, my brother-in-law, Stanley, took the initiative and entertained everyone wonderfully. The birthday celebration ended, and the guests left the house with smiles on their faces. I was happy that perhaps for the last time, I was able to celebrate with them. No one knew about my condition; I didn't even mention it to Jagoda.

Nevertheless, I was convinced that the end was near. My wish was to finish this book, which I had begun writing in 2005. The last hope of turning my fate around was our beloved Pope John Paul II. I turned to him with a request of intercession to God Almighty to extend my life for the next two years, so that I might finish my humble memoir. I prayed for my family as well that the Good Lord might keep them in His care and give them strength when I wasn't there anymore. On November 15, Robert called me very worried and told me that he dreamt about the pope that night. My son asked him what would happen with those who are unbelieving. John Paul II took him in his arms, comforted him, and answered that human deeds are what counts. Robert woke up covered in sweat.

I could not understand why, that same night, I had a dream about Robert. However, right before I fell asleep, I experienced an incredible fear, which took hold of me and pierced my soul. It was the first time in my life that I had such a feeling. I felt that something incredible was happening to me. I had the feeling that something was coming out of me but was grasping onto me and trying to remain inside of me. I was afraid, but I didn't know of what. Shivers ran down my spine. I began to pray to John Paul II. I asked for mercy and intercession to God that I might once again be absorbed into that perfect light, which had brought me boundless joy.

Christmas time approached, and the very thought of medical examinations terrified me. I wished to be present, as in previous years, at the Christmas party, at which Jagoda's entire family gathered. Maggie and Ron flew in from Arizona with the children, and Robert always came with a female friend. I awaited the arrival of the guests from Arizona on December 17, 2005.

Sarah had changed a lot; she was thinner and even more beautiful. Anthony had changed the most. He matured, became taller, and he fascinated me with his wisdom and interesting outlook on life, despite his seven years. Erica charmed us with her beautiful green eyes and light blond hair, as usual, a beautiful girl.

How pleasant it was to have each of them run up to me one by one to hug and kiss me. The house was filled to the brim with squeals, commotion, and chatting. When on December 27, Maggie returned to Sedona with the entire family, the house became empty, and it was incredibly sad. We had gotten used to a different pace of life. Meanwhile, everything suddenly changed and access to the bathrooms was easy again. It was somewhat strange, and we had to once again become accustomed to the new reality.

We welcomed the New Year 2006, by watching television programs, which aired New Year's celebrations in various countries. Jagoda was impressed with the fireworks displays and by the performances of famous bands, singers, and actors. Unfortunately, this didn't delight me as usual because the chest pains and numbness in my left hand clearly indicated my heart problem. I wasn't thrilled about going to the hospital because the very thought of it filled me with disdain toward everything surrounding me.

Nevertheless, under pressure from my wife, I called Loyola, and on January 9, I underwent another angioplasty procedure. The doctor was astonished beyond belief at how I was still alive. It turned out that the previous year's heart surgery, performed on February 22, was unsuccessful. One of the bypasses wasn't connected at all, and the other stopped functioning most likely following the operation. This explained the feeling of being "on the other side of the river." The doctor, in an attempt to save my life, inserted three stents, but only into the bypasses from eight years ago because the more recent ones were not suitable for opening.

I posed three questions to the doctor who was discharging me from the hospital: "Doctor, why am I alive?" Instead of an explanation, he spread his hands and remained in that position for a moment, without an answer.

Secondly, I wanted to know how blood was able to reach my heart if everything was 100 percent obstructed. This time the doctor responded right away, "The blood had to find a way to your heart, otherwise you wouldn't have lived."

The third question had to do with how long the stents were meant to keep me alive, and what I heard surprised me because his answer was, "Two years at most."

Right away, I was reminded of my request to John Paul II, in which I asked him to prolong my life for two years.

The next angioplasty procedure was scheduled for February 7. On January 9, only one of the arteries was unclogged, while at least two had to be cleared for normal heart function. Unfortunately, I was feeling awful. I felt extremely strong pains in my chest, as if it were on fire, and the pain spread to my back. As if this weren't enough, I experienced a very painful infection in my left ear. The family doctor prescribed penicillin, which was supposed to help me after five days. During the visit, I decided to ask the same question that I asked the doctor who discharged me from Loyola Hospital, "Doctor, why am I still alive?"

This time the reaction and the answer to my question was different. The doctor looked up then pointed her hand in the same direction and said, "Someone up there is watching over you."

I thought that it was only thanks to my Guardian Angel, whose patience was surely running low. After all, how many times could he save me from such serious troubles? Nevertheless, I did not doubt it, and after leaving the doctor's office, I said out loud to myself, "Angel of God, my guardian dear, to whom God's love commits me here, ever this day, is at my side…"

On February 7, at seven o'clock in the morning, my usually infallible wife took me to the hospital for my second angioplasty procedure. During that time, I received a call from my daughter, who was on her way to the airport in Phoenix to fly to Chicago. A moment later, my son-in-law called me from his house in Sedona, and I was greatly surprised when he told me "I love you."

After a five-minute pause on the line, I heard the voice of my grandson, Anthony. In a breaking voice, nearly weeping, he uttered these words, "Grandpa, I don't want you to die." Just then, his voice broke down, and he couldn't speak any more.

After hearing those words, something stirred inside of me. An internal impulse released a great will to survive and an incredible desire to live. I imagined Anthony going to First Communion and carrying a golden chalice, which his great-grandmother, Zofia, bought for him, so that he may present this gift for a mission.

After the procedure of inserting three stents into another artery, I was connected to a monitor and was resting in the hospital bed. Next, the telephone rang, and when I picked up the receiver, I heard the voice of my seven-year-old grandson, Anthony, once again, "Grandpa I heard that you are alive, and you can't even imagine how happy I am."

An extraordinary joy entered my heart. I simply got such wings that I felt I could fly around the globe. It was hard to believe that such a small being could strengthen the soul of an adult, but that's exactly what happened in my case. The next day at eight o'clock in the morning, I was released from the hospital.

Deteriorating Health Continued

On May 30, 2006, I had strong chest pains, which radiated all through my back. I called my family doctor, and fortunately for me, another patient was not able to make his appointment. I was given that timeslot and seen that same day. The doctor examined me and ordered the nurse to perform an EKG. A moment later, I was told that I needed to go to the hospital immediately.

The doctor and nurse wanted to call an ambulance, but I refused. The ambulance would have taken me to the nearest hospital, but I wanted to go to Loyola. My doctor didn't want to let me leave her office. She agreed to it only under the condition that a family member would take me to Loyola, the hospital that treated my heart condition. I called my son, and it turned out that he just happened to be on the south side of town at a friend's house. He came right away and took me to Loyola. I couldn't move on my own, so my son placed me into a hospital wheelchair and pushed me to the reception area. Before our arrival, Dr. F. Leya arranged for my admission to the hospital without the use of an emergency room. Unfortunately, I was forced to wait for two hours, since beds in the cardiology unit were not available. Finally, at eight o'clock that evening, a space opened up in room 3364. Once there, I asked a nurse to bring me a few sheets of paper and a pencil, since I wanted to take notes. That is why I'm able to so accurately relate what happened hour-by-hour.

Every hour, my blood was drawn for various tests. The tests showed that I had had a heart attack, the third one in my life. In order to confirm this, three blood tests were needed, and all had to be positive. In addition, other tests were performed, and I was wheeled from one place to another until four in the morning.

I wasn't able to rest, and at six in the morning, two doctors paid a visit and began a routine check-up, which took nearly an hour. At 9:30 a.m., I was taken to the lower level for a CT scan. I waited in line until 11:40 a.m. When an additional IV was connected, I informed the nurse of my allergy to iodine. I noticed her face turned red, and she immediately stopped the iodine. She ran to the other room to check on the time that I was given the medication that neutralizes the effects caused by iodine allergies. It turned out that the medication wore off an hour before, and the tests were stopped.

Another test was performed at 1:00 p.m. Before this test, an IV with iodine was connected, after which I felt chest pains and a heat spread through my body. Unfortunately, after the test, as I sat in a wheelchair back in my room, the chest pains intensified. I informed the lady attending me of this. She had wheeled me from test to test throughout the hospital. She was doing all that she could in order to get me back to my room as fast as possible. To make matters worse, we were forced to wait a long time for the elevator. Once I was back in the room, I was immediately given nitroglycerine under my tongue. In addition, an IV was hooked up to me containing some sort of medicine.

I received many telephone calls that day. Most etched in my memory is a conversation with my grandchildren. To end the conversation, Anthony said, "Grandpa, just don't die! I don't want you to die. I love you very much."

Then Erica cheered me up just like Anthony, and she finally said, "Grandpa, I love you more than a thousand times!" The will to live entered me once again; this time with more strength.

On June 1, 2006, just after midnight, I was informed that a coronary catheterization would have to be performed. The procedure was to take place in the morning, but I wasn't taken away until nine o'clock that evening. It was the second day that I wasn't given anything to eat, since I was constantly undergoing tests. Despite this, I didn't feel hunger because I was being given many liquids through IVs, which suppressed any hunger. The chest pains worsened, and I was given nitroglycerine under my tongue.

Before the procedure, the doctor informed me that this would only be a check-up of my arteries, but most likely, everything would be fine. After all, in January and February the arteries were fixed by inserting three stents into them.

"It will only be a formality," he announced.

Following the procedure, he came to see me again, but I saw profound anxiety on his face. He only said, "Both of the arteries were 100 percent obstructed. Please do not worry because this time I will do everything so that you won't have to return to the hospital for a long time."

I didn't even ask the doctor why I was still alive because I knew that John Paul II interceded for me, and I would surely be able to live the two years, for which I asked. Once again I thought, *I have a wonderful Guardian Angel, as long as he doesn't miss anything because that'll be the end of me.*

The doctor on duty comforted me that he would come up with a medication that would keep me alive, so that I would not have to undergo any complex procedures.

Days passed, and no decision was made. It was a very complicated matter. Only the IVs with a few drugs and liquid nitroglycerine kept me alive.

Although I had recently attended confession, I asked that the nurse permit me to see a Polish-speaking Catholic priest. Earlier an American priest visited me, but he wore a tie, and despite his assurances that he was a Roman-Catholic priest, he didn't inspire my trust.

It wasn't until a priest, Father Zbigniew Pienkos from Our Lady of Czestochowa Church came, that I could speak honestly. I asked directly, "Father, what do you think about my situation, which I just presented to you? Please don't think that I am blaming God for sending me so much suffering at once. I have never thought in such a way. After all, I have to suffer for my sins."

The kind priest's answer surprised me. He explained that I might not be suffering for my sins. Perhaps someone had chosen me to repent for their sins, seeing as I would be able to better suffer through them. I was happy that perhaps this was true, although the sins that I accumulated throughout my life were many. Later I confessed and took Holy Communion.

After I parted with the priest, the nurse informed me that the next morning, June 5, 2006, I would undergo open-heart surgery. The doctors could not find another solution. This was going to be the third surgery of its kind. The most recent one took place on February 22 of the previous year.

I surrendered to God's will and was convinced that, as I wrote my request, these were the last words of my life: "God, permit me to once again see that wonderful light, which I was granted the chance to see before. I forgive everyone and ask forgiveness for my wrongdoings, unto my loved ones. John Paul II, I ask for your intercession though Mary, to whom you devoted your entire life, and to her Son, Jesus Christ, that I may view the face of our Creator. God, keep me in your care and take my soul to the Heavenly Kingdom. Amen."

At five o'clock in the morning, I was taken to the operating room. The surgery was performed by a professor of Loyola University, who was recommended by my doctor. During the surgery, I had a strange vision. I saw myself lying on the operating table and being operated on. Right by me stood my mother at age forty. She was wearing the same blue dress in which she was buried. I was convinced that she came to take me with her, so I tried to strike up a conversation, and I said, "Mom!" Just then, she disappeared.

The surgery was successful, and so I'm able to continue relating the rest of the events.

After the surgery, I completely lost my appetite. I was disgusted by all food. The very thought of food made me nauseous. I couldn't even look at anything that reminded me of something edible. Fearing that something could happen to me, my wife brought me specially pre-pared goodies from home. As soon as she told me what was in the bag, I began to vomit. Two days later, it all went away, and I was able to take in at least small amounts of food. Soon everything returned to normal.

On the fifth day following the surgery, the documents were pre-pared for my discharge, and Jagoda came to pick me up. Suddenly, the nurse burst into the room and told me to lie down on my back and not move. She forbade me even to move my hand.

"What happened?" I asked.

"Your heart began to beat three times quicker than it should."

"What does that mean?" I asked another question.

"A doubling of your heart rate is sometimes fatal, but a tripling..." she paused. "Please don't even move a finger, just relax," she added and hooked me up to an IV with new drugs. Then she explained that the heart sometimes reacts this way because during the surgery, the doctor touched it with his hand.

The hospital stay was extended by two days, so that my heart could stabilize. Although after two days my heart functioned normally, I was held in the hospital for another day to ensure that the arrhythmia would not return. While discharging me from the hospital once again, the nurse said, "You were lucky that you didn't leave for home when you planned because you wouldn't have arrived there alive."

Was it by sheer chance that this happened? I thought. How wonderful it was that this time too, my Guardian Angel didn't leave my side even for a moment.

After a few weeks of recuperation, I began special exercises at the rehabilitation center. Under strict supervision, where a nurse was able to keep an eye on my heart through a monitor, I performed the recommended exercises. The rehabilitation sessions took place three times a week for twelve weeks. I didn't feel well from the beginning, and I had to rest after each exercise. The nurse would stop the exercises a few times and ask me to take a break. The monitor most likely indicated some abnormalities. I finished the sessions, but my well-being wasn't improving at all.

On the night of October 6, John Paul II appeared in my dreams once more. I was riding my bicycle on a routine trip when, near the trail behind the house, I saw the lonely pope sitting at a table. I was incredibly surprised to see him by himself. After all, there were always enormous crowds surrounding him. Then I thought, *How unrewarding old age is that a person is left alone and abandoned.*

I decided to stop and talk, but I wasn't sure if the Holy Father would agree to it. I took the risk and was surprised when we struck up a conversation. He even invited me to sit at the table.

In the first phase of the conversation, I was timid and nervous, but as time passed, our conversation became more of a friendly discussion. At one point, I had the courage to invite him to dinner at our house. I was happy when he answered, "I will come, but please tell me exactly when I should come." I was relieved that he didn't refuse and accepted the invitation so readily.

Then there was a shift, and I saw that a musician was playing the guitar for the Holy Father. The group of people became larger. Among them was my father, who took the guitar from the musician and began to play it. Suddenly, I remembered that I didn't set a date for dinner with the Holy Father. As I was about to propose a specific date, I woke up.

From the dream, I inferred that John Paul II was watching over me. The date of the dinner though wasn't yet set and that could have been either a warning of impending danger or a good omen for me. I would like to indicate that I took this note on the same day in which I had this dream, and I didn't know what would happen in the future.

I am not a fan of believing in dreams, but I had predictive dreams a few times, which surprised me. One time, when I worked at the Cromwell Paper Company (the job I had when I first came to the

United States), I had a dream that they were going to build offices, and a wall was going to be put up right beside the machine on which I worked. I told my assistant about the dream. Usually, once a week, he would remind me that he didn't see any signs of construction. "Apparently, your dream will not come true because we would have to take apart this giant machine," he joked, pointing at the one that stood where the wall was supposed to run through. I explained that it was only a dream, which had nothing to do with reality.

It wasn't until a year later that the dream came true in its entirety. One day, I noticed some strangers measuring and surveying the area around my machine. At first, I didn't connect the two. However, they began to break apart the concrete floor in the exact place I visualized in my dream, I asked one of the workers performing the task what they were intending to build. His answer surprised me, "There will be a wall here because we are expanding the offices. Your headquarters will be transferred here from the downtown location."

I suspected that something was amiss with our factory, and a financial crisis was coming. I wasn't surprised when later the factory closed. I had worked there for nine years and six months, but I didn't get a factory pension because I was just short of the ten years needed to receive the pension. Luck just happened to pass me by.

I would like to indicate once more that, for a time now, I am taking notes of events as they happen, and what I describe below comes from one of the events that took place on the same or previous day.

I was quite surprised that, after the heart operation, my well-being worsened from day to day. I had frequent chest pains, and my hand felt like it was wilting. I was sure that it was because of my heart, but please believe me, I did not have the slightest desire to go to the doctor, or to the hospital.

May God's will be done, I thought, and I didn't even tell my wife about my symptoms. Nevertheless, on November 29, 2006, at eight o'clock in the evening, I had very strong chest pains. Jagoda was at work, so I called my sister-in-law, Chris, just to chat and mentioned the symptom.

Chris reacted immediately, "I will be there soon," she said and put down the telephone.

Only a few minutes passed before she was in front of my house. I stepped out to greet her, and I began talking to her with no intention of going anywhere. Then Chris said loudly, and in a demanding voice, "What are you waiting for? Get in the car right now!"

An order is an order, I thought, and after closing the front door, I got in her car. The pain began to intensify on the way to the hospital. I instructed Chris that if I were to lose consciousness, she should park the car on the shoulder of the street and call an ambulance. Loyola Hospital is thirty kilometers away from my house, and getting there takes longer than it would for an ambulance, which doesn't have to stand in street traffic.

We arrived at 9:15 pm. I was admitted right away and tests were started. On December 1, 2006, nearly five months after my open-heart surgery, I underwent a coronary catheterization. I signed a document informing me that one in every thousand patients dies during the procedure. I had signed the document many times, but this time I sub-consciously thought that I would be the thousandth patient.

I overheard a conversation between two doctors, one of whom was to assist during my procedure. They stood at a computer in front of my bed and were most likely reading my medical history. After look-ing at it for a long time, and there was a lot to look over, one of them turned to the other saying, "You've got a good case here, and you'll have the opportunity to learn a lot of new things because he's got everything messed up in there."

This time it really is the end, I thought. I wasn't upset about it at all because perhaps the sedatives had already begun to work. A moment later, I was approached by Dr. Robert Dieter, who informed me he worked with Dr. Fred Leya, and that he would be performing the pro-cedure.

He asked me, "Do you trust me?"

I looked into his eyes, and I responded that I did because I truly believed in him.

I was pushed into the operating room on my bed, and they moved me onto the operating table. The surgical room is always cold. Upon my request, they covered me with two warm blankets and even put a hat on my head. I felt comfortable.

In my mind, the procedure lasted quite long, and at one point, the doctor stopped it entirely and walked away. After some time he returned, and turning to me directly said, "I have to tell you that the situation is very serious."

Oh well, I thought, *my premonition was correct after all. I would be the thousandth patient.*

Despite this, I turned to John Paul II with the request for interces-sion and extending my life for the remainder of that year. It was strange, but it just happened that a year had passed since my last request.

The procedure seemed never ending. I knew that the doctor was doing everything to save my life, and I was incredibly grateful to him. When the doctor once again approached my bedside, he announced that the surgery was finished.

Just then, I began to feel weak. I had the feeling that I was dying. I only had enough time to tell the nurse standing the closest to me about this. I thought, *God, take my soul into the Heavenly Kingdom,* and I lost consciousness.

Later the nurse related the entire surgical procedure to me. The procedure was started at 8:15 a.m. and ended at 1:15 p.m. It lasted five hours, with a half-hour break after a three-hour attempt to save my life. Actually, after the first three hours, the doctor saw no possibility of repair and concluded the procedure. Nevertheless, he took advantage of the half hour break to get another opinion with other doctors, so he returned. After informing me of the gravity of the situation, he went into the arteries again. The repair took another two hours, which proved successful.

When I lost consciousness, the doctor took the initiative of saving me. It turned out that I had a heart attack, the fourth in my life.

I regained consciousness, covered in sweat. My boundless faith in the doctor paid off because, thanks to him, I'm alive.

They wheeled me to my room and released me after four days. Unfortunately, after a few days, the chest pains were permanent. The doctors claim that the maladies were caused by the wires, which were used to close the chest cavity several times after my numerous open-heart surgeries. They were forced to cut open the chest in a different spot each time, so the old ones simply remained.

I even permitted myself to joke about it and asked my family doctor very seriously, "Doctor, maybe during the last operation they didn't have the correct wire, and they bought some barbed wire on sale at Home Depot and sewed me up with it! Maybe that's the cause of the pain."

The doctor first thought that I was serious and began to explain that hospitals don't get medical supplies from that store. A moment later, she remembered my sense of humor and began to laugh and I with her.

On April 30, 2007, I found myself in the hospital once again. All this time I was haunted by the question, why did the Lord God give me so many chances at survival? After all, even as a boy, he saved me from many hopeless situations and still saves me until this day! What did I do to deserve this? I don't know the answer.

Despite the many difficult moments, I lived through immeasurably happier moments. If one were to place on a scale all of the good and the bad times in my life, the good would surely outweigh the misfortunes.

It is with great pride and joy that I think of our upcoming forty-third wedding anniversary on June 14, 2007. Despite our times apart, suffering and misfortunes, we lived in love and respect so many years.

My wife, who vowed at the altar a life for better or worse, never disappointed me. I know that I will not be able to repay the debt of gratitude that I felt during our married life. It was thanks to her care and help that I survived death twice. She nearly ran one car into the ground bringing me to and from hospitals, thereby saving my life. She called an ambulance at night when I fell nearly lifeless to the floor. I don't know how she heard my feeble voice in her sleep calling, "Jagoda, I feel weak," because I only regained consciousness as I was carried to the ambulance. (That time I slept in another bedroom.)

There aren't words to express my gratitude for the concern and care which she has for me and continues to provide me always and everywhere.

Jagoda, thank you from the bottom of my heart for everything, especially for the pain you endured with me. Through marriage, you are part of my body. May God bless you and repay you for everything you have done for me.

To me the greatest "success," however, is the fact that in two days, on June 14, 2007, we will celebrate the forty-third anniversary of our married life. Despite our time apart, our suffering, and misfortunes, our marriage has lasted so many years. Perhaps the words of the song, "Love will forgive anything" are justified; they ring true.

We have two wonderful children and three grandchildren, whom we love deeply. The family, both from my wife's side and mine, was always helpful to us and supported us in our every need.

I thank my friends, who personally, by telephone or letter or email, encouraged me, cheered me up, and lifted my spirits.

I want to especially thank my brother, who's Holy Masses in my intention most likely helped me most. On February 22, 2005, just before my unsuccessful surgery (during which I felt absorbed by light), he went to Czestochowa and celebrated a special Holy Mass before the miraculous painting of the Holy Mary in my intention, and he asked for her intercession for me. Because John Paul II was the Holy Mary's advocate, they both interceded for me and miraculously brought me back to life.

I also believe that my Guardian Angel watched over me always and everywhere and in many, what seemed like hopeless, situations, and never abandoned me.

A few times, he saved me from certain death when I was still a boy. Overlooking my carelessness, he watched over me when I jumped from a moving train or a speeding tram. He saved me from death during my several open-heart surgeries. He was with me whenever something bad was about to happen.

That is why with great humility I repeat, and will repeat until the end of my days on Earth, "Angel of God, my guardian dear to whom God's love commits me here, ever this day be at my side…"

My wife and me in Sedona, Arizona.

A heavenly vacation

By Henry Czajewski

On July 14 our European trip started in Paris, where we celebrated my birthday. On July 24 we were in Rome, where my wife and I and a group of travelers had a special audience with Pope John.

My brother, who is a priest in Poland, arranged this audience with the Pope for us. He also flew to Rome to meet us. In the picture my wife is presenting the

Pope with vestments which my mother sewed and embroidered.   These will be used in a poor country for Mass.

We talked with the Pope for about three minutes. It was an experience we will never forget. On July 26 my brother said Mass at St. Peter's Basilica to celebrate our 25-year anniversary.

This is a trip my wife and I will long remember.

After we gave the vestments, we were blessed on our twenty-fifth wedding anniversary. The article above was published in the local newspaper.

My daughter and her family.

Childhood Dreams Come True—
Travels around the World

As I have already mentioned, what I liked to do best as a boy was to read travel books. I was dreaming and traveling through the characters in my books, journeying in my imagination to various parts of the world, and having the same adventures they did. During that time, the thought that my dreams would come true never crossed my mind. Nevertheless, human lives are a great unknown, and none of us can say what will happen in the future.

Thanks to my brother, my dreams already had begun to come true during my college years when we began to journey around Poland. Then I traveled through Poland far and wide by train or official car, coming to know it well, as I took business trips with various delegations or for training.

The first trip I took abroad was to East Germany, under the occupation of the Soviet Union at the time. I went there by myself, as it was a business trip for my company, but I wanted to bring more marks (the German currency) with me in order to supply myself with goods that were not available in Poland. I submitted an official request that my children would be traveling with me, who were also permitted a monetary share of marks. At the register, they noticed that in my identification document there were two children reflected, and there was only a ten-day difference between their birth dates—March 19 and March 29, mistakenly of the same year.

"How did that happen?" asked the cashier surprised.

If I had admitted that the same birth years were written into the document, she would have demanded that I go to the commission to make the correction. Meanwhile, I was to leave the next day and had not enough time to make any corrections. Without a thought, I replied, "That's easy, ma'am. One of the children was born through one woman and the other child was born through another. That says a lot about my manliness," I added.

All of the people behind me in line burst into laughter. The disoriented cashier paid out the money without a word. As I left the register, the other women, especially, were staring at me. I, like a "real man," left the office with my head held high.

With the extra cash, I bought my children many toys. Maggie was most thrilled with a doll that blinked her eyes because there weren't toys like that in Poland yet.

Two trips to the United States left me with unforgettable impressions. The first was the voyage on the *Batory* and the second, the flight there, during which my childhood dreams began to shape themselves into reality.

When I left my country permanently, through no other choice, I missed Poland very much. I wished to visit my family as soon as possible, but this was not possible until I obtained United States citizenship—I was certain that the Security Office had not forgotten about me. After my wife and I passed the appropriate exam and took the oath, we became citizens of the United States. We then received our passports. Not having seen our family and friends for six years, we were happy to fly to Poland, where we were able to spend time with them. Ms. Paluszko, the former nanny of our children, was especially delighted.

I usually flew back to Poland every two years, and after I was no longer able to work, I even traveled there twice a year. Unfortunately, my wife could not always accompany me because she could not get time off from work.

One time, when my wife and I both went to Poland, we took a ferry from Gdansk to Sweden. We took my sister, Anastazja, along with us. At the border crossing in Sweden, a guard stopped her because as a citizen of Poland, she was required to bring a certain number of Swedish koronas. Standing in line behind her, I announced, "She is with me," and presented my American passport.

The guard stamped her passport without a word and let her through. These were times of communist rule, and I was filled with pride that, as an American citizen, doors were open to in any country in the world.

One year, on my way back from Poland, we stopped in London for five days. We were able to purchase tickets for a wonderful pageant called "The Royal Tournament." It was worth coming to London, if only for the pageant itself. Then we took a special trip in a small open minibus around London's most interesting sites, while our driver and guide told us about each of them. We visited the wax museum and, of course, stopped at a few luxurious shopping centers. I liked Englishmen very much. After all, they were true gentlemen. I was surprised by the politeness of all of the English with whom I talked. Even a poor man who stopped us began his talk with niceties, "Excuse me sir, would you be kind enough to give me a dollar, if you can?"

During the first five years in America, we often took trips to Wisconsin Dells, a popular tourist destination still to this day. In the summer, even twice a month, we drove to the Polish retreat center in Yorkville, where both children and adults were able to enjoy a swimming pool and many activities. Soccer and volleyball games were organized, and for those who wished to dance, a band played. These family trips were a dream come true for a novice traveler, although as a child, I had no idea that such a lifestyle was possible.

Both my wife and I have wandering souls, and we love to visit interesting places. After our first visit to Las Vegas, we returned there four times. This city of entertainment and gambling must be one of the most beautiful in the world. Each time we stayed at a different hotel, and without a moment to spare, we discovered new attractions. Another time we made it to Canada, where we toured beautiful Montreal and Toronto. These cities reminded us of Europe in their atmosphere.

To this day, we reminisce of our two-week vacation in New York, where we made it a priority to tour the Statue of Liberty.

We went to Florida two times, and we can't get enough of that beautiful place on this earth.

Our trip to Mexico was unforgettable. In the beginning, we had a few frightening moments, since an airplane emergency occurred. The airplane began to ascend into the sky and then suddenly fell toward the ground. We only survived thanks to the good judgment of the pilot. We were transferred to a different airplane, and we successfully landed in Mexico. We relaxed in Cancun in a high-class hotel with wonderful service. Our stay there was made better by the mariachi band that played Spanish music. The water in the ocean was clear, and I couldn't imagine a more beautiful beach.

Each morning before breakfast, when Jagoda was still asleep, I took a walk. Each time I left the hotel, I repeated the words, "How beautiful is this world that God created." I was simply captivated by the place.

Yet the most wonderful trip, which is impossible to forget, was our trip to Rome for the twenty-fifth anniversary of our wedding. My brother, along with Father Turek, who was the rector of the Olsztyn Seminary at the time, arranged a private audience for us with Pope John Paul II. We had boarded a plane to Rome a few days earlier, stopping in Paris on the way on the day that just happened to be my birthday. We went to the hotel restaurant to celebrate the day. With beautiful music and French songs playing in the background, reminding me of the careless and youthful high school years when I studied French, we ordered various drinks and gourmet meals. At one point, I asked the waiter for the check. "You don't have to pay," he replied. "Please just give me the number of the room you are staying in."

We enjoyed the night for a long time, not worrying about the bill. We devoted the rest of the time to touring Paris. When it was time to fly out to Rome, I went to check out of the hotel. The receptionist gave me the bill, and I think she noticed that my face became pale because she asked, "Is something wrong?"

"No," I answered and paid the proper amount.

When I returned to the hotel room, I joked to my wife, "We have to return to Chicago because we don't have enough money for the rest of the trip." It turned out that the night at the restaurant cost us a lot of money. We didn't worry about it, since we lived by the saying, "you only live once." It was our life's motto.

In Rome, we met my brother and the entire pilgrim group, led by Father Turek, which came to the Eternal City by bus. After a warm greeting, we headed out to tour the city. Each corner of the city held a rich history. The most wonderful were St. Peter's Basilica and the Vatican Museum.

The monastery at Monte Cassino left a lasting impression on me. The very drive there awoke a surge of emotions because the monastery lies at 517 meters above sea level. Just near its peak only the brave are able to look down the side, as the precipice is terrifying. The monastery was completely destroyed in World War II by a bombing campaign on February 15, 1944. A land attack of the allied forces followed. Finally, on May 18, Polish soldiers were the first ones to hoist a red and white flag atop the still smoking ruins of the historic abbey.

During the conquering of the hill, over a thousand Polish soldiers died a historic death. In the cemetery in which they were buried, the immense number of Polish soldiers made an incredible impression on me. I took a stroll around the alleys of the cemetery, reading the last names of the perished and their places of birth. I concluded that the entirety of Poland was buried there.

Along the alley leading to the cemetery, there stands a monument with the words, "For our freedom and yours, we, the Polish soldiers gave: to God—our spirit, to the land of Italy—our bodies, and to Poland—our hearts."

By the raves on the plate there is a verse, "Passerby, tell Poland, that here lie its sons, loyal till their last hour."

The conclusion arises by itself. The cemeteries with Polish soldiers are strewn across the world, and we Poles are so undervalued in a global sense.

The first meeting with the pope took place on July 23, 1989, in the hall of Paul VI. I was fortunate to be able to stand by the barrier, shake hands with John Paul II, kiss his ring, and exchange a few words, "Holy Father, I'm from Chicago. I sincerely greet you and bring greetings from all people of good will from that city."

Then the Holy Father smiled at me, and looking me in the eyes, he answered, "Thank you," and then in a pensive manner he repeated several times, "Chicago, Chicago…" and moved on.

The next day we attained an honor that people usually only dream of. We had an audience with the Holy Father in Castel Gandolfo, where we were blessed by him on the occasion of the twenty-fifth anniversary of our marriage. On this occasion, Jagoda presented a vestment purchased by my mother for missions in poverty-stricken countries.

On the next day in St. Peter's Basilica, we renewed our vows. My brother blessed us, assisted by two priests. The entire pilgrim tour from Poland took part in the celebration. After leaving the Basilica, we invited everyone to dinner at a restaurant. Then, at the camp-ground where we were staying, we finished our celebration as if at Cana of Galilee. After returning to Chicago, an article appeared in the local newspaper about our meeting with the Holy Father entitled, "A Heavenly Vacation."

I was impressed by Niagara Falls, whose vastness cannot be captured in any photograph, not even in the best-made film. It is meant to be seen, and one should actually feel the enormity of the falling water.

Thanks to Maggie and Ron, we had the opportunity to see the Grand Canyon twice. It was a small distance away to Sedona, from where they lived, and we took the trips from there. Sedona is a beautifully located place. On each of my stays there (I have been there several times), I discovered something new, and each time those beautiful red mountains captivated me. Sedona is often compared to Lourdes, not only due to its beautiful location, but I heard that the two towns have similar health benefits. From Maggie's house, a beautiful view of the colorful mountains stretched across her bay windows. I flew from Chicago to Arizona on a regular basis. Sometimes Maggie would call me on a Monday and ask, "Daddy, can you come for a visit on Wednesday?"

Of course, I could, and I flew to Phoenix, where a limo picked me up and drove me 210 kilometers to Sedona. In this case, Maggie covered all of the costs, so the pleasure was all mine.

During the following trip to Poland, I went with my brother to Lithuania to a health retreat center in Druskienniki. What I liked most were the morning strolls through the woods and the smell of tree sap, which simply indulged my senses. I enjoyed the treatments and medical care as well. One time, as I passed by a bench on which a couple of people were resting, I heard a conversation in English. We started to chat, and I made a connection with a man who resided in Florida. From then on, the American often visited our room. He was cheerful and told jokes by the dozen. Because he wasn't aware that my brother was a priest, he told even the more "salty" ones. I had a good laugh at both of them. It wasn't until I returned to Chicago that I called him in Florida and explained that my brother was a priest. "Why didn't you warn me?" he asked, surprised.

"I couldn't because I had double the fun," I replied truthfully.

On our itinerary were trips to many towns and interesting places. I enjoyed Vilnius a lot. The painting of Our Mary of Ostrabrama impressed me incredibly. The cemetery and grave of former Marshall Jozef Pilsudski prompted me to reflect and filled me with hope that his successor would be born in Poland and would lead Poland to glory. Just as the prophecy says, Poland will become the land that flows with milk and honey.

Thanks to Maggie, I had the chance to see a good part of the world several times. Thanks to her, I saw Texas while taking care of some of her business at the same time. Another time, I flew with Sarah to Paris for a whole seventeen days. Maggie sponsored the trip for Sarah for babysitting her younger siblings. On the other hand, I flew there as Sarah's caretaker because she was still a minor. During that time, my brother and his friend also came to Paris, and the four of us visited as many sights as we could. Our guide throughout Paris was none other than Sarah. At breakfast, we discussed what we were going to see that day, and Sarah's task was to get us there. We followed her, not worrying about getting lost. We usually took advantage of the metro.

We also took a train to the south of France to Lourdes. In addition to the Sanctuary of Our Lady, the place where the Holy Mary appeared to a girl named Bernadette, we visited a cave located near the Spanish Pyrenees. It was amazing. A friend, with whom I shared an office in Bialystok, helped us in Paris. I met her through sheer coincidence during this trip. She had lived in Paris for over fifteen years—how small the world is.

We spent many joyful moments with my son on a vacation, during which Robert was both the driver and the guide. We drove the entire length of the United States on Interstate 80, which extends from New York to San Francisco, stopping at as many sites as we could along the way.

Unfortunately, I fell ill in San Francisco and per Maggie's recommendation, Robert first took me to the hospital, and later, after some tests, drove me to the airport where I took a plane back to Chicago. At the Oakland airport, I must have been perceived as a terrorist suspect because I didn't carry luggage. I had only a one-way ticket, and Robert answered all of the official's questions, even though the law forbids it. I was too weak, and they knew it. I underwent an additional search by security officials, although I didn't have anything with me. Even right before boarding the plane, I was turned back. Three policemen searched me thoroughly, even though they had already done so when I walked through the metal detector. I was finally the last one to board the plane.

I thought, *Finally, they caught a real terrorist red-handed,* and despite the fact that I was very weak, I smiled to myself. Oh well, situations like that happen in life.

I visited Paris for the third time as part of a pilgrimage to Fatima and Lourdes. This time, Jagoda accompanied me. At my request, the manager of the Chicago travel agency allowed my brother to serve as the spiritual guide of the trip. On the way to Portugal, we had a layover in Paris, where we were joined by my brother. We flew on a plane to Lisbon, where a rented bus was awaiting us. Fatima was first, the unforgettable place of worship of Mary. Then we drove through

Spain to Lourdes in France. On the way, we stopped at the most interesting spots. We had many unforgettable moments, we admired unforgettable views and places, and before our return to Chicago, we spent a few wonderful days in Paris.

On my next trip to Poland, I went with my brother on an organized tour through the countries of the Benelux, during which we visited cities in Germany, Luxemburg, Belgium, and Holland. "Europe is beautiful," I remarked when I returned home.

I've described the places that I had the opportunity to be in and admire what God created for man on one hand, and on the other, what the human mind was able to achieve. Of course, I haven't described all of my trips because that wasn't my intention. I elaborated on only a few of the most important ones to show that my childhood dreams turned into reality. Unfortunately, since 2005, I haven't been able to travel, but I thank God that he permitted me to enjoy life up to this time, and I lived through many beautiful days.

Henry Czajewski, June 16, 2007.

From left to right my grandchildren; Anthony, Erica, Jack, Jordan, and Sarah, Christmas 2009.

My grandchildren, Anthony, Sarah, and Erica, 2004.

Jacek's parents, Robert and his wife Sarah.

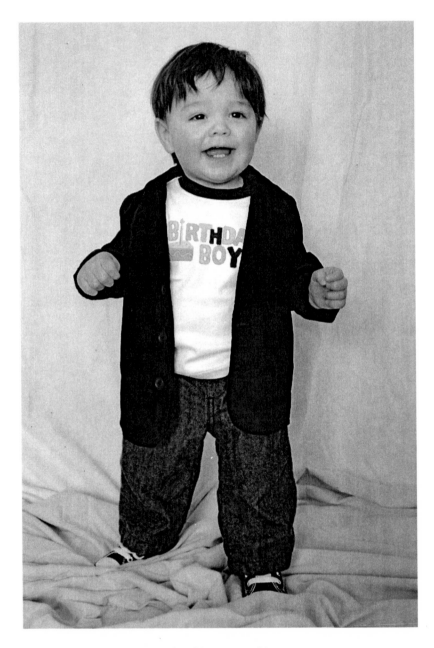

My grandson, Jacek Henryk Czajewski, one year old.

Epilogue

On March 5, 2007, I received two phone calls from Maggie from Arizona. In the first, she informed me that Ron was in a car accident in Phoenix and was in the hospital. An hour later, she called a second time and said that Ron had passed away. The sad news fell upon me like a lightning bolt. I was certain that it was just a nightmare, and I would soon wake up. Unfortunately, it was the tragic truth, not a dream. I personally lived through it quite painfully.

A thought occurred to me as to why I was still alive, despite such complicated experiences, and Ron, despite his forty-three years, had to pass from this world. *God's judgments are a mystery,* I thought.

On June 21, Maggie flew in to Chicago with Anthony and Erica for nearly three weeks. I knew that my grandchildren loved me because they expressed it many times during our numerous telephone conversations. However, having direct contact with them was completely different. Anthony and Erica made me feel it in every step. They hugged me and kissed me dozens of times a day. Anthony even expressed his wish to sleep with me. He held my hand the entire night. One time, he came up to me, kissed me on the cheek, and said, "Grandpa, I love you. You're the best grandpa in the world."

Erica, on the other hand, said to me, "Grandpa, I love you a billion times."

One day, Cindy, Ron's sister, called me and told me these crucial words, "Henry, God spared you for your grandchildren's sake because he knew that they would need you during such a difficult time for them."

I agreed with her whole-heartedly, and I thought that those were exactly God's "judgments" to which there is no repeal.

I planned a trip to Poland for August 2007, in order to publish my memoir. As a bearer of the "Status of the Aggrieved," I would be able to take advantage of the right to inspect the contents of my file at the Institute of Remembrance in Gdansk. I would like to note that I had forgiven all of my persecutors already, even though I wanted to see the partial file. The Communists were able to destroy a large part of my files, although those that were preserved were proof enough to grant me aggrieved status. For this, I am personally grateful to Dr. Prof. Leon Kieres.

My quiet wish is to fly with my brother to the Holy Land. Before death, I would like to set my foot on this most important, for me, place on the globe. Because my brother has been there many times, he will be my guide.

I hope that this time, too, my Guardian Angel will keep me in His care.

USA, Chicago, June 30, 2007

Afterword

Since my last angioplasty on December 1, 2006, during which Dr. Robert Dieter saved my life by inserting a stent, I feel constant pain in my chest. The persistent pain and discomfort are side effect of three open-heart surgeries, two of which were performed within one year. Not even medication is effective for relief. It is in this difficult time that I completed the Polish version of my book. I wrote while conquering the pain. Despite these obstacles, and at times my inability to focus, I succeeded in finishing my book.

In 2007, I decided to risk my life by traveling overseas to Poland, where I published my book. All of my friends, family, and particularly, my wife, deemed the trip as a willing suicidal act. I believed, believe, and will not stop believing, that John Paul II and my Guardian Angel continually watch over me. I was not disappointed even then. I flew out of Chicago at the beginning of August, and I handled the twelve-hour flight to Gdansk and the stopover in Warsaw tolerably well.

My childhood friend, currently a professor at the University of Cardinal Stefan Wyszynski, Dr. Jozef Dolega, gave me a verbal guarantee that I would be able to publish the book during my short, two-month stay in Poland. As a director of the Catholic publication, *Episteme,* he did everything to meet the deadline. With Father Dr. Jaroslaw Sokolowski, we formulated a general outline of the book and added photos.

During one of the daily morning Holy Masses celebrated by Father Sokolowski and my brother Father Romuald in Osowiec, my well-being was far from good, and I was close to losing consciousness. It took the last of my strength to leave the church. I turned my gaze toward the cemetery, and at that moment, I experienced a kind of spiritual relief that I would be buried in this area. Sweat poured down my body, but I felt better as a cool breeze literally brought me back to life. I survived.

I held on to the belief that I would see my book published and then submit to leaving this world, in the hope of being given the chance of being absorbed by the light, which would be a beautiful ending to my life in this world. I prayed, and I continue to pray, that I may attain this, and that the Merciful God not dismiss my sinful soul, that my shortcomings will not close the gate to the Heavenly Kingdom.

On September 21, 2007, the mayor of the city of Gdynia, to celebrate the occasion of the fifth anniversary of the Andrzej Wajda's School of Film Production, organized a screening of the best productions of the school. At the screening, I had the honor to personally meet one of the most distinguished film directors in the world, Oscar winner Mr. Andrzej Wajda. Not only is he an extraordinary director, but he is a wonderful man. If it had not been for the long line awaiting his autograph, our conversation would not have ended so quickly. At the end of the conversation, I suggested that he visit me in Chicago.

"I would gladly take you up on the offer, but on account of my three bypasses, I cannot risk flying on a plane," he answered.

Then I was compelled to tell him the story of my illness. I briefly mentioned my three open-heart surgeries and four heart attacks. He was very surprised because he must have thought he was speaking with a ghost rather than a live person. Nevertheless, I had to walk away because the line of people waiting for an autograph got longer. We bid a warm farewell, and I felt that I was saying good-bye to someone close to me. I walked away with my head hung low, in reverence and honor of the man so meritorious to the good of Polish culture.

The next day, the premiere of perhaps not his last film, *Katyn,* took place, which I did not miss either. The film touched me deeply. The murder of twenty-two thousand Polish officers, professors, and employees of institutions of higher learning, eight hundred doctors, fifty clergymen and women of various faiths, who were shot in the back of the head by Bolshevik executioners, was true genocide. This fact was diligently concealed for fifty years. The crime was executed in a period of just six weeks, April to June 1940, under Stalin's personal orders. The murdered officers were prisoners of war. They were detained following an insidious attack on Poland by Soviet Russia on

September 17, 1939, based on a secret agreement between Hitler and Stalin. It was the famous Ribbentrop-Molotov Pact.

It was strange that the entire democratic world remained silent about this, even after the end of the war. No nation officially reproved the horrendous crime, most likely not wanting to irritate the "polar bear," as Soviet Russia was referred to at the time. It wasn't until United States President Ronald Reagan called Soviet Russia by name, describing it as the "Empire of Evil," that the truth was released.

After the end of the film, everyone left the screening room with tears in their eyes. No one dared to lift his or her head. Staring at the ground in immeasurable pain and grief, everyone returned home. I was pained by the fact that the director's father, a Polish Army officer, was also murdered in *Katyn*. His son waited for the historical moment in which he was able to produce the film and show the world this brutal and lawless genocide. This was possible because in 1989, Poland was freed from Soviet Russia's sphere of influence. In my opinion, it was simply a miracle that this moment was able to happen at all.

I was very happy when the following year, 2008, I saw Mr. Andrzej Wajda's silhouette stepping out of a car in Hollywood for the Oscar awards ceremony. I thought that perhaps the conversation with me contributed to Mr. Andrzej Wajda's change of heart, and despite his illness, he decided to fly even further than Chicago.

The time came when my book was published. Two days before my departure, my brother, and my godson, Darek, picked up the print run. I was very moved when I took the first Polish version copy of In The Shadow of My Guardian Angel into my hands. It was already my second authored book. This book however I dictated it from the heart and transferred the feeling onto paper.

For Darek, who drove the car the entire time, getting through the five-hundred-kilometer stretch of road was not much of a problem. When I thanked him, he surprised me very much by answering, "For such a great uncle, I would do anything."

I don't know why I deserved such words. Among other things, perhaps he deemed me deserving when I was patient with him, while I listened, and grasped the significance of his life's secret, as he revealed it to me a few days earlier.

Unfortunately, a few months later, on January 11, 2008, I received sad news. My godson, the deliverer of my book, ended his journey on this earth at the young age of forty-six. Now I will take his life's secret to my grave.

I would like to refer to a certain dream I had on the night of March 16–17, 2008. Right before the dream, I turned to John Paul II with the request to give me life instructions, which would pave the way to heaven. Something extraordinary happened. I dreamed of Kazik, my late childhood friend. When I saw his silhouette, I heard an alarm on the street and an announcement that everyone gathered there would die in a moment as a result of a bomb. No one had a chance of getting out alive. Instinctively, we all formed a circle and taking one another by the shoulders, we began saying the Lord's Prayer in unison. When we got to the words "Forgive us our trespasses, as we forgive those who trespass against us," I noticed my brother in our circle. I thought that his prayer was probably most pleasing to God, and at that moment, I woke up.

I felt that somewhere, deep in my heart, a thorn remained that did not let me forgive those who trespassed against me. Just after waking up, I decided to fight with my weakness, so that the sin would not leave a mark on my soul. This is why I ask everyone whom I have harmed to forgive the wrongdoings I have committed, consciously or unconsciously. Now, following the example of the Polish bishops' proclamation to the nation of Germany, I wish to say, "I forgive and I ask for forgiveness."

When Anthony and Erica celebrated the sacrament of their First Holy Communion in April 2008, I flew with my son, Robert, to Sedona in Arizona for the occasion. Before receiving the sacrament, they both presented the golden chalice given for that occasion by their great-grandmother, Zofia, as an offering for missions. I was greatly moved seeing my grandchildren granting the wishes of my mother.

On May 5, another celebration was to take place. This time my wife, Jagoda, joined the guests to celebrate my eldest and beloved granddaughter Sarah's graduation from Embry-Riddle Aeronautical University, which is among the most renowned universities in the United States. Sarah was one of the most successful students, both in high school and at the university. She was just twenty years old upon graduation from Embry-Riddle, since she finished a year ahead of her peers from both high school and the university.

My greatest comfort and satisfaction is that my grandchildren reciprocate my love, which they do not hide and which they show on each occasion.

I wish to thank my wife who threw me a wonderful party for my seventieth birthday in July 2008. It was a complete surprise, and I was pleasantly astonished when upon entering my house, I saw many guests, who sang, "Happy Birthday…!" to me in unison. This time, Chris, and her husband, Stanley, helped to organize the event. Stanley's job was to "drag" me out of the house, so I wouldn't catch on to what was brewing. He managed it perfectly. Thank you, Chris and Stanley for helping my wife and organizing similar celebrations for her fiftieth and sixtieth birthdays.

I am living to this day, April 15, 2009, through the intercession of my Guardian Angel and John Paul II. Unfortunately, for over a month, my health has been deteriorating. An accident, which nearly ended in death, most likely affected and added to my state greatly.

For more than three months before this accident, I had a strange premonition that something would happen to me. From the moment I woke to the moment I fell asleep in the evening, I was constantly under the influence of this strange state. I was sure of my impending death. I confessed to my wife that something would surely happen to me, that I expected "the worst," as some people describe the death of a human being. I have never had this feeling before, which bore through my subconscious thoughts daily. A week before the accident, I had an urgent matter to tend to. I wasn't entirely sure if it was legal and that it wasn't going to be the cause of a sin.

Quite literally, two days before the accident, I asked my Guardian Angel and John Paul II to give me a sign as to how I should handle this matter. An incredible thing occurred. A day before the important impending situation, October 1, 2008, I broke my foot as I fell off a ladder. It happened in my backyard. I was alone. My wife was at work at the time. I felt an incredible pain. Falling to the grass, I slipped out of consciousness. I had my cell phone in my shirt pocket, but despite the fall from the second rung of the ladder, the telephone remained in its place. Thanks to this, I called my neighbor when I regained consciousness. Luckily, her daughter ran over promptly, and a moment later, the neighbor and daughter administered first aid. They called an ambulance. The ambulance came within a few minutes, and I was rushed to the nearest hospital. There, when I gathered myself, I remembered the matter, which I was supposed to finalize the next day, on October 2. Due to the accident, it no longer became necessary to face the circumstance. Despite my pain, I was happy that now the matter was finished, and I didn't have to fear its consequences. From then on, the strange premonition that something would happen to me stopped afflicting me. I feared death was awaiting me, but it turned out that I only broke my leg.

After becoming familiar with my health history, the doctor immediately referred me to the intensive care unit. They performed an x-ray of the foot, which proved to be completely crushed. I spent three days in the hospital, then eleven weeks in a cast. A complete and comprehensive operation could not be performed, due to the impending removal of blood thinning medication ten days prior to surgery. After consulting with the hospital where I underwent my heart surgery, this doctor concluded that withholding these medications would be detrimental to my life. The saying would have come true: "the operation was successful, only the patient didn't make it." The doctors gave me no hope that I would be able to walk after they revised and simplified the surgery. Fortunately, their prognosis was incorrect, and despite the pain, I moved rather well without walking aides.

I am immune to pain, and now, in the plural form, pains don't make a great impression on me. I was encouraged by the fact that on November 23, 2008, not even two months after my accident, my grandson was born. This time the father of our wonderful grandson is my son, Robert. He and the baby's mother, Sarah, gave him two names, Jack Henryk. I was very glad that the second name he would carry is the name of his grandfather. When my cast was removed, I was able to see my grandson at last. Although I had to enter their house on my knees, it wasn't a problem. After all, I went to see my newborn grandson. My wife and I said with one voice that no other grandchildren in the whole wide world are more beautiful than ours. I was very happy to have the chance to hold him in my arms, even for a moment. My wife was thrilled and didn't let him go until the moment of our departure. Now Jack Henryk visits us with his parents.

I wish for only one thing, to see the baptism of my grandson. This will be the most wonderful gift my Guardian Angel and John Paul II can grant me.

I am happy that I have two wonderful children, who endowed me with the most beautiful and smartest grandchildren, whom we love very much.

July 5, 2009, was to be an extraordinary day for me. It was the day of my youngest grandson's, Jack Henryk's baptism, the son of Robert and Sarah. Three days before the baptism, on Friday, I experienced a strong pain in my chest. I didn't regret life, but I feared that I would not be able to make it to Sunday and not be granted the chance to attend such an important celebration. A few hours after taking some medication, the pain nearly subsided. The entire time I wondered if the One on High heard my request directed to John Paul II and my

Guardian Angel, and if I would survive these three days. I made it to the moment, and it was one of the most important days of my life. I experienced the baptism of each of my grandchildren in a similar way.

A few days later, I had another painful attack. July 9, 2009, Dr. Fred Leya saved my life again by inserting one stent. I had a strange feeling when, after the procedure, I saw the doctor's happiness in his face, who told me that the procedure was successful. What can I say? I experienced a miracle again. This time, in what seemed like a hopeless situation, the Guardian Angel had not abandoned me

I hope I will be able to continue my next project, my book, *Emigration,* which I just began writing one month ago. Before my gallbladder surgery on March 10, 2010, the anesthesiologist told me that he would be prepared to administer emergency treatment in case I should have a heart attack during surgery. I took the risk because my chest pain was so severe. Unfortunately, having gall bladder surgery was not my choice, but as always throughout my life, I relied on my Guardian Angel.

As I write these final words today, March 9, 2010, the day before my surgery, I received news from Poland that my beloved brother, Romuald, had passed away. This is some of the worst news that I have ever received in my life. I am convinced that God took his soul directly to heaven. He spent his entire adult life in the service of God and the parishes he served. He will be deeply missed by our family. Dear brother, I will remember you for the rest of my life.

I do not know how many days I have left on this earthly vale, but surprises are not over. The many unexpected medical emergencies that I have experienced have interrupted almost my whole life. I had a firm belief and illusory hope that after the surgery in March I would have a moment of respite from medical problems. Unfortunately, in May, my health began to deteriorate sharply. I experienced intense chest pain daily. I suffered cardiac arrhythmia and had to take nitroglycerin every day. For a long time I felt antipathy toward the hospital, and I resisted having to return to that place. For the next two months, I was convinced that there was no salvation for me. However, under strong pressure from my wife and my family doctor, I called my cardiologist. He ordered me to come to his office immediately. I was examined by two doctors. An hour later, I ended up on the operating table.

My medical treatment took place once again at Loyola Hospital on July 6, 2010, after less than a one-year break from a similar procedure. This time doctors inserted four stents into three veins. The doctors said that the veins were 99.9 percent obstructed, which really means they were completely blocked. Dr. Ferdinand Leya prolonged my life again, and I will be forever grateful to this wonderful doctor.

Why am I living? That is the ongoing question, and I don't even have to indicate who is behind this miracle.

I was convinced that the stents the doctors inserted into my veins would be so efficient that other treatments would no longer be needed. It turned out that was only an illusion on my part. Unfortunately, one of the bypasses must be redone because there isn't any room left to place another. There are already "just" eight bypasses in place. I need to get the next open-heart surgery performed soon, which will be my fourth procedure. I refuse to give up and become discouraged, even though severe chest pain prevents me from living peacefully. Again, my Guardian Angel may keep me alive. And this time as well, I hope that He not will leave me, but will stand by me.

Acknowledgments

Thank you to:

Maggie, my daughter, who put her whole heart into guiding the translation, many times re-translating, to make my intentions clear. To you Maggie, I am incredibly grateful that you took on such a task. Although you are always busy, you committed yourself and helped me in this most critical of times.

My son, Robert, who helped in the translation.

My neighbor, Christine Daniels, who worked diligently and tirelessly as one of my editors.

Wendy Weidman, for her wonderful work in editing and designing the front cover of my book.

The translator of my book, Ms. Marta Kazimierczak. She also translated my first book, *We the Children of War*.

My cousin, Michael Gosiewski for translating the document, "Aggrieved status of the Institute of National Remembrance." (The commissions for the Prosecution of crimes against the Polish Nation).

I wish to finish my story with the prayer to the Guardian Angel.

Angel of God, my guardian dear,

To whom God's love commits me here,

Ever this day (night) be at my side,

To light and guard and rule and guide.

Amen.

Chicago-Orland Hills, September 1, 2010

Henry Czajewski

269

My wife and me in our home.